CHUCK BERRY

CHUCK BERRY

THE AUTOBIOGRAPHY

HARMONY BOOKS / NEW YORK

Photo credits: Pages 49, 78: Harry A. Davis; 124, 125: Don Bronstein; 142: H. S. Rhoden; 157: Johan Hesselberg; 173: Irving A. Williamson; 229: Bob Gruen/STAR FILE; 235, 238: Richard Mossler; 257: J. P. Ravelli; 260: Mark Richman; 269, 271: J. P. Ravelli; 295: copyright © 1986 Michael G. Bush; 300: Linda Edwards; 301: © Samuel Teicher, Songwriters Hall of Fame; 302: copyright © 1985 Michael G. Bush; 303: copyright © 1986 Michael G. Bush; 305: © Samuel Teicher, Songwriters Hall of Fame; 308: Andy Dalton; 320: Luann Wing

Published by Harmony Books, a division of Crown Publishers, Inc., 225 Park Avenue South, New York, New York 10003, and represented in Canada by the Canadian MANDA Group.
HARMONY and colophon are trademarks of Crown Publishers, Inc.
Manufactured in the United States of America

Design by Ron McCutchan

Library of Congress Cataloging-in-Publication-Data

Berry, Chuck.
    Chuck Berry: the autobiography.

    Includes index.
    1. Berry, Chuck. 2. Rock musicians—United States—Biography. I. Title.
ML420.B365A3 1987   784.5'4'00924 [B]   87-11825
ISBN 0-517-56666-4

10 9 8 7 6 5 4 3 2 1

First Edition

TO
THE MANY
WHO NEVER KNEW,

AND
TO ANY
WHO'VE WANTED TO

KNOW
WHAT IS TRUE
PRAISED OR TABOO

HERE
ARE A FEW
THINGS THAT I DO
EXPOSED TO YOU
FOR YOUR REVIEW

CONTENTS

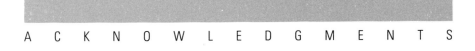

A C K N O W L E D G M E N T S

Acknowledgment is not enough to express the gratitude due Francine Gillium who launched my serious intentions to write this book in the beginning. Likewise the experience of Michael Pietsch was the essence of perfection that brought my intentions, during the project, into a marketable perspective. Esther Mitgang helped me closely in picking the pictures and educating me about the publishing process. Francine, Michael, Esther, and the entries of Yvonne Cumbie, whose computer compassion compiled the construction through to completion, all made it come to be the book form of a message of the memories of my music from ''Maybellene'' to ''My Ding-A-Ling'' and more.

All of the above could not possibly have surfaced without the patience that Themetta has shared with me.

Foreword by
Bruce Springsteen

*[Now here's a guy who speaks what God loves, which is
the truth. How he got it down so straight I'll never know,
but it's just like I had written it.—C.B.]*

I met Chuck Berry once.
    We played at the Maryland Armory in the early '70s, and
we got a call from the promoter. My manager said, "Gee,
you know, we're going to open on a bill for Jerry Lee Lewis
and Chuck Berry." We thought this was like *forget it!* I was
twenty-three or twenty-four, and these guys were our heroes. So
we were really excited. The promoter said, "He's getting a band
that's going to back Chuck Berry up." And we said, "No, no,
don't get one of the local bands, tell him we'll back him up."
    I think my first album might have just come out around that
time. So we went down to Maryland. We drove there from some
overnight gig—I forget from where. We started our set, and the
audience was strange, because it was a big place. It was about ten
thousand seats. You had young kids who had just got turned on to
Chuck Berry. He was having another surge of popularity at that
time. Then you had Jerry Lee Lewis who was in his country phase,
so there was a lot of real country music fans there, too.
    We came out, and we played about a half hour, which was gen-
erally the allotted time in those days if you were an opening band.
We went over pretty good. Then Jerry Lee came out, and he did
his set, you know. Standing on the piano.
    Chuck Berry . . . not there. I forget what time he was supposed

to go on, but it was getting close to that time. And no sign of Chuck. The promoter was getting really nervous, and he came up to me and he said, "Look, go on back out there, because Chuck Berry's not here. I don't think he's coming." I said, "I'm not going out there. They're waiting for Chuck Berry and we're not going to go on again."

Now it was five minutes before the show was timed to start. The back door opened, and in he came. And, he was by himself. And, he's got a guitar case. And that was it. I guess he pulled up in his own car. He didn't have anybody with him. He kind of walked by me and went straight to the promoter's office. I think the rumor was he would get eleven grand. At the end of the night he'd give a grand back if the band was okay and if the equipment worked. I don't know if that's true, but that's what we heard. So straight into the office, and then out of the office, and he came into the band's room.

We were all really nervous. There wasn't supposed to be an extra guitar player, so I came up to him and I said, "Gee, is it okay if I play?" And he said, "Yeah, yeah you can play." And I said, "Well, Chuck . . ." And he said, "What?" And I said, "What songs are we going to do?" And he said, "Well, we're going to do some Chuck Berry songs." That's all he said. So we went, "Okay."

We got out on stage. The lights were up. The crowd was going insane. They could see him. He walked on, opened the guitar case, and tuned the guitar in full view of the crowd. The place was going nuts. I felt like I had never been on stage before. I felt amazingly nervous. I was twenty-three. I had been playing for about nine years by then, but I felt *really* nervous. The lights went down, and we're going like, "What are we going to start with?"

He's kind of not paying attention to us, and then all I hear is "da-na-na-na, na-na-na," and that was it. We were in a state of total panic. We're trying to figure out what song we were playing, what key it was in! Chuck played in a lot of strange keys, like B flat and E flat. Everybody turned to our bass player, he was kind of the historian of the band, and he had the right key. So we picked up the key, and we were doing pretty good, I think. I forget what song it was, but we were playing away, and the crowd was going nuts. Chuck ran back and said, "Play for that money boys!" But we forgot to tell him we ain't getting any money, we were doing this for free.

Anyway, the night ended. There was a big brawl in front of the stage, and the lights came on. I think his amp blew up, and he just kind of walked right to the side of the stage, and packed his guitar in front of the entire auditorium. They were going crazy, and we were, I guess, doing "Johnny B. Goode" by now. We were just playing that rhythm. He waved, and that was it.

He walked out. Walked back into his car, and he was gone. I doubt that he remembers. We were probably just another one of the bands he was using on the road at the time. It was an incredible night. It was just the kind of night that when I'm sixty-five or seventy, I've got to tell my grandkids. "Chuck Berry, yeah I met Chuck Berry. As a matter of fact I backed Chuck Berry up one night." "You did?" "Yeah."

It's a story you're always going to tell.

> "Bruce Springsteen Interview"
> from *Hail! Hail! Rock 'n' Roll*
> a Delilah Films Production
> a Taylor Hackford Film

Every fifteen years, in fact, it seems I make a big mistake. You can read the story of the lean, mean, and in-between years in the chapters ahead.

Depicting a condition or experience briefly in a song is elementary, I found, compared to trying to arrange a lifetime between pages. Most of what you may read within these pages was started during the "time" I had to spend in Lompoc Prison Camp in 1979, which has a chapter to itself. At Lompoc I finished a course in typing that enabled me to complete over 250 pages while there. It may be obvious that the book displays certain longings, as I was away from the satisfactions (of a rolling stone) that a man in isolation yearns for in such places, but that's a part of me as well.

Returning to my home and office, I began to rewrite the entire script, and thus purchased a word processor to speed the process. I also began to talk about writing this book on TV shows I appeared on and word was out. Regardless of the WP machine, I was a year and a half getting the first four chapters rewritten. With my personal appearances continuously in calling and other enterprises requiring my attention, another two years passed before I had finished rewriting up to chapter eight. All the while I was making excuses for its incompletion in the interviews I gave.

In 1987, after nearly eight years of writing and rewriting like a slave of my own criticizing, I decided to let it go as it is, raw in form, rare in feat, but real in fact. No ghost but no guilt or gimmicks, just me.

Every fifteen years, in fact, it seems I make a big mistake. You can read the story of the lean, mean, and in-between years in the chapters ahead.

Depicting a condition or experience briefly in a song is elementary, I found, compared to trying to arrange a lifetime between pages. Most of what you may read within these pages was started during the "time" I had to spend in Lompoc Prison Camp in 1979, which has a chapter to itself. At Lompoc I finished a course in typing that enabled me to complete over 250 pages while there. It may be obvious that the book displays certain longings, as I was away from the satisfactions (of a rolling stone) that a man in isolation yearns for in such places, but that's a part of me as well.

Returning to my home and office, I began to rewrite the entire script, and thus purchased a word processor to speed the process. I also began to talk about writing this book on TV shows I appeared on and word was out. Regardless of the WP machine, I was a year and a half getting the first four chapters rewritten. With my personal appearances continuously in calling and other enterprises requiring my attention, another two years passed before I had finished rewriting up to chapter eight. All the while I was making excuses for its incompletion in the interviews I gave.

In 1987, after nearly eight years of writing and rewriting like a slave of my own criticizing, I decided to let it go as it is, raw in form, rare in feat, but real in fact. No ghost but no guilt or gimmicks, just me.

This book is entirely written, phrase by phrase, by yours truly, Chuck Berry.

Within these pages is information from as far back as my records and memory extend through the years of my life. I've written much about my involvement with other people, in and around the music sphere of show business, and about people having close relations to my life and personal affairs. Within are also incidents that, through the course of my life, have influenced my personal behavior and beliefs.

In brief (though it's taken over seven years so far to write!) this is the history of my life. It carries from birth to 1987, a breath over sixty years, preceded with a bit of my roots. The dates, deeds, and descriptions are as real, thorough, and as precise as my records and memory can deliver.

In 1959 I wrote some forty pages of this book but abandoned it during the height of my popularity. That manuscript was ultimately lost in a fire that consumed my office building in 1969. The urge to proceed always came back whenever a boost in my career prompted new interviews. Usually it was not the ''boost'' that was elaborated on in the articles resulting from the interviews, but instead the naughty-naughties I would commit from time to time.

we forgot to tell him we ain't getting any money, we were doing this for free.

Anyway, the night ended. There was a big brawl in front of the stage, and the lights came on. I think his amp blew up, and he just kind of walked right to the side of the stage, and packed his guitar in front of the entire auditorium. They were going crazy, and we were, I guess, doing "Johnny B. Goode" by now. We were just playing that rhythm. He waved, and that was it.

He walked out. Walked back into his car, and he was gone. I doubt that he remembers. We were probably just another one of the bands he was using on the road at the time. It was an incredible night. It was just the kind of night that when I'm sixty-five or seventy, I've got to tell my grandkids. "Chuck Berry, yeah I met Chuck Berry. As a matter of fact I backed Chuck Berry up one night." "You did?" "Yeah."

It's a story you're always going to tell.

"Bruce Springsteen Interview"
from *Hail! Hail! Rock 'n' Roll*
a Delilah Films Production
a Taylor Hackford Film

S omewhere in Kentucky, as best is known, in the southern-
most region of the state, during the year of 1839, on the
Wolfolk Plantation, the wife of Master Wolfolk inherited the
prosperity and programming of the plantation at the time of
his death. The freedom it gave her proved to be a blessing to the
slave workers in that she didn't push them to the maximum of
production. In fact, she seemed to have favorites who, at her
whim, would be treated leniently. It was believed that her manner
of administrating the estate resulted in her conception of a mixed-
blooded female child. The illegitimate birth of the child was well

total authority over the administration of the plantation. Once she
returned, Mistress Wolfolk announced that she had bought the
baby at a reasonable figure in New Orleans during a visit with a
French skipper who had in the past brought other sales up to her
husband. She announced that the child was to be called Cellie, that
she was special to her, and that she would be a privileged servant
catering to her alone. That made Cellie a favorite among the others
as she grew up to be unusually smart. But according to the plantation hands' rumor, verified with other whispers-of-experience, it
was believed that a certain one of the house servants was the father
of the child.

The Wolfolk Plantation was adjacent to another called the Johnson House Plantation, whose population had just been increased with an infant slave boy of slave parentage named John Johnson. As word has been passed down, John Johnson and Cellie Wolfolk first met on the Johnson House Plantation when they were in their late teens, during a harvest when Johnson House would borrow help from neighboring plantations. John had for years had his bright eye on the light-skinned Cellie, looking at the beauty of her. He dreamed of marrying Cellie as soon as he could. John was seen often working at both plantations, they said, for the chance only to be near her.

John's Master Johnson was a good master and, though seldom present on the plantation, was sympathetic of his slaves and their welfare. Master Johnson became aware of John's enthusiasm, and, living true to his Baptist faith, he went to his neighbor and discussed John's hope to marry with Cellie. When Master Johnson returned he told John the good news that he would be permitted to marry Cellie in a year and a half. He explained who Lincoln was, bringing new laws that likely would cause them to lose all the help from the results of the war. John thanked the Lord for his master's kindness.

John shifted from one plantation to another, adding to his required field duties during the wait. Cellie's mistress kept her promise vivid by allowing John occasional visits to Cellie but she had him see Cellie only within the "big house," where she served.

John Johnson and Cellie were permitted by the good Johnson House master and Cellie's mistress to move to Ohio. It was there they were wedded and housed, with the aid of Ohio relatives from the Wolfolk Plantation, and started a family of many children.

Mattie and Ella were the first two children to be born in the confines of Cellie and John Johnson's own log cabin, which was similar to the one John had known as a slave child. Though they were happy, John was unable to find enough employment to support them and they soon moved back to Kentucky to work on the plantation again for the Johnson House. The good master had died and his governing wife welcomed them to return and work for her.

Back living in what had once been a slave shack, with Cellie pregnant with her third child, John L. Junior, they were happy. In the evenings, while John was away doing extra work to make ends meet, his wife was taking in laundry and sewing to help. Both plantations were assisting them in getting ahead until one dreadful night three unknown white men made an attempt to molest Cellie. They were intoxicated and sought entertainment in trying to persuade her to submit to them sexually. Her screams caused lights to come on in the big house and saved her as the men fled.

Trusting the help of a neighboring male field hand to watch over his loved ones, John took the funds he had saved and traveled by mule and buggy to his sister's place in Missouri. There he rented a small piece of land just north of St. Louis, portions of what was once Fort Bellefontaine Farm, from a plantation owner named Mr. Victory. John purchased tools and built a one-room log cabin. He traveled back to Kentucky in the fall of 1870 and announced his accomplishments to Cellie. The attitude of Southerners was heated, and within days they packed and left Kentucky once again with their three children.

At their farm, in their cabin amid the rolling hills of Missouri, the sorrows and secrets of Kentucky soon faded. The one-room cabin sheltered the birth of two more children, Mary and Lucinda. The last child, Lucinda, was the child who became my father's mother.

Little knowledge of my dad's father's parents is retraceable. I only found that Dad's father's mother had come to Missouri from slavery in Memphis, Tennessee. She had come together (under slavery) with an Oklahoma Indian who was a gardener on a plantation somewhere in northern Missouri. The Memphis slave girl and the Indian garden boy were the parents that bore a son and named him William Berry, my dad's father.

I think Grandpa William Berry must have been quite a roadrunner during his days before marriage and likely after, too. We've heard he traveled extensively and had a knack for getting along with the opposite sex, especially a fair-complexioned damsel. Little info trickled down through the generations of any unbecoming activities but evidence of the fact lay in the apparently potent condition he still exercised beyond the age of seventy. He wore a perpetual smile, even in his sleep, and was said to have moaned (while asleep) a few details of his adventures.

We do know it was in competition with one of his companions that the strife to become acquainted with a soft-spoken schoolteacher arose. His rival lost out and William went on to win the love of Lucinda. Lucinda was also a very fair maiden of sixteen, shy and humble, living with her family. Without hesitation, William wedded and seeded Lucinda with child. They named the baby, born on April 9, 1895, Henry William Berry, who is my father.

In her enthusiasm and haste during recovery from delivery, Lucinda fell short of maintaining good health and never completely regained it. Henry was kept out of school to care for his mother while his father, not unlike during his days of being single, traveled far, to where and with whom they know not. At the age of twelve Henry William lost his mother, Lucinda, passing from her long illness. He was then sent to live with his maternal grandparents, John and Cellie Johnson.

My father was reared by his grandmother until his father married again and added two more children, Thelma and Clarence, to the family. Dad had a cousin Harry who was also reared on the farm where Dad worked as a field hand and each was hindered from schooling due to the need for money to support the family. They learned much from their elders but that did not take the place of going to school. Reaching adulthood the two of them left the Bellefontaine farm and moved together to a bachelor apartment in Bellefontaine until Dad got married to Mother.

The lineage of my mother can be traced to Muskogee, Oklahoma, in the early 1800s, where a Chihuahua Indian cook saw a fearless African out of the plains working bare backed and decided that such a man could fulfill her dreams of bravery. The Chihuahua maiden, named Susan by her tribal grandfather, was reared under native customs but often worked supplying food for the black slave workers of the Banks Plantation. The slave who had captured her fancy was named Isaac Banks.

This Banks Plantation was deeply rooted with rich, red-blooded Indian seed mixed with an equivalent amount of African origin. Isaac Banks was a thorough-breed African and was easily distinguished among the lighter-skinned Indian workers. Because of that fact, he was often snatched away from gatherings of whites and Indians and punished for being too familiar around Susan.

But Susan learned how to elude the no-nos that restricted her from seeing Isaac and arranged ways they could meet. Years of secretly corresponding brought plans of their elopement. It wasn't until she was twenty-three, with her mother's blessings, that she married into the arms of Isaac and ran off with him to Raymond, Mississippi. Isaac was a farmer at heart and sowed seed that brought a total of seven children.

In September of 1840, Isaac and Susan were blessed with their first child, a boy. They christened him Charles Henry Banks. Later came John, Will, then Joe. The next three children were girls, Lucy, Mary, and the last Anna. Charles Henry Banks was Mother's father.

The marriage of Susan and Isaac Banks occurred during the same time that a farmer named John Thomas was employed as a pullman chef on a train from Chicago to Memphis. John Thomas, while on one of his northern runs, had the fate of winning the appetite of Loretta, a rather well-to-do English woman visiting from Leeds, England. She could not pass up the magnificent taste of his dishes and sought to employ him as her own chef. Once she reached her daughter's home in Raymond, Mississippi, bringing the newly hired black chef, she not only decided to prolong her visit to the country but boldly declared her admiration for John Thomas as a person as well. She insisted her daughter place him permanently in their home as their cook. Loretta then celebrated his being with the family by suddenly taking him off for the entire weekend and returning that Sunday evening as his bride.

John Thomas and Loretta settled in Oklahoma and had a son bearing the name Boston. Loretta died of pneumonia when Boston was nine. John Thomas married a second time, to Mary Rafford, a German immigrant, and fathered a family of six. John Thomas was light skinned and it is prominent in the family memory that Loretta and Mary Rafford were Caucasian. Joanna was the first child of John Thomas and Mary Rafford, then came a boy named Missouri. Then born in 1867 was Lula, then Moses, Isaac, and last George. They were all born in Rentiesville, Oklahoma. Lula, their first child to be born in freedom, was the fairest of them all, which became advantageous to her later. Lula Thomas was my mother's mother.

Lula was courted by Charles Henry Banks and she became his bride even though she was twenty-seven years younger than he was. They lived together in Mississippi. Charles Henry was a heavy smoker, carrying his pipe almost everywhere he went, including the outhouse. He lived an out-of-door life and did very hard work. Charles and Lula reared a family of seven children, two boys and five girls. The firstborn was a girl named Mary, in 1893; then Martha Bell, on September 15, 1894; then Alice in 1897 and Ruth in 1898. The boys then got under way in 1903 with Kemuel; then another girl, Stella in 1905, and the last child was Edward in 1907. It was after the seventh child, Edward, that I was given my middle name.

Grandpa Charles Henry Banks worked up to the last six of his ninety-four years. In the spring of 1934 he left his pipe smoldering at his bedside, where he was found asleep forever.

Martha Bell Banks, the second oldest sister of the family, is my mother.

Uncle Tom (John Thomas Banks) invited Martha to St. Louis, Missouri, specifically to meet my father at a May Day gathering called Orphan's Home Day. When my parents met, Dad worked at a flour mill and had not long returned from a troop ship that was called back from the mid-Atlantic the day World War I ended. Dad was earning eighteen dollars a week and had a limited education but a tremendous moral outlook on life.

Mother had just graduated from college as a schoolteacher in her home state of Mississippi. The love bug bit 'em and after two years of courtship they had their wedding on May 14, 1919, in Antioch Baptist Church in St. Louis.

One year later in July, Thelma was born and named after Dad's sister. This put a legitimate end to Dad's suspicion that Mother contemplated helping out by activating her teaching career. We often thought that having a big family was Daddy's strategy to have Mother at home with their own children instead of out teaching someone else's. So nineteen months after Thelma, a boy child was spanked and christened Henry William Berry, Jr. He was a spitting image of Dad, egg-head and all. Henry Jr. was followed fourteen months later by the third child, Lucy Bell. Three years more and another sunshiny baby boy was born in the bedroom of the family's three-room brick cottage at 2520 Goode Avenue, a nicely kept area in the best of the three colored sections of St. Louis. There were more, but since I'm on the scene now the book has the rest. Enjoy it.

Wean Age

There were scattered clouds over mid-America and a mile-wide wind arrived from the north with the promise of another cold winter. In Missouri, it was taken for granted that the weather could be any way at anytime and thus was as hard to predict as the moment when a woman would go into labor. The most important lady in my life was lying in that condition, ready to give birth to a child for the fourth time. Her name was Martha and she was with her husband Henry who had summoned a doctor from his church membership to deliver the baby at home. Dr. Anderson Cheatem came and performed his duty under the eyes of the observing father.

At 6:59 A.M., October 18, 1926, at 2520 Goode Avenue, St. Louis, Missouri, U.S.A., I was born in the best year of my life. My mother tells me that before I was even dry, I had begun singing my first song; I started crying prior to the customary spank that brings one unto life. For the second show, at an age of five hours, I amazed my mother again by raising my body up with my arms. I tell you, I already wanted to look the world over. I was christened Charles Edward Anderson Berry.

Mother and Daddy were of the Baptist faith and sang in the Antioch Church choir. The choir rehearsed in our home around

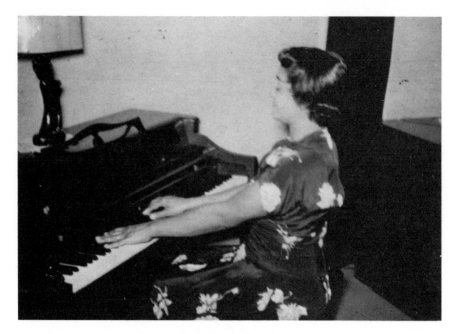

My mom, Martha Banks Berry.

the upright piano in the front room. My very first memories, while still in my baby crib, are of musical sounds—the assembled pure harmonies of the Baptist hymns, dominated by my mother's soprano and supported by my father's bass blending with the stirring rhythms of true Baptist soul. I was always trying to crawl out of my crib and into the front room to where the rhythm came from. Long before I learned to walk I was patting my foot to those Baptist beats, rocked by the rhythm of the deacons' feet focused on the tempo of the times. Oh! but the feeling it generated still stirs my memory of back when. Hallelujah!

Sometimes I wonder if that was the roots of my rockin' rhythm. More than once I later heard it said of black males: "Them boys are born with rhythm." Maybe it's true but I came to find out, so were white boys. I just didn't know then, as the two kinds of boys never had the occasion to harmonize. Up to then the whole world was "colored folk."

Our family lived a block and a half from our church and singing became a major tradition in the Berry family. As far back as I can remember, Mother's household chanting of those gospel tunes

My dad, Henry William Berry, Sr.

rang throughout my childhood. The members of the family, regard-less of what they were doing at the time, had a habit of joining in with another member who would start singing, following along harmonizing. Looking back I'm sure that my musical roots were planted in me, then and there.

Mother says that before learning to walk, I would frequently crawl straight toward the piano. The amazing huge black box that made many different sounds constantly bewildered me. At times somebody would leave it open and I would reach and find to my wonder a world of sound at the touch of my fingers. I can imagine the many infantile concerts I attempted at the piano only to be lifted up and carried away leaving an unfinished symphony. I would be placed back in the "icky" crib out of mischief, where only the sound of my mother's old washing-board carried the tempo of the hymn she'd be singing.

I actually believe I learned the majority of the first bunch of words in my vocabulary from listening to the lyrics of the songs that my mother would sing while doing housework. Whatever the chore, she'd unfailingly tackle it while belting out hymn after hymn. Sometimes she'd emphasize a passage in a song and the change in her volume and expression would frighten me. It was as if she'd suddenly discovered Jesus standing in the house enjoying the song.

I was also fascinated by a big wooden cabinet that also produced music. Thelma told me it was a Victrola, but we were not allowed to touch it. To me it was a box that talked and sang, making music by itself. I would sit on the floor and stare at it, trying to figure out how it worked.

After I'd become a little older, I got the chance I needed one day when Mother went shopping. I got a chair, climbed up, and by stretching was able to raise the top of the Victrola, look down into the turntable compartment, and study it. I'd seen Daddy place the needle of the horn to the edge of the record that was on the turntable. I did it and it played. Someone had left a fox trot on the turntable and when it sounded off, the jumpy rhythm floored me. I played it over and over until I heard a particular personal sneezing that signaled my mother returning. I hurriedly tried to put the Victrola back the way it was and thought I had. I'd managed to shut it down okay, but I'd forgotten to remove the chair I'd used to reach it. That afternoon I received my first whipping, which was known as a "whoopin'" then. She scolded me, "Be sure your sins will find you out," a verbal chastisement I heard for many years after, whenever I was caught in mischief. Mother pointed her finger, which I knew meant for me to get across the chair. "You're going to learn to keep your hands off things they have no business on." Whack . . . Ouch! Whack . . . Really ouch! Another whack and I swore it would never happen again in my life.

Times then were becoming very hard though Daddy still had the job working in a flour mill on North Broadway in Baden, Missouri. While we didn't have much money, we always seemed to be able to get by. Mother never worked out of the home, but fared extremely well in managing the money Daddy earned. She was a natural-born economist. Lights were turned off when you left the room even for a moment; it all counted in the kilowatts used. "Eat all that I put on your plate or I'll serve you less next meal," she preached. She hand sewed our clothes, washed, ironed, shopped, punished and praised us according to our need. We all pitched in with the house chores, doing what task each was capable of. We made up for whatever we lacked with the wealth of a good family relation and love that we all shared when not fighting.

During the weekdays Thelma, Henry, Lucy, and I would play in a little playhouse that Daddy had built for us. It was the size of what a garage for a motorcycle would be and was furnished with household pieces that he'd also made of wood scraps from the flour mill. All the kids in the neighborhood came to our backyard to play in our playhouse. It was built along the fence (which reminds me) near the walkway that led to the other "little house," a two-seater near the ash pit where we would sit near the alley.

I must have been born curious and often wondered about things that it seemed others took more or less for granted. While I was still not two years old I had begun to ask questions that often aroused my folks to wonder what I was thinking most of the time. One such question was why everybody went to the toilet (that's what we called the house that was "out") by themselves, yet somebody always took me when I needed to go. This particular wonder was satisfied when Thelma came running into the house one evening shouting that as she sat down on one of the two seats, she heard noise coming up through the other opening.

Daddy went to check it out and returned telling us that somehow a chicken, likely belonging to Mrs. Bonner, the next-door neighbor, had fallen into the hole and was making noises in its struggle to escape. No one to my remembering ever rescued the chicken but it was then that Thelma told me that she or Henry went with me there to avoid having to pull me out from where the chicken was. From then on I welcomed the precautious accompaniment.

It was different at night, when we used a porcelain bucket for such functions, out of sight in the kitchen closet offset. Even then, I remember being accompanied and held under my arms when I would have to use the container. Daddy later made me a form-fitted seat to use on the "slop jar," as we called it, after I once tried to solo and slid too far in. After they devacuumed me, I was cautious on the slop jar, but sought other things to get in to.

A brighter seat of my memories is based on pursuing my rubber ball. Once it happened to bounce under the kitchen table, and I was trying to retrieve it while it was still bouncing. Usually I was reprimanded for disturbing activities when there was company in the house, as there was then. But this time my manner of retrieving the ball created a big laugh from Mother's choir members. Stooping with full-bended knees, but with my back and head vertical, I fit under the tabletop while scooting forward reaching for the ball. This squatting manner was requested by members of the family many times thereafter for the entertainment of visitors and soon, from their appreciation and encouragement, I looked forward to the ritual.

An act was in the making. After it had been abandoned for years I happened to remember the maneuver while performing in New York for the first time and some journalist branded it the "duck walk."

From the beginning of my world, I was taken along to the Antioch Baptist Church where I was placed in the Cradle Roll Department to be a child of God. Every Sunday, without fail, the family (and I mean all four children and both parents) went to church. Daddy would leave before the rest of us because he was the superintendent of Sunday School, a position he held for thirty-six years. The rest of us, with Mother, would walk to Sunday School and stay over for church services.

Our three-room cottage was a (shall I say a hangout or) domicile or maybe a divine den is better, anyway, it was infested on Sunday afternoons with dining deacons that Mother would cook dinner for. Once dinner was called, a habitually l-o-n-g prayer ensued, then the deacons sat down to the table of steaming food and started in, each with a verse of the Scripture before a bite would ever ascend to a lip. Moreover, the deacons as they tarried discussed church affairs during the meal. All this had to pass before we children would get to the table for the remaining round of the dinner. I never thought this system was good economics.

One of the warmer sights of an early summer's night was the blaze from a roaring fire that engulfed the next-door neighbor's shed. It seemed everybody in the world came over to our house and stood around on the lawn to watch the flames. The red fire engines came ding-a-linging up Goode Avenue, stringing their hose toward the burning shed. I remember, as the firemen raced toward the bright blaze, their faces were lit up like lightbulbs. The firemen were the first white persons I had ever seen up close in my life. Not knowing them as Caucasian, I thought they were so frightened that their faces were whitened from fear of going near the big fire.

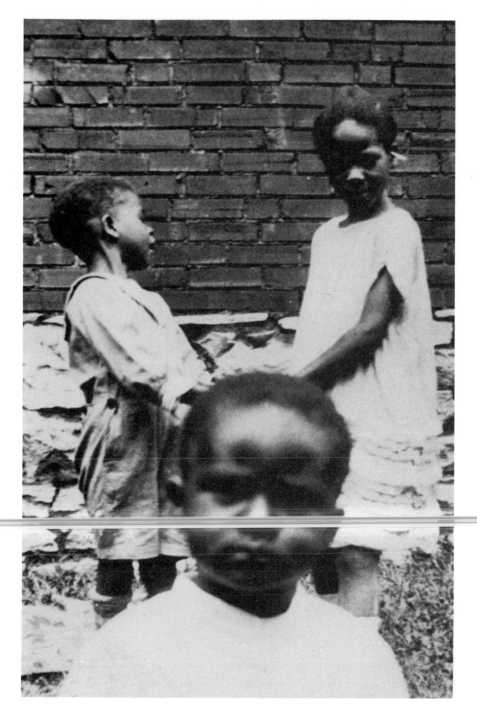

Me at age two, as I jumped into a photo
of my brother Henry and my sister Thelma.

When I questioned Daddy about them being scared to death and turning white, Daddy told me they were white people and their skin was always white that way, night or day. There were people in our church that were bright skinned but not that bright. I never forgot the whiteness of their faces, which was amplified by their expressions in the flickering glow of the flames. Naturally their faces reflected more greatly the changing surges of light from the fire. I assumed for a long while that all "white folks" (as Thelma and Henry called them) actually glowed like lightbulbs.

I was a healthy child other than during a period when I caught pneumonia and came nigh to the point of death. Had it not been for Mother's wit in sensing the condition early and choosing the proper care, it would have been hello and good-bye for me. Otherwise I grew up with the care from frequent visits to Barnes Hospital for checkups.

When trips to Barnes Hospital were inconvenient, Mother had their visiting nurse (who reminded me of the fearful firemen) come on a house call. This nurse had a lengthy pointed nose that seemed to dance as she spoke. She chastised me whenever I would mess with gadgets in her nurse bag. Mother supported her in paddling me when I was into any mischief and I grew to fear the white nurse lady in the navy-blue-and-white uniform.

I became determined to satisfy the nurse's instructions, and it wasn't long before the noticeable change in my mischievous nature brought a hug and kiss from the nurse. The feeling of her lips, the same lips that forgave me after once punishing, has yet to leave my memory. In fact there are things today that I realize are related to the sting that was embedded in my character then. There are times when, just talking to a female Caucasian, the jolt of that memory inhibits me from holding on to my train of thought. My mother's nurse had a profound effect on the state of my fantasies and settled into the nature of my libido. I'll tell you more later.

Around age three I got to where I felt big enough to go outdoors by myself, but Mother wouldn't let me. Thelma, Henry, and Lucy had started school so there was no one to watch me. I was kept in the house with Mother, listening to her sing. I also went out when Mother did; my rein was Mother's coattail and my destination was wherever she wore the coat. Whenever Mother crossed a street, if it was my left foot that last stepped off the curb then my right foot was next to touch down on the opposite curb in free-swinging flight.

Beg as I would, I wasn't allowed out. Mother would come back with her slogan, "Safety first, young man. A stitch in time saves nine, go and take a bath, you'll feel better." That bath became the path to wrath. I stayed so clean that whenever I did get out to play I wallowed in the dirt to bestow an equilibrium. We had two wash-tubs in the kitchen, one of which Mother washed clothes in and the other we used for bathing. I would help fill the pots and heat the water, then fill the tub and splash around in it, run in the front room and change into clothes Mother had laid out, and be back out in the dirt. Sometimes before an interval in her household chores could allow her to monitor the fraud, I would skip the bath and hit the dirt dirty. But Mother was a saver for sure and she soon caught my act by checking the soap. She issued out just enough of a piece of soap for one bathing to each of us from the nickel bar of OK-brand soap, and she could tell when mine hadn't been used.

Not long after the shed fire the Berry family moved across the street into the upstairs of a two-family brick duplex, also with three rooms, but with a major difference: this house had a full bath, inside the premises! We also had a great view of the neighborhood from the second floor. We were then on the same block as the Sumner High School. Cottage Avenue School was our elementary school, a collection of six frame portable buildings erected in the recreation yard of Sumner High. The six buildings each housed a grade of elementary schooling units, built to accommodate the overloaded classrooms of the black neighborhood children. The years of the twenties must have been rocking as well as roaring based on all the five-year-olds reeling in to register for schooling.

We could also see from our house the block that the great white city fathers had allotted as the colored neighborhood recreational grounds. It was known as Tandy Park, and designed to be at the disposal of the community as a playground. Including a tennis court and a three-foot-deep swimming pool, Tandy Park was equipped with a combination football and baseball field that was used by leagues that were unheard of beyond the neighborhood. Rumor was that the city fathers had created this to satisfy com-plaints and at the same time keep the colored people in places of

schoolwork that we did in the kindergarten class while Thelma, Henry, and Lucy were doing their homework, so the class was boring.

My second-grade teacher, Miss Richardson, never smiled, only puckered her mouth occasionally and blew out puffs of stern academic data that polluted the immature atmosphere there should have been in a second-grade classroom. I didn't know she would not enjoy too much monkey business even though I was one of her best students.

One day I cut out some letters of the alphabet, spelling *St. Louis,* and pasted them to my forehead. I placed each letter on backwards so it could be read forwards by the teacher. I marched up to her desk unrequested and stood wordless, presenting my essay to her. She rose without comment and led me by the ear directly to the principal's office. There I stood, only thinking that my achievement must be magnificent to warrant the gaze of the principal's eyes.

The principal, Miss Wells, who tipped the scale at 155 pounds and had a mustache and enormous breasts, decided that punishment was in order and personally prepared to administer six licks with a rattan. I was ordered to bend across the oak chair where she took aim and came down across my bottom with the first stroke and brought me to salvation. A whipping is a whipping, but a rattan is a round piece of soul-stirring, hair-raising, will-weakening wood. Even from my father, I had never known a lick to provoke my will to behave as much as that walloped by Miss Wells. And to make matters worse, my brother Henry saw Miss Richardson taking me there.

Honor thy parents and thy principal so thy lashings shall be limited while in learning under the laws thy leaders giveth thee. This was my prayer thereafter. I was two weeks at doing chores for Henry before he released me from the threat of telling Mother or Daddy what had happened. I floated through the second grade without incident thereafter.

Somewhere in between my whippings, the church members performed a stage play entitled *The Dream of Queen Esther* at the Amytis Theater, one of the three "colored theaters" in the city that we were able to go to. The entire family was present and seated in the second row center of the theater. My father, in cos-

was next to touch down on the opposite curb in free-swinging flight.

Beg as I would, I wasn't allowed out. Mother would come back with her slogan, "Safety first, young man. A stitch in time saves nine, go and take a bath, you'll feel better." That bath became the path to wrath. I stayed so clean that whenever I did get out to play I wallowed in the dirt to bestow an equilibrium. We had two wash-tubs in the kitchen, one of which Mother washed clothes in and the other we used for bathing. I would help fill the pots and heat the water, then fill the tub and splash around in it, run in the front room and change into clothes Mother had laid out, and be back out in the dirt. Sometimes before an interval in her household chores could allow her to monitor the fraud, I would skip the bath and hit the dirt dirty. But Mother was a saver for sure and she soon caught my act by checking the soap. She issued out just enough of a piece of soap for one bathing to each of us from the nickel bar of OK-brand soap, and she could tell when mine hadn't been used.

Not long after the shed fire the Berry family moved across the street into the upstairs of a two-family brick duplex, also with three rooms, but with a major difference: this house had a full bath, inside the premises! We also had a great view of the neighborhood from the second floor. We were then on the same block as the Sumner High School. Cottage Avenue School was our elementary school, a collection of six frame portable buildings erected in the recreation yard of Sumner High. The six buildings each housed a grade of elementary schooling units, built to accommodate the overloaded classrooms of the black neighborhood children. The years of the twenties must have been rocking as well as roaring based on all the five-year-olds reeling in to register for schooling.

We could also see from our house the block that the great white city fathers had allotted as the colored neighborhood recreational grounds. It was known as Tandy Park, and designed to be at the disposal of the community as a playground. Including a tennis court and a three-foot-deep swimming pool, Tandy Park was equipped with a combination football and baseball field that was used by leagues that were unheard of beyond the neighborhood. Rumor was that the city fathers had created this to satisfy complaints and at the same time keep the colored people in places of their own in their own neighborhood. Nevertheless, we had Tandy Park and also a nice backyard behind the duplex that I could play in.

We had been living in the house for less than a month when one afternoon two big men leaped from the alley, over our ash pit, and crouched in the landing of our cellar doorway. I froze and watched them take out a huge wad of dollars. Suddenly, they leaped out and ran away, jumping back over the pit and down the alley. I ran to the cellar entrance to see if they had left anything behind. Minutes later two policemen came through the back gate and asked me where my mother was. I called her and listened as the policemen told her of the robbery of an insurance man that had taken place just around the corner. I volunteered that I'd seen the men and that they ran that way. That announcement resulted in me being kept upstairs and indoors for all of three days, not to mention the six licks I got that evening to remind me to "attend to my own business." Again a lesson.

Mother thought much of the new house and her new four-legged Quaker gas stove and the 1929 console Philco radio that kept the home filled with music and voices. I was fascinated by the radio with its illuminated orange station dial that brilliantly dominated the room while we listened in the dark. With a twist of the wrist I saw how Mother could switch from city to city and song to song with one knob. I was allowed to change stations but it took more than a couple of strappings to get me to realize that I shalt not enter into the back of the radio to try and find where the sound was coming from. Daddy and Mother both explained to me how the voices and music were coming from the radio station "through the air," but that was not enough. I looked with sincerity and found nothing in the air coming into the radio. I hadn't disbelieved them but figured they were giving me a brief consolation answer. It wasn't the sound of Kate Smith singing or Amos and Andy talking that titillated my curiosity so much as how that dial that shone like a beacon of magic brought them into the radio. I paid time after time for monkeying with the back of that radio. I was sure that within it I would discover a world of goodies. My behind so deciding was most overriding and soon put asunder my feeling of wonder.

After a while, Mother finally let me solo in the sandboxes across Cottage Avenue in Tandy Park as it was so near our home. She could see me from the kitchen window as I played on the high bars, swings, and the three seesaws. The three-foot-deep empty kiddy swimming pool, the whole playground, and the baseball diamond were mine alone while school was in session.

The swings were a challenge. I had seen the bigger boys pull themselves up to the top of the slanted poles that braced them and I was determined to ready myself to compete with the older boys. Over and over I tried to reach the top but never made it. One particular time when I was nearly to the top, I was bestowed with a stimulation in my loins that surprised but pleased me. Though I had been confident of reaching the summit of the slanted round pole, I became more stimulated with each boost of my body. Totally exhausted I stopped and held fast to the pole, too close to the top to retreat and start over again. When I resumed my effort an extremely intense, pleasant sensation surged through the midst of my body. The feeling was so effective that I lost altitude and slid down in ecstasy the short while it lived and found myself almost at the ground as it simmered away. I was too weak to make another attempt and gathered my little sand shovel and started across Cottage Avenue home to rest.

I told Daddy the whole experience but his explanation that it was only fatigue was in no way convincing. My curiosity demanded I try climbing the swing poles to find the source of such a pleasant experience. Thereafter, every play time I had I went there to try for the summit. I'd climb and climb and climb but it seemed that until I became tired, the feeling would not approach. No matter how many times I'd try to induce that feeling I'd obtained the first time it wouldn't return even after I mastered reaching the summit.

When Mother took me to enroll in Cottage Avenue School, I was a month short of being fully five years old because my birthday was in October, and the faculty wouldn't let me register. Somebody did some talking and in three days I was in class. I entered kindergarten very enthused to discover the new world of school. My very first teacher was Miss Bosquick. She was tall, very masterly, and had a slight mustache. I had already been doing the schoolwork that we did in the kindergarten class while Thelma, Henry, and Lucy were doing their homework, so the class was boring.

My second-grade teacher, Miss Richardson, never smiled, only puckered her mouth occasionally and blew out puffs of stern academic data that polluted the immature atmosphere there should have been in a second-grade classroom. I didn't know she would not enjoy too much monkey business even though I was one of her best students.

One day I cut out some letters of the alphabet, spelling *St. Louis,* and pasted them to my forehead. I placed each letter on backwards so it could be read forwards by the teacher. I marched up to her desk unrequested and stood wordless, presenting my essay to her. She rose without comment and led me by the ear directly to the principal's office. There I stood, only thinking that my achievement must be magnificent to warrant the gaze of the principal's eyes.

The principal, Miss Wells, who tipped the scale at 155 pounds and had a mustache and enormous breasts, decided that punishment was in order and personally prepared to administer six licks with a rattan. I was ordered to bend across the oak chair where she took aim and came down across my bottom with the first stroke and brought me to salvation. A whipping is a whipping, but a rattan is a round piece of soul-stirring, hair-raising, will-weakening wood. Even from my father, I had never known a lick to provoke my will to behave as much as that walloped by Miss Wells. And to make matters worse, my brother Henry saw Miss Richardson taking me there.

Honor thy parents and thy principal so thy lashings shall be limited while in learning under the laws thy leaders giveth thee. This was my prayer thereafter. I was two weeks at doing chores for Henry before he released me from the threat of telling Mother or Daddy what had happened. I floated through the second grade without incident thereafter.

Somewhere in between my whippings, the church members performed a stage play entitled *The Dream of Queen Esther* at the Amytis Theater, one of the three "colored theaters" in the city that we were able to go to. The entire family was present and seated in the second row center of the theater. My father, in costume and makeup, playing the role of Mordecai, made his first entry about midway through the play. I didn't recognize him strutting across the stage until he spoke his line, shouting: "Oh, Sire! Sire! Someone's approaching the castle!" Immediately, I stood straight up and shouted back, "There's Daddy! There's Daddy!" Mother yanked me back down in the seat (Mother is strong) and rendered me a dandy fanny chastisement.

What really became burned in was not behind me but what lay ahead through the inspiration I acquired from my dad's and my big sister Thelma's way of dramatizing things. The ability to construct a statement, manipulate a situation, or just do a job as well as they did it became my ambition. All the poems that Daddy used to recite to us after dinner settled in my bank of memories and encouraged me to create my own rhymes and ditties.

Late in the second grade our family moved again. Daddy found a five-room brick bungalow with full bath, full basement, central heating, and a front and backyard just two blocks away at 4420 Cottage Avenue. We thought it was a palace to have closets and front and back porches. The rent was twenty-five dollars a month. Mother dug in her savings and added new pieces of furniture that included a new Whirlpool washing machine and a pedal Singer sewing machine that (to my delight) I was invited to pedal while Mother sewed. Daddy had some white people install a telephone which brought a million questions from me about its function. There was too much to learn and nobody had enough time to explain these things to me.

My sixth birthday party took place on our back porch while choir rehearsal was being held within the house. Afterward, I overheard the adults saying the Berrys would soon have a baby child. I wondered who would bring him and asked where he would come from but nobody gave me answers. It was such things as where the newcomer would sleep that bothered me because there was no room left. My father's cousin Harry had separated from his wife and moved in with our family, causing us to have a full house. Cousin Harry moved in to the actual bedroom and Mother and Dad took the larger dining room for their bedroom. Thelma, Lucy, and I had a room with one full-size bed for the three of us and Henry had a partitioned-off room in the basement where he and Cousin Harry's son, Harry Jr., slept. Harry Jr. was ten, closer to

Henry's age but closer to my class in school.

Thelma was thirteen then and Lucy eleven, both much larger than I. I slept at the foot of the bed while Thelma and Lucy slept at the head. When the two were quarreling, Thelma would sleep at the foot where I would snuggle close to her backside as I'd done as a tot. It felt secure to be close and also much warmer being next to somebody when the room was chilly in the cold seasons. A warmth of pleasure similar to the playground-swing feeling would sometimes arise within me when snuggling as the embers faded each night in the furnace.

The games that Thelma and Lucy introduced to me included one I particularly failed to win that they called "Stinky Feets in Faces." The game was merely putting your feet near the other's face as the other tried to reciprocate the feat. Being shorter than they I soon realized my legs lacked the length to ever have victory. I smelled no future in the game, losing by two feet each time, and it became their manner of punishment when I was not at my best behavior in their view.

That same Philco console radio that lured me into chastisement so many times was bringing "The Shadow Knows," Flash Gordon, Fats Waller, Bing Crosby, and Louis Armstrong right into the living room. But until the kitchen had been cleaned from supper, the table cleared of homework, Barney our police dog fed, and the wood and coal in and the ashes out, we were not allowed to turn the Philco on.

We took turns sharing the punishment if Mother caught us listening without permission. The beautiful harmony of the country music that KMOK radio station played was almost irresistible. Kitty Wells, Gene Autry, and Kate Smith singing love songs were popular then, along with the piano playing of Fats Waller and old World War I songs like "My Buddy" and "Fraulein," which I suppose will never leave my memory.

The only time the Philco was at rock 'n' roll volume was during the glorious gospel singing early Sunday morning. It was customary for singing choirs like Wings Over Jordan to be heard, with Mother above the volume of the radio and Daddy joining in harmony. The Victrola with its Bluebird fox trots and waltzes was fast losing its attraction as I was beginning to hear alluring boogie-woogie sounds on the radio.

Sadness fell upon the family for the first time in my life when my mother was crying over the death of her mother, Lula. Mammaw was sixty-six and well as a spring chicken when she died suddenly. When they took me to the wake and walked me by the casket, the image of her powdered face coupled with the change from the embalming, I guess, frightened me to no end. They pulled me away from staring at her and seated me never to forget the look of Mammaw's face. I have tried to look upon no one deceased since. I don't advocate sorrow, I pursue happiness in all avenues of life, and so I shall avoid all funerals, even my own.

My new baby brother Paul Lawrence Dunbar Berry arrived December 18, 1933, christened after the most loved poet in our family. The newcomer brought a special excitement to 4420 Cottage and a noticeable change in the position enjoyed in the household. Mother had to keep me out of school for a week to help her recover. At seven years old, I learned to fry eggs, make toast, fix oatmeal, and prepare baby bottles of milk. I ran errands and such, helping ease the load while she convalesced.

While Mother was asleep one day, I looked in her big doctor book and saw photographs of the male and female anatomy depicted in detail. I spent hours, every opportunity I found, studying that book. It was my first discovery of where and how a baby was created and born. Although I couldn't begin to read the technical terms in the text, it gave me my first knowledge of the differences of man and woman. I had never seen, though I'd sincerely tried, the always hidden part of a female, even in a picture. I had no idea there was an absence of what I had, yet I had tried many times to peek and see the difference. Then I realized I'd never heard a girl speak of having "one."

My curiosity, coupled with my imagination, got me in trouble constantly but made school a special place for me. I was intrigued about places learned about in geography and often daydreamed about how the rest of the world beyond Missouri was making out. I dreamed of far-off places like Kansas and Illinois, never with the least thought that I would ever see them.

My fourth-grade teacher, Miss Walker, was nicknamed by the pupils "Shorty Bo-Bo" because she totaled in heels only five feet one inch. Miss Walker was very stern and if challenged with misbehaving, even mild chatter, would warn us that if we didn't stop the talking she would cut off our tongues and let them slip back down our throats. The look of her face gave proof she would. I tried to imagine what my tongue would feel like slipping down my throat and decided to obey her rather than risk learning it. When provoked, she would threaten to sit on our head if we were caught a second time. Analyzing that was worse than having the tongue cut because Miss Walker had an enormous bottom that shifted when she stepped and rolled when she walked. Her threats were taken seriously by all not wanting to fall victim beneath her huge bottom, breathless. I was one of her better students, doing well in arithmetic, world geography, and general science. In her class I learned much, helped a lot, stirred little, and talked the least.

During fourth grade, the family moved several blocks across the neighborhood to a larger duplex on Labadie Street my father was purchasing. The building had four rooms with bath and basement, and a second floor with the same number of rooms, which could be rented out. I immediately asked for a space in the basement to fix a place of my own like Henry had when he was ten.

One evening I came through the gangway of home and heard water running in the bathroom on the second floor next door. The light from the window was casting down on the roof of our porch. Temptation told me I might finally see a girl's parts so I hurried to the roof and creeped toward the open window to redeem my dream. There, through six inches of the raised shade, I saw, for the first time in my life, the bare buttocks of a woman about to step into the bathtub. I froze, instantly excited, and crouched stunned and amazed at my long-awaited view of the opposite sex. She even turned around momentarily and allowed a direct view of her front part as she came over to pull the shade down.

The shade was pulled too far and detached itself from the roller at the top and tumbled down. The falling shade exposed me stooped on our roof in full view, five feet away, caught dead center by the bathroom light. Face to face, the woman let out a scream that petrified me. It lasted through the flight of my jump from the roof to our backyard where my brother stood looking up at where I'd come from. He knew what had happened and the seriousness of it and helped me into the basement of our house. In less than five minutes I was summoned upstairs, given a sincere lecture on the shame of my actions, and taken to the basement and punished.

The Berry bush on the steps of
the Labadie Street home, 1956.

This one I remember well, as well as it was administered.

Dad worked sometimes for Drozda Realty Company, run by a German family who owned and managed multiple-unit apartment buildings throughout St. Louis. He started out working on menial jobs, cleaning vacant realty properties that were foreclosed and readied for resale. As trust in him grew, he began fixing screens, fences, and porches and doing concrete patching until they gave him jobs in the interior of homes, repairing kitchen cabinets and windows, hanging sinks and closet doors, and so on.

This helped tremendously in that time when work was still scarce, especially for a black man. The pay was nowhere near that of what even a nonunion white carpenter was earning per hour, but Dad took as much work as he could to compensate for the lack in dollars. Not knowing of union wages and with the cost of living constantly rising, Dad worked for seventy-five cents an hour for years before either of the Drozda brothers favored him with a dollar per hour. They refused his plea for a raise, declaring that his chances of such opportunities elsewhere were nil. They would remind him that he was not in the union, which then, by every union charter, a black man could not join.

Dad worked for them from 1935 through 1964, when he was about to slide into his seventieth birthday. After all the verbal compliments from the Drozdas through the years, when Dad retired, they gave him a necktie. Guess what color? No, white.

I always begged Daddy to take me along with him on his jobs. Once I went along to help him repair shower stalls at a country club in Glen Crest, Missouri, and I wandered around. This place to me was beautiful, like the Garden of Eden. All the people there were white, but stolen away in couples, busy at their happy games. Couples were smooching here and there in secluded spots away from the path. Some were far beyond hugging and kissing. I wandered to the slope leading to the little creek running through the country-club grounds and discovered I wasn't alone. There was a white man sprawled on a blanket beside a lady, who was not resisting the presence of his hand beneath her dress. They heard the crunching sound of me approaching and looked up to discover me (at age ten) standing there stiff as a board. The man laughed and invited me to come forward.

I was afraid but dared not disobey for fear of being in trouble for even being there. I was looking where the lady had failed to cover herself when he asked me who I was. I told him who, where my daddy was, and what we were doing at the country club. Then the lady asked me my age, whispered something to the man, then told me to come over to them. She told me I was off limits and had violated the law, that if I wanted to avoid being arrested, I was to do as I was told or go to jail for trespassing. I didn't quite understand "trespassing" but *violated, law, arrested,* and *jail* were all known to me as extremely grave circumstances. I stood silent in tears as she again whispered something to the man then told me to bend down and hold her feet in my hand and rub them. I was surprised she allowed me to do that, in fact I was not hesitant to respond in lieu of her threat of jail.

At my anxiousness the lady spoke firmly, repeating the threat, and I came before her and rubbed her feet as the two of them began chattering in undertones. I overheard the lady say that I was a "good one" and I thought I was about to be released to go back to where my dad was. I remember the lady laughing as the man watched her in awe. I was shaking like a leaf on a tree when she insisted sternly that I kiss her feet before she let me go. They were

Me, age eleven,
in my basement photo darkroom.

smiling, seemingly satisfied, when they ran me off with a further threat of arrest if I told my father where I'd been.

When I returned, Daddy was rounding up for the day yet never questioned me about where I'd been for nearly an hour. We gathered the tools and left. All the way home I saw the lady's face before my thoughts, a face that I have been curiously apprehensive of seeing again.

Things were pretty bad for us during the Depression. Daddy was only working three days a week at the mill, and jobs were failing everywhere. The wood Daddy brought home from the mill that he used to make things out of now had to be used in the coal heater for fuel. The little piles of coal Mother bought were handled like groceries. All of our clothes were made at home after Mother got her sewing machine. After school in the evenings at home I would hear Daddy discussing President Roosevelt and the world adult affairs.

Dad heard of a used GMC truck for sale, which he could pick up for thirty dollars from the U.S. Mail Depot. He was contemplating going into business for himself, selling vegetables on a route that would include the houses of the Antioch Baptist Church members. There was a big announcement in church that week, and the show was on the road. By the end of the first month Daddy was able to return the ten dollars he'd borrowed from Cousin Harry to help buy the truck.

Once the huckster business was set up we all pitched in to help Daddy on the truck. Allowances for spending change were not invented yet; we had to help out on the vegetable route and the money we made went for our clothes and personal supplies. The vegetable route for me was fun. At 6 A.M. we would begin by picking up bushels of produce at the farmers' market. By the late morning we'd be back in the neighborhood driving through the streets selling from door to door shouting the familiar cry of the street merchant. I loved to open my mouth wide, pitch my head into the air, and sing out, "Apples, tomatoes, potatoes . . ." Whatever came to mind, we sang it.

Most of all, I wanted to drive that big truck, even though I was only able to hold on to the steering wheel while sitting in Dad's lap as he actually drove. My legs were still too short to operate the clutch, though I knew how. I knew for sure though that someday I wanted to have my own truck, or maybe a car, that I could drive and travel in. If only I could reach the clutch! "Our Father, Who art in traveling, hallowed drive Thy car, to kingdom come, on earth, if I can't in heaven." Such was my motivating prayer throughout my wean-age years.

Teen Age

I was at home in the living room of 4319 Labadie, at 6:58 in the morning on October 18, 1938. Alone and quiet before the fireplace, I knelt to pray. I had been taught that all my sins up to then were to be washed away in that prayer and the remaining days of my life would be my responsibility to bear. In one minute, according to the Baptist training I'd had, when I turned twelve, I would be sure my sins would not only "find me out," but also I would be held accountable for them on the Great Judgment Day.

What puzzled me most was how so many people in all the world could be monitored for that Judgment Day when it took a week or more for the teachers to get a couple hundred children sorted for just a semester of classes. The Lord Himself could do all things, I was told, but it had me thinking. Were there any really true plumb liners? I hadn't known of any in our house—even Mother and Daddy claimed they were not without sin—and there were definitely few in our neighborhood that I could observe myself who (except those having one foot already in the grave) were living without sinning.

I also wondered if I was the only black plumb liner, would the white plumb liners there in heaven accept me as a fellow-liner or would there still be back-seat busliners there too? Nobody ever talked about it around home or school or even church, only that all God's children would be there in love.

I remained kneeling a few minutes to receive some kind of answer to my prayer as this one was most important, but like times before, nothing happened.

Later that day I was working with my father and I had a pair of step stringers to hand saw out to repair a second-floor porch. Every downstroke of the hand saw sounded like shrieks from fallen sinners as they looked up from hell seeing me tumbling toward them.

My determination to avoid that hell-bound trip snowballed by the hour. The step tread and risers were sawed perfectly without a sinful stroke. I avoided the routine chitchat on the job that my brother and I had been in a habit of carrying on. I could observe sin after sin being committed all day long by Daddy and Henry, in my determination to avoid sinning myself.

That evening was boring, sitting on the front porch after work, watching more sin happening up and down the street. I had never dreamed sin was so popular until I chose the path of righteousness.

The very next day, October 19, I sinned twice. I wasn't strong enough to go holy cold turkey. Now what?!? According to my understanding and the lack of response to my prayers, it would be Judgment Day before I knew which trip I'd be taking. That night I prayed anyway. It seemed to me that day was the longest day of my life.

I sinned again and then again. Still I prayed forgiveness each time without realizing whether forgiveness was or wasn't granted. As my sins grew in number I began to postpone the separate prayers for each and accumulated them for the weekend in Sunday School. I was yet to receive an answer to a prayer. One thing that I did realize from praying was that consciousness cultivates caution.

My twelfth was my most Christian and most boring year of my life. Try as I did day after day to cling to righteousness, I was washed around in suds of sinful surroundings.

No matter how holy I tried to be, I was still a robust five-foot-eleven virgin buck whose curiosity was leaping beyond the birds and bees into the animal world of my manhood. I was not only beginning to wonder about the sexual "no-nos" that I had been cautioned against, but was searching for yes. Relief from the temperatures that grew when I came near a warm-hearted girl did not come from holding hands or kissing. I sought more. I would unconsciously dream up relief without any control and sometimes without memory of it save the evidence the next morning. I was still afraid of sinful activities regarding girls but still dearly wanted a girlfriend. But as bad as I wanted one, I had blockage that inhibited my longing. It was a shyness and an inability to talk to girls unless they would take the lead in the conversation as had the nurse, Miss Walker, and the woman on the creek bank.

Using methods of approach that I saw other guys have success with always failed, and the blockage did not diminish. The longer I was unsuccessful the stronger my desire became for what I was craving. It seemed other fellows (the sinful ones, especially) could start and hold a conversation so easily. Some were so bold. They'd right out ask a girl to kiss them or go out steady. Some had the guts to ask a girl to go "all the way"! I knew that was sin. I presumed they must have also known, but they "did it" anyway.

When I tried with girls who were said to have "gave up" it was pitiful how they would run my pleas around in circles, leading my lure into laughter, leaving my lust to lack. I thought I was nicer than many who were scoring relationships yet the same girls would go with those types of guys rather than me. I was doomed to be a loner with a reputation of "being nice," and in my heart I was rapidly becoming a gentle satyr.

Throughout my early teen years I was around a relative who was a photographer. This fellow was Harry Davis, a high school student at the time who was highly endowed with a talent for science along with a sincere love for photography. He became interested in my sister, Lucy, and although it never developed into matrimony, Harry favored the family with hundreds of photos in his effort to only photograph Lucy. Lucy was young and doing so well in school that her popularity brought his courtship to the verge of worship.

Harry fused the rocket that launched my journey on the road to a love of science and photography, which has cost me over three quarters of a million dollars in electronic equipment, from my pencil-crystal radio set up to my twenty-four-track recording

Me with my high-school camera club. I'm the one
stealing a picture of the photographer.

studio, and from a Brownie box Kodak to the three-quarter-inch video-mixing editor set I now possess. He availed me of his photographic studio and science books. He was instrumental in my learning to trust in only proven facts and not to base decisions on foolish or even fictitious findings. I learned in his darkroom how to take, develop, print, and enlarge photos.

I became so interested in the scientific discoveries of man and the processing of photographs that the desire for a girlfriend became secondary. However, my fantasies were rekindled by the many pinups that came through Harry's customers for developing. To see a picture fade into view beneath the dark red light, especially of a nude, was amazing. This never ceased to be a pleasant view to behold.

Every Sunday after Sunday School I would make straight to Harry's darkroom, in the attic of his home, to watch him develop his week's collection of film from his customers. When he'd be busy with work other than photography, I'd pull a book down from his shelves and read about the mechanics of rockets, the dimensions of space or about hypnotics, chemistry, you name it, all the things that intrigued me. Since I remembered much that I'd read, my teachers marveled at my advanced knowledge in math and science and couldn't understand why I appeared totally ignorant in history, civics, and such.

I looked upon Harry as a professor, and his attic studio as school. Finally Harry suggested I get a box Brownie Kodak, with which I began taking pictures of my own. I set up my own darkroom down in a corner of our basement and began processing my own pictures.

Around this time Lucy took seriously to singing and her voice was said to be comparable to Marian Anderson's. The rest of us had started sneaking in records of blues singers like St. Louis Jimmy doing his "Going Down Slow," "Worried Life Blues" by Big Maceo, "In the Dark" by Lil Green, "C.C. Rider" by Bea Boo, "Please Mr. Johnson" by Buddy and Ella Johnson, "A Tisket a Tasket" by Ella Fitzgerald, and you name it. But Lucy stuck with stuff like "Ave Maria" and "God Bless America."

Lucy, becoming more and more sophisticated in music at school and home, was constantly gaining recognition for her singing accomplishments. Playing and singing her classical songs consequently gave her priority above any of us to play the piano at home. Mother, Thelma, Lucy, and I were allowed to use the piano whenever available during the "piano-playing hour" set aside at our home. Lucy would invariably sit there playing and singing her hi-fi classics forever, even when her throat was sore, which greatly limited my growing enthusiasm for picking out my favorite boogie-woogie numbers. I got so mad at her one day that I broke wind in one of Mother's old fruit jars, put my hand over it, came back, and set it out on the piano in front of her to pollute her playing. I got possession of the piano immediately but soon after paid a dear price for the prank.

When I began to listen to boogie woogie and swing my desire to hear anything without a beat diminished. I became a fan of Tampa Red, Big Maceo, Lonnie Johnson, Arthur Crudup, Muddy Waters, Lil Green, Bea Boo, Rosetta Thorp, and later Louis Jordan, T-Bone Walker, Buddy Johnson, Nat Cole, and Charles Brown, all of whom were black artists whose songs were only played by the black radio station in East St. Louis. Whenever Thelma,

Henry, and Lucy bought any records they favored Duke Ellington, Count Basie, and Tommy Dorsey, whose recording "Tommy Dorsey's Boogie Woogie" was the tune that launched my determination to produce such music. The music of Harry James, Glenn Miller, and a lot of the white bands were beginning to "get down" then and show up on the jukeboxes and black radio programs.

Henry was dating a high-school classmate, Gladys Whitehead, who encouraged him and me to join a spiritual singing group she was a member of. After we joined the Jubilee Ensembles, Henry persuaded Lucy to join also. Even though Henry was four years older than I, his invitation to sing with the Ensembles brought us closer together. I came quickly to be the leading male support in the bass section of the choir and soon was singing solos at the different churches that we had programs at. The best of my solos with the Ensembles was, ironically, "Tempted and Tried."

Now in the eighth grade I was lured from the leadings of righteous hymns to the lusting of Randell's hems. The shapely Miss Randell, my teacher, had my learning leaning toward her lusciousness more than her lessons. I was running a close second to being a first-class failure because I couldn't resist peering at the views she revealed when seated at the head of the class. Consequently the girl seated in front of me complained to the teacher when my knees rubbed her bottom. Once Miss Randell detained me in the classroom during the noon hour for annoying the girl and declared I should assist her with the chore of putting textbooks in the case. I was handing them in stacks of six, through and under her arm, while she, standing on a chair, accepted them. The back of my hands would brush against her breast, which she tolerated until my condition triggered a reason for her to smile and excuse me for lunch.

Some two decades later, during the apex of my career, I visited her classroom. After introducing me to her pupils, she beckoned me into the hall and anointed me with a casual kiss on the cheek. Feeling she must have remembered the "excuse," it did not fail to bring memories of school days.

Across the street from Simmons Grade School a sandwich shop had opened. Every noon hour it was jammed with seventh- and eighth-graders of the "in" crowd, who would lunch quickly and then dance unsupervised to the jukebox. Just a dozen nickels

Simmons Grade School Graduation, 1939.
I'm in the top row, fourth from the left,
far from sexy Ms. Randell, who's at the extreme upper right.

dropped in the slot would produce thirty minutes or more of Count Basie's "One O'Clock Jump," Glenn Miller's "In the Mood," Tommy Dorsey's "Boogie Woogie," or a good blues by Muddy Waters. This also allowed a chance to get closer to the girls and dance. Dancing was the most direct avenue I had to get next to a girl to befriend steadily. Still, even when I danced, I was slow with shyness when it was in the vein of trying to suck face.

It seemed that the only way I could ever get a serious conversation going with a girl was when I was telling jokes. But following the climax of my joke, I found that the girl took me as a joke as well. They developed a nickname for me—"Ol' Crazy Chaws Berry," as they pronounced it.

As graduation from Simmons Grade School approached, I purchased my first tailor-made pair of "drape" pants, in fact, my first tailored anything. Drapes were the style and the wider they were at the knee, the sharper you were styled. Henry was wearing thirty-two-inch knees with ten-inch cuffs. Mine were twenty-eight inches with twelve-inch cuffs, just two inches short of being a zoot suit and costing twelve dollars instead of eight. The style was an economical issue; the more you ordered in the knee width the more they cost. My graduation clothes stayed in the "will-call" until three days before graduation.

The morning that the graduation photo was being shot, I arrived at school just in time to make the lineup and forgot to brush my "stick-ups" (bangs) down. You can't win 'em all.

I worked hard with my dad during the long hot summer before entering high school. My skate-truck days were over and my ambition was bent on getting a bicycle. The only manner I had of owning a bicycle was getting parts piece by piece and assembling them. It took three and a half weeks of dollars and dealing before I had it completed to ride. With the bike I ventured to parts of the city unknown to me, expanding my scope of what life was in other neighborhoods. I began to wiggle from under what few remaining restrictions Mother and Daddy had at our home.

Still, my greatest fortune in my teen years developed through observing the qualities of my parents. Such things as my mother's economic ingenuity; managing with what little she had, to do as much as she did. Things said by my father, such as, "Take what you have and make what you want." "What a man believes; thus is it so." He also introduced me to, "Young men dream dreams while old men see visions."

Little Paul was standing in the truck once, peering out the windshield while Daddy was driving on the highway, and told Daddy it appeared to him that the truck was mashing down the hills and raising up the lowlands. Dad asked him to explain what he meant, and I, realizing the illusion, began answering for him. Dad stopped me with words never forgotten: "We may know what Paul means but only his explanation will confirm if *he* does." So Dad did know, I realized, and was seeking the extent of Paul's imagination. I thought that through such strategy Daddy showed more smarts than many persons with degrees.

Paul monopolized the cuddling of the parents until Mother gave birth to Martha Luvenia, making a family of six children, which it remained. The first thing I noticed about the new baby was that she was lighter skinned than Lucy, who had been the brightest in the family. What all this color ratio really meant was nothing, but we kids seemed to harp on it. I was beginning to think of people in the form of poetry: "If you're white, you're all right. If you're

CHUCK

yellow, you're fair fellow. If you're red, you're low bred. If you're brown, don't come 'round, and if you're black just stay back.''

A tall, handsome, popular football player had married Thelma and they had a son soon after Martha was born and we all tried to digest two-year-old Martha being the aunt of Thomas Allen Rooks.

I'd been following Dad around since I had been eight years old and finally he began training Henry and me at working for a salary. The Drozda Realty Company benefited from loading Dad with repair-work contracting jobs far under regular cost. Occasionally Dad would have a conflict with union carpenters, but once they talked to him and found he was a religious man and, what's more, humble while being questioned, there was never any trouble. Dad had a way of showing he was "in his place" and not a trouble-maker.

It was always in the white neighborhoods that the realty company would contract Dad to work. We painted kitchens, fixed windows, and did whatever needed doing in apartments. During the day, the women of the houses would usually be alone or with only a kid or two to take care of. Dad always checked out the resident as Henry and I gathered the tools for the job.

When we worked at a household with a lone female at home, he would always caution us to be careful and to avoid looking at her or even making glances that could be construed as "advances" or "insulting" to the "white lady," as Dad always put it. I was curious as to why he showed such concern only around the white women and not when we were working in the "colored" homes. Why were the coloreds "women" and the white "ladies," any-way? When I asked him, Dad said there was no actual reason for the difference in statement, it was only the custom of habit acquired from frequent conversations held with so many white men.

I remember once we arrived at a job at eight o'clock prompt to replace some broken windowpanes. I was just behind when Daddy knocked at the kitchen door and the door opened wide. From behind Daddy I saw the white lady turn, inviting us in, clad only in a bra and brief panties. I remember Dad standing still as the lady walked back through the house, repeating herself louder and beckoning for us to follow, informing Dad that the realty company had phoned to say he was coming. Daddy was blocking my view and grunting undertones of skepticism as he hesitatingly followed almost a mile behind the lady. It was the first time I'd ever seen a white female in scanty attire. The lady's garments were so thin, I saw the outline of her body nearly as plain as if she were nude (a sight I still enjoy).

Thereafter, each time the woman passed the room I looked. Dad noticed my efforts to get a better view and quelled my ambition with a lecture on the danger. Only when she first directed us to the repairs did Dad ever look upon her person. She finally dressed, bade farewell, and went off to work, leaving me frustrated for weeks, thinking of what she may have thought of the effect she had on us (especially me).

Henry and I soon discovered that some of the housewives on jobs where we worked weren't nearly as careful in dress as they appeared in public, nor were they nearly as dignified or snobbish and cold to a black person when alone as they were when their male companions were around. Henry and I developed little codes for alerting each other to someone approaching or to a good view. We would signify an observer or Dad coming by calling out the number "twenty" and a good view from beneath a high porch or a window as "fourteen." Of course we always had our tape measures in hand at the time we used the signals. With the code, we could do our work and at the same time check out the eyeball action.

After several years of working with Dad coupled with the expansion of my findings in other neighborhoods on my bike, I told Daddy I was contemplating other employment. The monotony of being under the same rule at job and home was rising to a level of stalemate. Along with that I was unable to buy all the supplies I needed for my darkroom and decorations for my bike with the pay Dad was training me at.

I managed to get a part-time job after school at a neighborhood Kroger's grocery store. Mother had always traded there and, unlike a supermarket, it had a personal atmosphere that was warm and neighborly. Each customer would come up to an open place at the counter and the one clerk would go around and gather each of the requested items, bag and ring them up, then take the next customer in line. The butcher cut and served all meats and kept his cash register himself. I made fifty cents for working just two hours an evening emptying trash and loading shelves with canned goods. Without my knowledge, Mother had made arrangements with the two store clerks whereby she would be credited for some of her meats and groceries as part of my pay.

It went well until I decided to pull a fast one. I was into my second dozen of eggs, pocketing two at a time, when Ray, the manager, surprised me with a shocking pat on the shoulder as I stood smiling with two eggs I'd lifted from the display crate. I didn't see him come up behind me until it was too late. He'd been skipping around checking inventory and suddenly, "What do you have in your pocket, Charlie?" he asked, pointing to the bulge there. "Nothing," was what came out of my mouth. Ray swung his arm and slapped my pocket. "Sorry," he said. "Did I crack something?" Then the front of my trousers were gooey and looked like I'd wet them. "Now go home and tell your mother how it happened," he suggested and sent me home. I told my mother what happened and I got a going over but continued to work at Kroger's, only cleaning and taking the trash out thereafter.

I was going through many new experiences that brought radical changes in my life-style. Besides giving me a raise in salary, Daddy began treating me more maturely with responsibilities and trust. I was attending church more often than my immediate friends but still constantly slipping away from the family tradition of spiritual life. I felt that I couldn't be a true Christian and possibly cope with the conditions of the environment I was in. The holy temple I was reared in was beginning to fade from influencing my behavior. The only temple my immediate friends knew about was upside their head.

One Sunday evening after the BYPU (Baptist Young People's Union) and just before night church assembled, Jewel Wilder, a thirteen-year-old stepdaughter of one of the church deacons, suggested that we go around to the rear of the church where we could be alone. I had been returning goo-goo eyes at her for weeks in hopes to someday reap the fruit of her charms. So between the two services we hurried to the backyard of the church, where we immediately embraced. I was in the vineyard of hope that she, as fast and bold as she seemed to be, would put an end to my virginity that night once and for all. What I needed was a little encouragement from an aggressive girl.

I handled her flow of kisses all right, until she reached to gain possession of the untouched master of my desire—then I grew like a weed. I was not prepared in one way, though ready in another, as she had observed during the kisses. Sin itself had much to do with my inability to go through with the act and with frustrating fear I flew back around to the front of the church and entered the services. The sermon seemed miles away.

Not six months later, Jewel's older sister Doris seemed to challenge my shyness. When the charm of Doris came forth, I yielded to her suggestion when BYPU turned out and followed her to her home two blocks away. She settled us on her back porch and asked me did I want to go with her. She led the way after that and guided me to satisfaction. I was manmade in an instant.

I learned later that all during my "first show," the next-door neighbors viewed but did not interrupt the amateur performance. Instead, after the show, they reported the act to Doris's father. Her father was a deacon of our church and he reported the incident to my father at prayer meeting that following Tuesday. The ball was rolling and I was sure to catch it.

Dad called me into his room that memorable Wednesday and softly asked, "What's this I'm hearing?" You didn't ask what he was referring to, you straight away told him what he wanted to hear from you. I did just that and as usual when wrong doings came up at night, was sent to bed, to await the punishment. Three days passed before he beckoned me to go to the basement.

On my way downstairs, I could hardly remember ever even wanting to be with a girl. My father used a leather razor strop and the licks from it were hard to bear. When the strokes come to more than one, the name of the game was shame and pain. I felt the razor strop reach home. The beginning had begun and I reached back with both hands to see if I had actually lost my base. A little late for the first lick but on time for the second, I tightened the muscles of my buttocks in preparation for the contact. I tried to jump out of the way of the strop but Dad, like a professional boxer, swung jabs, hooks, and roundhouses with superb accuracy. This was the most unholy mischief I'd committed and I knew I would burn before it was over unless I spaced the hot licks by dodging. For those of you who have never experienced corporal punishment, it is sheer hell without tightening up and thinking of ice cream or something nice while the heat is on. When the temperature at the base became unbearable I came nigh asking Dad to stop so we could talk things over. I had already sworn never to yield to temptations again. Breathing heavily, he came toward me, with an expression I'd never seen him wear. The strop was limp at his side and his eyes looked tired and moist with sympathy.

I realized then I had won the round and somehow wished that I hadn't. For some reason, I sensed that something was also lost. Something like the difference between shelter and exposure, between favor and refusal, between father and son. I may have gained his recognition that I was then a man, but I was refusing the shelter that his guidance had afforded all my life. Judgment would henceforth be my own responsibility and consequently seemed frightening.

Since I was enjoying having a girlfriend now and then, I was eager to stay in high school, where they gave the students greater freedom and responsibility than we'd had in grade school. Opportunity and temptation were anywhere you let them be. New ideas, ideals, and eye dolls were there to be held.

The first liberty I took was an appearance in an "All Men's Review" program. It was a musical stage performance arranged by the student body class of 1941 at Sumner High. I'd chosen to sing a popular hit tune, "Confessin' the Blues," a recording originally done by the late Jay McShann. Because nobody in the school band knew it and there wasn't any sheet music for such songs, a student guitar player named Tommy Stevens agreed to be my accompanist. I thought of choosing that blues number because everybody was playing it on the jukebox across the street and nobody was singing any blues in the show. I knew it well from singing it around the parties in our neighborhood, being the life of the party, which I truly enjoyed. Tommy had played out at nightclubs for money and was well prepared to back me, so I went for it.

Without thought of how bold it would be, singing such a lowly blues in the rather sophisticated affair, I belted out the purple pleading tune with crooning cries. It was probably the nature of the song that startled the audience more than anything else, but when I began laying out the love lyrics the school auditorium exploded with applause. I remember the feeling I had at that instant: "Jeez! What'd I do?" The audacity of singing a blues song on a school program, where classics like "Danny Boy" and "Old Man

River" were usually rendered, was less than the least of my concerns, but "How dare you?" showed on the faces of a couple of faculty members. I realized as I was performing that the audience will respond if you give them what they want to hear and that regardless of your ability (meaning texture of voice) to deliver a song, they will enjoy the feeling that you put into it. At the completion of my selection I was complimented again with a tremendous ovation. As I remembered my dad doing in his play, I bowed away and exited the stage backwards, watching my pathway through my legs. I feel satisfied that stage fright, if it ever lived within me, was murdered during that applause.

Long did the encouragement of that performance assist me in programming my songs and even their delivery while performing. I began noticing and clocking every response I could detect from then on. I added and deleted according to the audiences' response to different gestures, and chose songs to build an act that would constantly stimulate my audience.

I guess the most important result of that performance was the inspiration it gave me to play a guitar. Tommy, with the tremendous drive he produced during the song, was to be commended no less than I for the success of our selection. It was then that my determination to play guitar and accompany myself while singing became an amendment to my religion.

The personal blessing that the All Men's Review performance brought was the popularity it generated with girls who before had never bothered to speak. I felt I was becoming a member of the "in crowd" although I was left out when it came to a steady girl-friend.

Clarence Richmond, a classmate of mine, became more friendly and loaned me his father's abandoned four-string tenor guitar to learn on. It was my first touch of the strange instrument and it kept me busy exploring the many songs I could pick out on it. I practiced for hours to be able to strum chords while singing. The first song I practiced and sang with was to be the backing for many, as it was the chord changes of the blues. The "three change" matched a million songs of which a couple dozen I already knew the words to. With a little change of tempo or a different stroking of the rhythm, another couple dozen were added, for example, "Worried Life Blues" and "Going Down Slow."

The guitar was slowly intoxicating me. Every lyric that left my lips seemed unworthy of the sound that the strings produced behind it, so I sometimes would not even sing, it sounded so good. Consequently my picking and chording progressed far more rapidly than my voice. I was learning to play better than I could sing. I wondered sometimes if I would ever be good enough to become a professional musician, but the thrill of what was developing so far satisfied me beyond any serious thoughts of the future.

My fifteenth birthday, Halloween, and Thanksgiving had come and gone with little excitement until one Sunday afternoon at a neighbor's home, while plunking on their piano, I heard President Roosevelt announce that the United States was declaring war on Japan. To me this meant little because war talk was everywhere. I continued practicing the boogie that I was playing. The president followed on with the news that the Japanese Empire had attacked Pearl Harbor and, at that moment, the harbor was in flames. I was three years too young to register for the service and four years too afraid. Had I been eighteen at the time, I would have hurried back to Africa.

The effects of the war were quickly felt throughout the home front. Materials such as rubber, copper, gasoline, and soap became scarce, and some were even rationed. There was a shortage of goods, but there was an abundance of jobs and everybody worked for the war effort. The suburban rich people were panicking because the maids and domestic workers were all leaving them for higher-paying jobs at the defense plants. The government not only paid well but seemed to discriminate little in employment or advancement in rank. As a result, maids, gardeners, and garbage technicians got the chance to revisit their former employers in the suburbs where they tooted their Cadillac horns while driving by, "Just coming out to say hello!" Everyone wanted to get in on the big money being made, including me, but one small factor stood between me and a good-money job—high school. I learned many things out of books, including how to read guitar music, but why did I have to miss having a good job now just to learn more for a better one that might or might not come? Remembering my father's vain toil to reach for the better life, I decided to stay in school.

The war caught Henry and Harry smack dab in the middle of the draft. Within months the draft took Henry to Pensacola, Florida, then directly to New Guinea, where he later rose to the rank of lieutenant, technical administrator of the Latrine Division. Remember, it was in the early forties and Henry was a black man, but he did climb to the rank of lieutenant of the crap crew.

I didn't miss Henry being in the army since just before leaving he spent most nights out courting Marion Gregory, whom he married prior to leaving for the service. Marion's younger sister, Mildred, was my age and we became dance partners until I found out she thought little of romancing a relative. Second to being killed, the absence of romance seemed the greatest sacrifice of being off in war.

Fun and money were coming more and more close to home week by week, and everyone was buying many things they'd always wanted. Parties were numerous and I was daily getting old enough to go to 'em. One such was a neighborhood block-unit dance that took place across the alley from our own house, where a twenty-one-year-old woman named Alma took a liking to me and we danced nearly all night. She was a student of registered nursing and very mature. After noticing her watching me, I asked her to dance and continued to dance solely with her, becoming extremely excited. She marveled at the effect her close movements had on me while we danced and would glance up into my eyes as if to shame me for my lack of self-control. She continued such gestures, bringing sounds in response to the anointment she was luring from my loins. When she suggested we go for a walk to cool off, I hardly could help but agree.

We left the block dance and walked up the alley to my father's garage and entered. I was burning with desire and Alma knew it. Age and experience allowed her to handle my condition and she preached patience for better places that passionate pleasures should be planned. I soon was dekindled as the people from the dance were passing the garage going home and Alma advised we leave and return to the dance. I was all but in love.

The next neighborhood dance came and I hoped to be with Alma. This time, I talked a little stronger, getting her to promise not to stand me up. Alma was leading the way so we danced a while and slipped right across the alley to the back of our garage. She must have been anticipating the serious move, I thought, because there was no music or dance going on in the garage. Daddy kept the garage latched, so I had to leave Alma waiting outside while I climbed over the rear fence and ran to my room to get a sheet and pillow. All was quiet on the alley front when I returned and leveled our old studio couch from setting on its end and prepared it with the bedding for the rendezvous.

I unlatched the garage door to welcome my awaited promise only to discover Alma had returned to the dance. Sadly I returned, too, and saw her standing alone. She told me that she had become afraid in the dark and came to shelter. Once again we returned to the garage, stole inside, and this time sat on the snow-white studio couch hugging.

The three-hundred-watt garage light suddenly came on. Standing beneath it with arms folded were my mother and my father, looking like Joseph and Mother Mary. My father spoke, "You'll never turn this garage into a bordello!" I nervously shoved Alma toward the latched garage door but, as I was unlatching it, I received my first bite of the strap Daddy had brought. I didn't want Alma to know I still got whippings, although my teeth were gritting as the licks fell from the strap. Not wanting to emit any sounds of what was happening while Alma was passing through the door, I hummed aloud.

Daddy had wasted no time in whipping me and the fourth impact of the strap changed the pitch of my hum from bass to treble. Much less than romantic I shouted in pain, "I'll see you later, Alma!" turned from her and darted away from the next swing of the strap. Mother was coaching Daddy, as usual, saying, "Lord knows how long he's been doing this. Henry, he's just getting out of hand." Instead of savoring Alma's solemn loving I was suffering Daddy's solid licking.

After that, Alma thought it best I follow my parent's advice and not see her. I then began exploring the city on bikes with my two friends, Lawrence "Skip" Hutchinson and James Williams, to take the place of brooding over my loss of Alma. Skip and James both had found little funky jobs but I mostly picked up the tab for us. We also kept extra change in our pockets by siphoning gasoline from the trucks kept in a coal yard close by our neighborhood. We felt patriotically justified in servicing ourselves from that business because it was the only one that did not extend credit to the black community, plus the owner was ornery.

One evening we found the yard gate unlocked. Prior to this we'd been hopping the nine-foot fence with one five-gallon can. This time we strolled in with three five-gallon cans, taking James's bike in for a quiet exit. While we were filling the first can, somebody drove up, stopped, walked over, and stood for a minute at the gate. When the siphoning hose finally had filled the three gas cans we mounted the bike and proceeded toward the gate, only to discover that it had been padlocked with a chain.

James was on the handlebars holding two of the cans as I broke speed seeing the gate had been closed and locked. We both lost balance and tumbled off to the ground with one topless gas can losing its contents as it rolled away. James went for the truck-tire tool to try to pry the gate as I went to retrieve the spilling remains in the gas can. When I picked it up and turned, a snaky trail of flaming gas was on its way toward me and the can. James was slapping his flaming hands against his trousers, shouting "I'm on fire!" He'd been smoking and the rolling can had passed over the butt. Immediately, we both split away from the line of flame to the fence. James's clothes were out but still smoldering while we were climbing to the top of the chain-link fence. Skip was over the fence and headed home when we reached the top. The trail of fire reached the can at that time and the blast was definitely felt on the seat of our pants as we dropped outside the sidewalk. Some drivers-by saw us descending and running from the blast so we kept going and three cans and the bike were lost.

Reaching home via the alley we heard the fire engines in the distance approaching and doubled back to watch from a block away. We later regretted the prank many times, walking by the coal yard seeing James's charred bicycle chained high above the office-building door with a sign on it stating OWNER PLEASE RE-TURN TO CLAIM SAME.

I hadn't been to Sunday School or church in weeks and I became conscious of the risks I was taking and the direction I was headed, but the mischief didn't stop. It only took a decided drop in quality and quantity. We settled to hubcap ripping and parked-car creeping, dimestore clipping and window peeping.

To mention the power of peers, on a trip to Chicago with my friend Ralph Burris, I submitted to his suggestion of sharing a "roach," which was what the butt portion of a marijuana cigarette was called then. After puffing the butt end and snorting as Ralph said to do, I sniffed as he did but remained cold sober. Even then, at the price it cost for just a roach, it didn't fit my economical judgment of pastime frolic which was all I thought it was then.

Once I purchased (I was large enough to appear of age then) a half pint of Paul Jones whiskey for ninety cents and went down the street to my grade-school-building boiler-room door to unwrap it, then stood there alone and drank it down. It like to burnt my throat up, but I emptied it, then went out on the basketball-court yard and got on the yellow markings and began walking the straight line. I'd heard you couldn't walk a straight line when you were drunk but then I figured it would take time to cause an effect and wanted to strategically observe the rate of change in my soberness that peers declared would occur as a delightful development.

I walked. I was still walking the yellow line perfectly when I noticed three bewildered spectators concerned about my sanity, having made three earnest trips around the court line. After realizing no change in the control of my walking, I began doubting that the feeling others boasted of would come to me, and I strutted on home. Before I could master the two blocks to reach home, I realized I was indeed sober as a deacon and duly sick as a dog. I just did make it to the basement sink and gave up the ghost.

The chili I'd eaten had colored the offering a reddish tone that I thought to be partially blood. I spent a couple hours hiding behind the furnace, suffering with a terrific headache, hoping my last hours would not be there. That experience drove me away from any other desire for any delight that intoxication was supposed to bring.

Around the same age I rode downtown on the streetcar to a burlesque theater in the skid-row area where they had women dancing on stage in what now are mere swimsuits. As I turned into the alley on my way to the stage door where I would enjoy peeping at the women coming on and off stage, I saw a man bending over a fairly well dressed drunk lying against the alley wall. The man standing reached stealthily into the pocket of the one in a stupor and lifted his wallet. What molded most to my memory was that the drunk man awakened during the lift but still did not have enough control of his movements to defend himself or resist against the robber completing the lift. I heard the drunk pleading pitifully, "Don't take my money." Witnessing that scene was the most touching and fruitful of my past in molding my determination never to fall into a condition where I would not have control of my senses at the highest level achievable.

My feeling about the incident is that the drunk, though within his right to indulge in alcohol, was stupid and careless to place himself in so vulnerable a situation. In view of the position the drunk was in, which in the first place could have been prevented, I had no sympathy for him. Whereas the thief, soberly taking a thoughtful chance to engage in gainful wrong, was to me clever and ingenious to find an opportunity so likely of gain.

I always say, "If there's no orange juice in heaven, excuse me but I'll just have to go through hell to get it." Now, after seeing so many people booze it up and some of my affiliates, namely Alan Freed and Clyde McPhatter, have problems with such, the indulgence bothers me none to pass up. Seeing so many regrettable things stem from intoxication, such as auto accidents, pregnancies, robberies, and last but not least, alcoholism itself, also led me away from indulging in liquor.

I finally lived to get the chance to be with Alma. Neither Mother nor Daddy was home and I prepared the garage and arranged for the rendezvous. Alma knew that I was quite passive and led me through the way she felt a man should satisfy a woman. I followed her requests, hearing her uttering the sweetest sounds I'd ever heard from a girl. The favors that she encouraged me to render were nearly as stimulating as the only way I knew of couples to be united, which after, I finally shared with her. It was Alma who showed me the way to manhood, and sharing my manhood reminds me of Alma.

From the first crystal radio set I got to the record player that Henry made for block parties, I was eager to learn more about radio. Once while I was shopping at a radio repair shop, George Lee, the shop owner, showed me a used table-model radio, more modern than any we had around the house, except the Philco. I couldn't purchase it outright but he gave me a chance to earn it by working evenings for him. There I learned how to dismount radio chassis from the cabinets and through questions I learned a bit of how a radio works. It became so intriguing that I abandoned taking pictures for a while and continued working there long after I'd purchased the used radio. The wonders of radio took me by storm and I wanted to learn more. At school I was sucking the seeds of the two subjects I liked and coughing up all the curriculum in classes I contested. I found no subjects that brought me inspiration, yet at the radio shop, doing something that intrigued me, I was wracking my brains to learn.

Mr. Lee had to close the shop on Friday and Saturday nights to play records at the then-black USO for dances. After a while, he gave me the job of spinning the records for the dancing. I was thrilled with the USO job because there were a lot of girls asking me to play their favorites during the dance.

My popularity began to really heat up when I finally got my first car. My sister Thelma, being twenty-one, cosigned because Daddy wouldn't. It was a 1934 V-8 Ford sedan costing thirty-five dollars, at ten dollars down and only five dollars a month, but some payments still were late. It was a young church member that had sold it to me, though, and he was patient. He was hopeful of getting closer to Thelma, whose husband, Big Tommy, had passed and Thelma and I had become pretty closely knit. I was a man Friday for her. One time a companion of hers wanted to stay at her home longer than she favored him welcome and I was summoned as bouncer. I had my petty problems at home with the parents, so the more I stayed with Thelma the better.

The car unfailingly interfered with my high-school studies, but I was proud to get the prestige and popularity of being one of only eighteen students driving to school and one of only two who actually owned their cars. My Ford had the key broken off in the ignition and anyone could start it. That was discovered soon after by the seniors during football practice. The consideration granted me for not complaining to the school authorities when they would drive it around locked me in friendship with them. I learned it was being used when some senior girl came up to me and laughingly complained that she had scratched her back on the exposed cushion springs, implying that I needed seat covers.

Later in the summer, Mother having forgotten that she was the same girl in the three-hundred-watt garage festival, Alma started visiting the family, mainly Mother. Alma was identical to my mother in build (though twenty-eight years different in age) and they struck a hardy companionship rapping about medics and domestic things. We would steal away trying to repair the defeat we suffered in the garage festival. Alma, being much more clever than I, left it totally inconceivable to anyone in the family that we were engaged in anything but my schoolwork while off alone in the house.

Thelma must have thought I was surely into something, because she was encouraging me to get circumcised before I got too much older. I didn't know it at that time, but Mother, with the influence of Thelma, had already talked with Alma about setting me up for the operation. Alma had suggested to Mother that if she could get on the ward where my circumcision would take place, she then could "look over" the operation.

The day came and into the clinic at Homer G. Philips I staggered, asked a few questions, and signed up to be scalped. When I reported to the operating room, Alma was standing there with two other nurses. We chatted a couple of minutes, but I didn't mention what I was there for. The doctor came in and told me to lie on the table. I did. Alma didn't move. Because of that, I thought then I would never speak to her again. Part of the time it was hard, but she handled it well. Alma was in her third year of practical nursing at Homer G. Philips Hospital and Mother often got medical advice when she would visit, but this trick on me severed any future between us.

My broken-down, ragged 1934 Ford had served me well but was traded in for a 1933 four-door Plymouth sedan that ran like a sewing machine. You could stretch out across the lengthy front seat, which was a promising advantage over the Ford's bucket seats. I had learned there was too much opportunity for rejection when moving to the back seat was suggested. Still I had no luck.

I had learned enough from *Nick Mannaloft's Guitar Book of Chords* to strum out the progression to most of the popular love songs while singing at backyard parties. Most of the guys in the neighborhood got their haircuts at the home of the three Harris brothers, Pat the barber, John the juicehead, and Ira the jazzman. Ira was the one who showed me many professional styles of execution on the guitar and reinstated my ambition to play the instrument. When it came to playing tunes by Muddy Waters, Tampa Red, Big Maceo, and Little Walter, I could shine like the sun. I would always take the guitar when I went to get my hair cut so Ira could show me more passages. I would chord for him while he took off on the solos.

Working along with Ira, I discovered that four out of every ten popular songs were based on the chords of the tune "I Got Rhythm" and thus were known as songs with rhythm changes. To name a few: "At Last," "So Long," "Sentimental Reasons," "Heart and Soul," "Blue Moon," and there are hundreds of others. Even more songs are based on blues chords than rhythm chords. Only a few songs, compared to the millions there are, have their own specific progressions, such as "Stardust," "Deep Purple," and "Silent Night." I determined that by learning rhythm changes and blues progressions, I would be prepared to chord nearly 80 percent of the songs that were played. With this in mind I worked until I had matched over ninety popular songs together with their lyrics and began to sing them before people as often as I had the opportunity. I even took the guitar on dates and sang to the girl I'd be with.

I traded in the Plymouth as a down payment on a 1937 Oldsmobile sedan that had a trunk. Our family car was a 1939 Buick Roadmaster, so I was cruising near domestic nobility in independence and popularity.

The job at the USO playing music was the hub of entertainment for the black soldiers on leave. The girls that came to keep the guys entertained got to know me well and I loved it. It was almost like being their idol, I'd say, compared to the feeling given by those hit-the-road-jackies that snubbed me in school. I was turning seventeen and most of the girls that catered the dances were from eighteen to thirty years old. I had an advantage over the soldiers being the only civilian, the youngest one there, and by being there constantly. There were two girls in particular who came to mold the cast that gave shape to my heart.

Cyreatha, a soft-spoken, chestnut-brown college sophomore, had taken a liking to me. I was overwhelmed by her interest and would have daily taken out her garbage just to be near her can. Speaking of beauty, she had little to share, but if charm equaled hours, she had years to spare. Cyreatha was classy like my sister Lucy, and though Cyreatha truly cared, she was determined to save our intimate relations for after marriage. I begged her while promising wedlock when she finished college, but she wouldn't yield. Her ways weathered my whims for weeks while some of the other girls at the USO were coming on strong to tease my loyalty.

A brighter-skinned, cat-eyed girl, well endowed with femininity and conversation, made her debut at the USO one night. She lost no time in conceiving the game the girls were playing upon me and Cyreatha, and she joined in. She was Margie, a major monument in my memorial of love. She came up to the record player and focused her eyes on mine and told me to play "I'll Never Smile Again" and, as it came to pass, my heart didn't for years. The very next weekend, for the first and only time in my life, I sought the love of one and abandoned the other.

As part of the USO girls' game with me they would lure me into taking each of them home in my car. Cyreatha never complained and actually thought it fun as she was always the last to be left off. The first night Margie made a move, she dominated the selection of tunes I was to play and openly called for me to plant kisses when she made requests. At closing that night, Margie asked me to take her home alone. Outside the building when all the girls gathered to pile in the car, Margie got in and yelled to the rest, "Sorry, girls, I have some special things I want Charles to do for me." I was surprised, since I'd been chauffeuring the gang home for weeks back.

That selfish suggestion was the first of many to come. I got in the car and followed Margie's lead to a food drive-in and to her home, where twice she quickly kissed me and whispered, "Be nice now and drive safe home." I did as she asked, for I was already in love with her.

The love of Margie drained heavily on my schooling. She was so far advanced from the makeup of the girls in school. On her twentieth birthday she accepted a small record player that I treated her to. She thanked me for it yet still refused me any physical comforts. She always told me "It will make you love me more, so please be patient." Both the reason and request seemed impossible. My tempo at school dropped to the pace of a snail and study time was spent in my car pining in front of the duplex where Margie lived.

When she became bored with the USO dances, I was the next to be discarded from her entertainment. She told me that her grandmother was Irish and wouldn't allow me to visit her upstairs residence. I could only hope to see her from my car window. She would come to the window every half hour or so and laugh or wave her hand. She told me finally that I would have to stop coming around parking in front of her house because people might get the wrong idea about her.

In the final months of the relationship, she allowed me to take her out in the afternoon to a drive-in. Afterward she conceded to riding around a while. I was approaching seventeen yet still not brave enough to exercise the male forwardness needed to seduce a hip girl like Margie. I just drove around, trying to think of a way to start getting her in the mood. We wound up in Baden, a black suburb north of the city, where I parked and started confessing how much I loved her.

To my surprise she listened and began asking me questions pertaining to the extent of my devotion. She asked whether my love for her exceeded my love for any other, and would I work hard and give her all my money? (I had a hundred seventy dollars in my bank account.) She further asked would I be jealous and would I do anything she asked to please her? After affirming these things to her, she gave me the first French kiss I knew of. Then she allowed me to fondle her and I became irremediably enraptured with desire for her. My destiny was to please her so that these privileges she allowed me could be continued.

She admitted that I would not likely render her the satisfaction she fancied but allowed me to lay my head on her lap. There she encouraged me to fondle further to a point where she must have reached some satisfaction because she pulled me upright and began

her, "How much do you love me, Charles?" I told her more than I did myself, and meant it. She then pushed me away, raised herself, and began tugging at her panties. Margie knew how difficult it was for me to make an aggressive move, and she kept my desire inflamed by flaunting the very cravings I sought. When she held her undies up, twirling them above her head, I knew the time was now or never. "Do you really want to make love to me, Charles?" she asked. Whispering yes, I was ready as a sturdy log twixt two rolling stones but still afraid to make a further move. When she asked me what was the matter, I embraced her in disbelief that I was about to enter the garden that she had spread before me. "This is how I'd like for you to please me, Charles. This is how you must if you really love me.''

What Margie wanted she usually got. She told me, ''I prefer to have this done by a female, but you can do it for now.'' I loved her without hesitation in fear of losing her. I did what she wanted until she whispered I was a nice fellow but I must take her on home.

I was saddened to hear her say that I should not expect to see her again and took her straight home. She was watching me as I sobbed most of the way, telling me that I should find a girl that liked me and be with her. That hurt. I wanted no one but her and she didn't seem to care for me nearly enough to let the relationship stay afloat. Once at her house, she told me to do as she asked and stay away from her house. She would phone when she wanted to see me. I did as she wanted.

That was the last I saw of Margie. After a week of waiting for a call, I circled the block she lived on, trying to get a glimpse of her. Later I began parking for hours to watch and still later I tried to raise someone at her front door and was told by the tenants downstairs that the people upstairs had moved to Chicago over two months before. I still parked and watched and began crying again. I'd lost her. I knew nothing of lesbianism.

> If there ever was a woman to whom my very soul I gave
> It was she, for I loved her and would soon have been
>> her slave.
> I would have stolen a thousand dollars and paid counsel
>> at a glance
> To keep me free in reach of her to beg another chance.
> If I'd gone blind and lost my sight, I'd use my hands to
>> feel
> My way until I'd found her, then before her would I
>> kneel.
> The only prayer I would have prayed is that she'd only
>> live
> Forever to receive some of the love I had to give.
> If she had happened to my home Lord knows what
>> could I say

Though it's not likely that she would, I waited day by
    day.
But it was October then and the things I was doing
To get to be near Margie, had me on the road to ruin.
I met my downfall and I fell, like many more before
Into the strong arms of the law and wound up in Algoa.
Then over three long years went past . . . but Margie
    still was there
Imbedded deeply in my heart, almost too deep to bear.
It wasn't long thereafter straight to Margie's home I
    went.
She talked to me sincerely, but I knew then what she
    meant.
She said there was no chance for me, she was happy
    with her mate.
"A girl," she said, "you knew back home, and once
    tried to date!"

When I learned of lesbian love, I knew how it felt to be in love
with one whom you could never satisfy. It was the very first real
love I'd ever known. When I hear the word *lesbian,* I think of
Margie.

Some people say, "Your first love is never really out of your
system." Well, the statement may be somewhat true because
seven years passed and I still loved her more than I could anyone,
and continued to until the feeling terminated one day in her basement apartment somewhere in The Bronx, New York. I never had
sexual relations with her beyond the attempt that afternoon in my
car.

In our first and only talk in seven years of being apart, she had
the audacity to inform me that I would still have to work hard and
bring her all of my earnings so that she could see that we lived
comfortably and that I could not be the type of man who wanted
his wife to stay at home and keep house like most women might
do. I was a bit in the know by then of the life she was indicating
she wished to live and knew I'd never be able to cope with her as
a mate for life as I had always hoped to.

As we kissed at her front doorway with her feeling she had me locked in to her for good, I left her with a smile, seeing her beautiful eyes for the last time.

That disappointment led me to be suspicious of many girls thereafter, where I otherwise would not have been. I did not care too much about loving anyone after that, or about what I did or wanted to be. I loafed around aimlessly and drifted. Looking back at myself then, I was the first in my family to try smoking, the first to play hooky from school, the first to venture away from home, and the first to go to jail. On the other hand, I was the first child in the family to own a Cadillac, the first to have a formal wedding, the first to fly to Europe, first to earn a half-million dollars, and the last one to admit I was wrong.

CHAPTER THREE

Kansas City

I t was the summer of '44 and I was hanging out with my friends Skip and James, struggling to reach my junior year. James was a dropout, strong, stocky, and as car crazy as I was. He couldn't cope with the strict religious rule of his home either. Skip had grown to be six feet, slender, loud mouthed, and lazy. He was a dropout, too, and as ugly as death eating a dirty doughnut. They were rebellious and lazy but they were otherwise my kind of guys. We were all fairly no good but we were together, bound by a common aim to get somewhere in the world: maybe California!

All week we curbed the riding around until the Oldsmobile tank was full, then my two friends and I were ready to fulfill a dream. We planned to leave our homes and go out for ourselves. The dream was to be in Hollywood, California, and the first live-in stop was to be Kansas City, Missouri.

We had the car in tip-top shape, with three extra used tires and tubes in the trunk and lots of tire patching. My strategy was that rubber wouldn't be the reason we'd crawl back home. Rubber then was like gold and you had to be a nun from abroad to be blessed with a new tire. We had packed four dozen doughnuts, a jar of jelly, two loaves of bread, one hunk of bologna, spare jeans, and repair tools for the 252-mile journey across the state to Kansas City.

It was high noon and I was seventeen years old. My running buddies and I got in my '37 Oldsmobile sedan and we set sail westward. We stopped in Wentzville at the Southern Air Restaurant to get some zoo-zoos (food). The colored lady cook came to the little window built in the back kitchen wall that solely catered to black patrons, and she asked what we wanted. She overfilled the paper plates of our order, which was the one good result that can be remembered about a jim crow café policy: getting more on our paper plates than we would have been served on china out front.

Regardless, we had a picnic there and likewise along the two-lane concrete snake named U.S. Highway 40 (now I 70), stopping only fourteen times in 130 miles before reaching Columbia, Missouri. Each of the four tires had a blowout that we replaced or patched. Since sundown had met us in Columbia, we hung in the city for the rest of the night, riding around until bedtime, then drove to the highway shoulder, where we parked and slept.

At sunrise we were rolling forty miles per hour, about thirty miles on the K. C. side of Columbia. We had expired our used-tire reserve at a filling station short of Independence, Missouri, after rolling in on a rim two miles. Another flat tire would have stranded us, but we cruised across 18th and Vine Street at eight-thirty that night and parked in front of the Street Hotel.

I had sixteen dollars left, a sore hand, red eyes, no spare tire, one rim ruined, was tired, hungry, and 252 miles from home. Already the feeling was creeping in that maybe I shouldn't have left home. We filled up with chili, Twinkies, and soda pop, then went to the Lydia Theater. At 11:30 P.M., we bedded down in a driveway at Swope Park. Where was the excitement we anticipated while preparing for the journey?

None of the glamour had surfaced the next morning with sides, necks, and backs aching. Jokes and laughter were at a minimum as I was cutting in half my expenditures for our food. By sundown that evening we were discussing how friendly and homey St. Louis must really have been. It was chilly sleeping in the car and we would have started back, but with two dollars and no spare tire, we had little enthusiasm for the return trip.

Skip suggested we let him out and somehow he'd get some money. James asked, "How?" He impatiently answered, "Just let me out and pick me up here in around fifteen minutes." James and I saw through his designs and I suggested that if he was going that route, we were going together. He explained what he intended to do and for us to wait outside and pick him up when he exited.

We drove around until Skip saw something that looked vulnerable; then he said, "Wait right here for me." We did and in less than a half minute, Skip came splitting out of the little bakery shop and jumped in the car. We sped away successfully with Skip's eyes as wide as quarters and him laughing like a hyena and waving lots of dollars. It seemed so easy to us the way Skip made the trip and doubled back with a stack that we talked about trying one more. Skip was taller, darker, and much uglier than either of us and I thought that that alone would give anyone good reason to yield to his demands.

My Christian background led me to suggest staying at the YMCA, where incidentally the police never dreamed to look for three downbound trainees in bandidoism. We bedded down like decent people and divided a stack of bills.

The following day we wandered around town, drove across into Kansas, ate hearty at nice restaurants, and then went to the movies again. That night, I planned the strategy and staked out our next job, a barbershop. I had been having much fun back home flashing around the remains of a pistol I had found in a used-car lot. Its wooden handle had been burned off in a fire and it had no magazine, but the barrel still left it resembling a potent 22-caliber weapon. I had to cover most of the gun to hide its uselessness, but it worked for scaring people.

After rehearsing my strategy, we drove to the barbershop and parked across the street, leaving James with the motor running. I led Skip in and announced the "holdup" to the proprietor, who at that moment was counting his take. We were in perfect timing as he was closing up.

Skip followed me in with a fish knife he had used for the bakery job and I eased toward the cash register. I said, "Stick 'em up!" and the barber turned and backed away from the register with his hands at his side. I stepped over and began raking coins into the pockets of my blue jeans. Suddenly Skip shouted, "Watch him,

Slick!" I looked over and the barber had moved his hand nearly into his pocket. Only then did I realize that he could have a gun, too, a real one at that. Jesus! I raised and leveled my lonely barrel and screamed, "I'll kill ya!" It frightened him, thank goodness, and he lifted his arms quickly over his head. I was nervous and shaking but kept on at raking more coins from the trays of the register as Skip shouted again, "Get the bills, Slick!" I was ready to give up robbing from not thinking first of the large money and, with Skip's shouting, I was as nervous as a billy goat on a freeway. I then grabbed one handful of bills, turned and abandoned all strategy, and split for the car out front.

James was sitting there looking like Baby Face Nelson, with the Olds running and ready for the getaway. We jumped in, slammed the doors, and headed for the YMCA. All I could think of on the way was that another two seconds without Skip's shouting, "Watch him, Slick," and I would have been pushing up daisies. That was my closest call from death.

Our take was thirty-two dollars at the barbershop and sixty-two dollars at the bakery. Following the barbershop we took off a night to convalesce. My nerves were wrapped around my liver. On the fifth night we, or rather Skip, collected fifty-one dollars robbing a small clothing store. We picked up several sport shirts on the way out of the clothing store and a half dozen sheets and pillowcases from the YMCA that night and checked out before morning. We finished loading in an alley, gassed up, and started back to St. Louis.

We admitted it was nerve-racking, especially James, who was a total wreck all through the two last jobs and constantly begged us to quit and go home. In Independence we bought a tire and rim, some snack goodies, and continued eastward. All day and evening I drove, until suddenly the Oldsmobile threw a rod on the outskirts of Columbia. It sounded like a gunshot; then the sedan rattled to a stop and died.

It was three-thirty in the morning and no one spoke until a car was approaching from the rear. James broke the silence with, "Let's get a push." We got out and waved, but one of the passengers shouted, "Go home, niggers," and they continued on. We tried asking for help for two hours, and got none. So we cuddled in the cold car stranded there on the open highway. It was pitch black outside and there was nothing but a shed and an old abandoned filling station with a dimly lit phone booth by it. It was so quiet we could hear ourselves think. Nothing happened.

Finally a 1941 Chevrolet coupe slowed and stopped. The only occupant, a kind, middle-aged gentleman, asked if we needed help. I was at the driver's side as he spoke and I pulled the door open, displaying my lonely barrel, and shouted an order, "Move over and let me drive." He must have known from the tone of my voice that I was inexperienced, and he only said, "Sure," and quickly shifted over, continuing on out through the opposite door.

I didn't anticipate him departing and shouted to him to come back, but he ran on from the highway toward the phone booth. I actually was saddened to leave the man stranded in what looked like prairie land, but my first thought was to get behind the wheel and start getting under way. I told Skip that James could steer the Olds while we two were pushing it. I pulled the Chevy in behind to line up, Skip got in the Chevy with me, and bumper to bumper we shoved off eastward driving fast, looking hard for home in St. Louis.

James didn't hear or see what transpired at the man's car because the Chevy's motor was running and its headlights were shining in his face. In the fright of taking the car we forgot James was still in the back seat where he rode. When we took off, all James could do was lean over from the back seat to steer the Olds as we pushed it. I accelerated the push to near forty miles per hour with the '37 Olds reeling and rocking but rolling toward home.

James was blowing the horn to stop us so he could change to the driver's seat but we thought he was signaling us to full speed ahead so we accelerated him more. James held the Olds on the road for ten miles, until close to Kingdom City, Missouri. We were sailing by a truck weight station doing forty-five miles an hour when we saw two state troopers standing within. In the Chevy mirror, I saw them leave the station and pull onto the highway. I told Skip they were coming after us. Skip said, "I know it, I saw 'em, throw that gun out the window so they won't find it." I did but they were getting closer and closer in behind us. The blinking cherry lights came on and in less than a mile there were three cars bumper to bumper with the one in the rear sounding a siren. I pulled over and stopped, bringing the holiday to an end. James was still rolling on down the slope as far as he could in the Olds away from us but the troopers stayed with us shouting, "Get out of the car with your hands up!"

The man we left by the side of the road had merely used the telephone I'd seen him run to, and evidently he had called the police, who had been waiting for us for ten minutes. The troopers pulled Skip and me over, frisking us without bothering about James in the other car. They were instructed to be on the lookout for a 1941 green Chevy driven by two black male suspects for highway robbery. James thought we had stopped on our own and had been waiting for us to pull up. When he walked back against the headlights of the Chevy, he finally saw us bending over the rear trunk deck with our hands cuffed behind us.

The state trooper asked him what could they do for him and James said nothing. They asked him his name and he told them and that he was with us. The troopers had not known there was a second car involved nor a third person but arrested James as an accomplice. The journey away from home had ended away from home.

We resided that Friday night back within the city limits of Columbia, in the Boone County Jail. Saturday passed and nothing happened. Our condition looked more and more gloomy each day. The county jail food tasted a year old and our stay seemed that it would outdate the taste. They let us call home on the fifth day. I talked to Dad, who had never before had any associations with the law or criminal procedures. I told him the entire story of our behavior as I'd also told the local authorities. Just seven days in jail sanctified me and I was ready to go straight. Trusting in the Lord and Bell Telephone, Dad received a call from some Columbia lawyer who asked Dad to send him $125 as a fee to handle my case. He further stated that he would handle James's and Skip's cases as a courtesy, since their parents were abandoning aid to them.

Dad sent the money. Nothing happened for twenty-two more days, until the sheriff took us to a small room where we met our lawyer, who advised us to plead guilty so that the judge could have mercy on us. He warned us that if we didn't it would cost the court additional money, plus cost us more than we could pay to him for defending us. I was submitting to everything and so agreed to that. Skip and James had no choice but to add their agreement. They

C H U C K

took us to a smaller room, then had us sign papers and answer questions. The troopers took me out to hunt for the useless gun and I cooperated in every way I could.

After we signed an affidavit, they told us we'd be in court any day and we were in the very next day. We three stood in the Boone County courtroom before his honor and received the maximum ten years the law allowed. The entire trial lasted nearly twenty-one minutes.

I had not heard from home since Dad wrote me about hiring the attorney and I asked the sheriff if I could call my father. He said our money was sealed in transport security and that he didn't have a dime, best I'd wait until we got where we were going. The Intermediate Reformatory for Young Men, better known as Algoa, was our destination, only two miles south of the Missouri State Penitentiary in Jefferson City. Phone calling was not allowed there. It was to be years before I made a call again.

Algoa

O n a white rock road two miles off the highway, a cloud hung heavy in my mind as I rolled up the long hill to the institution of Algoa. Twenty minutes after the sheriff registered the three of us as inmates we learned this place was called "the Hill." Built on a high Missouri River bluff, the layout was two rows of two-story brick dormitories facing each other, five in a row with a hundred-foot-wide lawn between. The big lawn had a three-story administration building combined with a hospital at the high end and a dining hall with a gymnasium above it on the low end. School and a Catholic church were on either side of that. In the center of the huge lawn was a tall siren nicknamed "the snitcher." The whole complex was on a hill nearly two hundred feet above the river below.

After fingerprinting, I was ordered into a Lysol bath that I thought was a punishment. They said it was necessary for sanitation but I survived. The medical examination showed me to be a robust, healthy juvenile but for having a positive return on a venereal disease test. I had to yield to mandatory injections over a ten-week period for cure.

By late afternoon we were put into isolation cells, called "the hole," to spend thirty days for what they informed us was orientation. The only thing I can remember while there was receiving a full Thanksgiving dinner instead of the skimpy tin plates of what seemed to be the leavings from the mess hall. So this, I pondered, was what I had to look forward to for the next ten years? Why did I do it?

In the hole, where you could talk but not see who you were talking to due to the solid steel walls with only a food hole in the door, the three of us learned there were only four other guys that had ten years besides ourselves. One of them was a sort of a ringleader named Slim Esters. Anyone bringing over ten years was sent on to "the Walls," better known as the Missouri State Prison. It felt like plumb freedom when I finished the hole and was taken to the dormitory.

All the guys, even most of the whites, looked up to Slim Esters. He was downright hateful to others compared to his attitude toward me. This became my greatest fortune, because he was the most belligerent bastard that ever reached six feet three inches. Of mornings, two beds away from mine, he woke up looking like a black gladiator lying against the back gate of hell. Nobody defied him. Frankly, I was scared of him but enjoyed the prestige that accompanied his association.

We learned fast to understand that James, Skip, and I were "fall pardners" having been convicted together and we had "copped a dime," receiving ten years, and our sentence was a "bum rap" since it was totaling thirty years for nine minutes' use of the guy's car. The "man," meaning judge, "threw the book at us." We were "short hairs and busted" (newcomers and brought no money with us) and were told if we wanted to kick back our "dime," we'd have to keep our mind off the streets, our hands off "ourselves," drink plenty of cool water, and walk slow.

There were three guards, called dormitory masters, per building. All the black inmates were governed by the three black men and the white dormitories by whites. There were black and white hours for the gym, black and white sides to the mess hall, black and white visiting rooms, and toilets all catered and tailored to custom. Black eyes watched white ones and white ones watched black but no one had any vision of change.

Saying "sir" to the white dormitory master was mandatory yet the white boys weren't required to answer so to the colored dorm masters. The punishments dished out to the black guys tended to be more severe than those for the same misbehavior by white boys. Recreational freedom, sanitation inspection, and visiting privileges were all more strict with us than with them. When white boys walked their families around the big yard during visiting hours, we were not allowed to sit or stand out front. The white dorms were not restricted and the residents watched the pretty black girls and ladies passing by.

Our day guard was a 180-pound southern black minister, Rev. Dave Scott, who fortunately (for my welfare at least) was quite illiterate. Within six months I had gained his confidence. I was chosen as his letter writer and read him his incoming mail after his former man Friday left. James became cook in the mess hall; Skip chose an outdoor job on the farm acreage, and I was given the laundry job in the dormitory, close at hand to Mr. Scott. I carried the clothes to and from the laundry twice a week and maintained the numbered racks near the gang shower where guys would switch soiled clothing for clean. In three months I made the rank of honor boy and moved to the sleeping quarters where the spring beds were and the doors stayed unlocked all night. It was a whole new ball game in the honor room where they had contraband lying open on their bed boxes and stayed up, smoked, and played radios after curfew.

Excluding the two evenings a week of the mandatory gang shower, my days were mostly at leisure. Wandering around I discovered large buckets of paint stored in the basement of the chapel, and I suggested to Mr. Scott that I would paint the dormitory walls if allowed. He phoned and got the superintendent's authorization and gave me freedom to do it.

Three weeks passed with the superintendent, Mr. Hudson, stopping by watching the progress. Before I'd finished, he brought other members of the staff, some with their wives, who came along for the chance to visit the black dorm. Dave Scott was from southeast Missouri, near where a notorious lynching of a black had recently happened, and was extremely humble to the white folk. In fact he still feared that the days of jim crow held steadfast. The inmates knew it petrified him when any white folks were within our dorm and would hide and peep under the women's clothes as they toured through the building. Dave only sat in the large entrance to the "recreation room" grinning and nodding. Truly an uncle tom, he believed the white folk always knew better and therefore would do no wrong.

Mr. Pruet, the rock-quarry foreman, was also from southeastern Missouri but was leather white and truly hated "niggers" beyond all passion. When he came by for his daily detail to work at the rock quarry, he left loaded with black backs from the dark dormitory, only taking a few from the fair fathers' flock. He was one son of a bitch that even half the white boys hated with heat. Black boys could never break enough white rock to satisfy him. Mr. Pruet never smiled. He constantly spat tobacco, sat in the sun, and watched you while he chewed.

A real racist also, I thought, was Mr. Preston, from the lynching city of Sikeston, Missouri, who ran the laundry and always gave me the impression he was eager to start something with any black. He would stare at a black boy; even Slim Esters avoided him. My most morbid days were picking up our laundry bundle from his department twice a week. I could feel the noose around my neck that it seemed he so hungered for in his gazing gray eyes. He couldn't have loved me much less, but then I couldn't have hated him a little more.

Every Sunday morning Dave Scott held church services within our dormitory. He demanded that each guy, and some were murderous, morbid-looking dudes, sit through at least one of his three sermons every Sunday. I organized a singing quartet to accompany his services. It proved to be right down the alley of most of the guys in that they'd listen to us but fall asleep on Dave. Little barrel-chested GG was alto, Steff with car theft was baritone, I was the bass (my nickname was "Wild Man"), and Po' Sam was lead. These names were the only ones I remember and are what we called each other. (A photo of the group is on the first page of the chapter.)

Po' Sam was also a professional musician. He played the guitar and blew tenor sax and had played clubs in orchestras around Kansas City. In the evening we'd take the guys home, singing and playing the blues before bed.

When our singing quartet got going with a catalogue of selections, we dominated the Baptist services, rocking the church with

80 percent of the dorm population hanging in through the benediction. You ain't seen nothin' 'til you witness a gang, who are supposed to be hostile, sitting there like apostles hearing a soul-stirring gospel. I'd been brought up in church but that was a weird beholding.

Our quartet was invited and started singing for the services at the white dormitories every Sunday. After the quartet stirred up a few white souls, with the help of Mother Robinson, the elderly white missionary who ran the services, we were given permission to go away from the Hill. She claimed great interest in the singing quartet's religious welfare after we agreed to let her take us to Jefferson City to be baptized. It was almost like going to Jerusalem. A couple more trips and the authorities were relaxed about us going off the Hill to sing.

I'd written Thelma about our quartet and she helped get a request to sing at a church in St. Louis. The approval and the day came and we took off early that morning in the state Chevrolet with our dormitory master, and not only sang at the church but visited my folks and had dinner at my home. The seventh trip away was on June 10, to Kansas City, where we sang and socialized with Po' Sam's family.

Summer was well on the way by then and it looked like I might survive a couple of years of the ten that were staring me in the face. I was into the swing of being incarcerated and getting along with the two main leathernecks, Pruet and Preston, and holding on to my neck. One major change was the arrival of a new superintendent and assistant superintendent. Mr. Scott warned us to beware because the new superintendent was named Cross, and most likely was. The assistant superintendent was Mr. Cockrell. Mr. Tom Cross finally visited to introduce himself and was thought by some to be rather gay, quite different from Mr. Cockrell, who seemed extremely intelligent, gentle, clever, and businesslike. Cockrell took time if he questioned a boy to consider the boy's problem and came up with good solutions. He, his wife, Katherine, and their two small sons took up residence.

It was known that I had painted the dormitory and by then had painted another. The glory from that, the singing quartet, the boogie band that Po' Sam and I had started, and my clean record on

A thirty-five-years-later return to Algoa, 1983.

the Hill qualified me for the job of house boy at the assistant superintendent's quarters. I'd been chosen by Mrs. Cockrell, who'd also introduced herself to Mr. Dave Scott and visited to see the painting.

Mrs. Cockrell brought a bit of light into my dreary life but frightened me with her friendly manner. It wasn't normal, to me anyway, being the recipient of such frank admiration of my character. She was one of the most frequent of the faculty to bring her own visitors to listen to our quartet sing. She was a model to any who saw her strolling around the Hill, even after dark, fearless of danger and carefree of criticism. Dave Scott's southern-born traditions kept him uptight whenever Katherine visited. She tried to bring him to relax but he maintained his place with his, "yas, ma'am, hy you, Miz Cockcrell?" Dave was nowhere when conversing with white folks and would hurry us to get the singers down to sing for the folks.

Katherine started bringing little snacks, leaving them with Mr. Scott, in appreciation of our quartet patronizing her personal visitors. My first knowledge of Mr. Scott's fear and concern for me was when he cautioned me in a trembling voice, "You better watch that white woman, she's gonna fool around and cause trouble." I

An Algoa benefit performance, 1983. The third window on the second floor was mine for over a year.

told him right out that she had not encouraged anything unbecoming between us and that I wasn't about to instigate any such desire. He said, "Dat down make no difference, iz what dez folk is thinking 'round here."

I was scared for sure then, realizing he probably didn't have as much pull as I with the heads of the faculty. I couldn't believe there was a rumor that she was visiting Mr. Scott because of her interest in me. My father, like Dave Scott, regarded fraternizing with white females as a no-no and had drummed it into my brother and me that it was dangerous even to look too long at "white ladies," let alone socialize.

It wasn't long before Slim Esters and the guys were ribbing me about having the best go on the Hill. Relating the truth of it all was to them just a show of modesty and a way of securing myself. As a matter of fact something was happening; I was in a state of frustration that I welcomed when around her. I carried the vision of her being and the memory of her friendliness back to the dormitory, where, after the lights were out, it was so easy for my fantasies to climax in reality.

Likely because of the rumors of visits and treats, Katherine stopped coming by my dorm but arranged that I be assigned to the task of delivering her laundry. Their laundry was done in Mr. Preston's laundry department also. Preston's eyes turned to steel when I brought the Number 9 bag and I feared he would ask me questions. On the very third call to Number 9, Katherine asked me to help her move two pieces of furniture in their living room. I had returned her many glances down at the dorm's recreation room, but never before had her eyes directed a gleam as they did when the furniture was in place. I breathed heavily as she walked to my end of the divan and reached for my face. She moved her fingertips down across my cheek and said, "Go back to Number four dormitory now and stay as nice as you are."

It is true I was scared and Dad's lectures were the only guide to safety I knew, but the lure and temptation were driving me mad with passion. Dave Scott did not advocate what was going on but didn't miss having me run down what had happened any day I'd go to Number 9 dorm.

I began hanging around the gym with the Algoa league for the chance to travel to St. Louis for the Golden Gloves tournament coming up. Sam had told us what liberties the trip would avail us but James and Skip didn't follow me in the elimination fights conducted to determine finalists for the Golden Gloves trip. My category, heavyweight novice, was free of opponents and I was set to go on.

The morning of February 3, 1946, Mr. Ellis, the dorm master who supervised the fight training, drove us into St. Louis. Mr. Ellis was to reside with my folks at 4319 Labadie and the other guys with theirs. Mother invited all for the rendezvous and dinners for the week of the boxing engagement.

The St. Louis Arena (now the Checker Dome) was the place of the fights. We checked in, sat around, and awaited our turn in one of the three rings set up for the elimination fight. My match for Monday night was not there for check-in nor by the time the fights started and I was free of the first contestant automatically. Tuesday night my husky Irish opponent took a look at my physique and announced to his manager withdrawal from our match. I secretly glorified his divine judgment, but in front of the Golden Gloves staff members spoke in disappointment. Monday and Tuesday night I went to several places where I had hung out in the past but I failed to find anybody I knew. Just on vacation a little while and it seemed like everybody I had ever known had left town.

I would have enjoyed Wednesday night more if I could have had a longer chance at a real stout Cuban boy weighing in at 190 pounds. Right off I went at him with determination, hope, luck, and no experience. Soon after the opening round I discovered he couldn't box a basketball. He made me look quite good. I became angry in the second round when he got a couple of nice licks in and I lucked up on some wild roundhouses that brought a cheer from the audience. In the third and last round, with the ultimate of my failing energy, I constantly bombarded him with roundhouses and aggressively chased the butterball around the ring until the referee called the fight. I bounced to my corner like I'd seen other fighters do, waiting. The ring announcer announced the decision and the referee grabbed my hand, raising my numb arm in victory. I won, but I had to be carried home and put to bed. It would have been painful had I seen a feminine form flutter forth that night. I was wishing I had trained more for the violent venture.

At breakfast the next morning, Mother thought they had half

killed me. Cradled safe in her kitchen breaking bread, swollen up around the face, I had to listen to Mr. Ellis rib me for not training as much as I should have. He was hip and let us do more than any of the dorm masters but was critical.

Thursday was my night off and I had to be present at ringside for press photos and interviews about my opponent, who would be the winning heavyweight of that night's bout. As I watched the bout that night, I realized there was no way I could stay in against either of the fighters and I began calculating how I could go about staying out. The press was firing questions at me, describing my opponent, and trying to provoke me to respond with an ''I hate him'' attitude. I lied like a dog, telling the reporters I would likely kill whichever one managed to survive the little spat I was watching and that the Golden Gloves representatives, with all due respect, must have had no better contestants than those waywards to match. I posed looking meaner than a junkyard bulldog, showing the few hairs that my nineteen-year-old chest had mustered. The big burly Italian brute, Joe Dazzio, lost to the monstrous black gladiator-built dude, Slillum Gillum. I knew in my heart I wasn't ready. The thought was worse than paying for my crime. What had I done? I'd had enough whippings in my life already, why did I have to fight before I could go back to jail?

Friday night they weighed me in, dressed me in a white robe with purple shorts, greased me down, and patted me on the back. While awaiting my bout, I slipped into my opponent's dressing room and asked him how long he had been fighting. In a guttery voice, three tones deeper than mine, while not even looking up, he answered, '' 'Bout three years, man.'' I thought how could my three weeks of watching in the gym compete with his status? I lowered my voice to the bottom of my belly and lied, ''Ought to be a good fight then!'' He said, ''I be doing my best.'' I didn't want to hear that. Jesus! I tried to think of something else threatening to say but nothing came to mind. I left his room close to being in tears, a nineteen-year-old robust wreck.

The time had come for my head to be on display and they took me by the arm and led me down the long ramp to the only ring set up for that night's competition. The gorilla I was to battle was prancing down the adjacent ramp, jumping along, punching and snorting. I felt like it was a death walk all the way from the balcony level to the ring, a hundred fifty feet of fearful feelings under four furiously focused spotlights.

In sheer bullshit, upon entering the ring I started jumping. I skipped out to the center, where the referee gave his final instructions, reminded us to protect ourselves at all times, and sent us to our corners. Even the referee looked in favor of him and I wanted, right then, to just shake hands and go home. But, seconds later "Ring goes the bell."

I shuffled with showmanship, as I had seen in gym sparring, around the side of the ring to meet my opponent. After half circling for a dramatic opening, Gillum came across the ring offering me a left jab in the face. I knew then he wasn't endowed with artistic ethics, to start hitting before I'd squared off to fight. I glanced complainingly toward the referee and received another set of jabs on my right jaw. I think it was the right side; I was already fast losing my memory as well as the hope to survive as he followed with a hideous right to my left jaw.

The referee raised a signaling "watch yourself" gesture with his finger and motioned to me to start fighting. I truly agreed and danced back to square off and get down to business but Gillum rushed me, backing me into the ropes, where I collected several blows to the gut, then on the nose, escaping only by a clinch that caused the referee to break Gillum's flurry. My nose was stinging and my jaws were numb. I lit into him with all three weeks of gym watching, throwing lefts and rights. My retaliation failed to make any connection, chiefly due to blinding blows he was slipping through on my face. Each time I went at him, he just dodged and inserted antagonizing jabs between my swings. I was hurting bad but furious from the embarrassing manner in which he was carrying the round on my jaws.

When the bell rang ending the first round, I hurried to a corner to find he was there. It was his corner and I lost valuable rest time getting to my corner. The Algoa trainer started yelling in my ear telling me I had to do better than what I was doing. Before he could finish fussing the bell rang for round two. They snatched the stool from under me and pushed me back out yelling, "Go get him." I got my guard up, determined to get some offense together.

If I could somehow just defend against his licks, I'd land some. My arms seemed longer than his but already they wanted to hang lower than my face needed them, so I rested the right arm while holding my left one out to ward off the pain. That worked okay and I could start hitting him with my right. But the licks didn't stop him. I felt left blows reach my guts after a couple of times that I tried it. I changed tactics and started dancing around and failed to see the onset of a sadistic straight right to the solar plexus. Gee! Did that hurt. I would have traded a week of solitary in Algoa not to have received it.

When my lights came back on I realized he'd started laughing. I became furious and I rendered a flurry of roundhouses. I tried to step on his foot while I delivered them, but while glancing down I found a sudden right cross to my face. A greasy glove, a black arena, and I was getting up off the mat on the count of six.

The dude didn't seem to use any sense of reason, no finesse, no practical style, no showmanship, he was just a street fighter and he was winning. He was hitting me anywhere, any kind of way. I heard a ring and he stopped hitting me all of a sudden. Thank God he withdrew the last blow I saw coming. The bell had rung ending round two.

I managed to at least get to my corner okay. My trainer was telling me, "Git on out there and knock him down. He ain't givin' you nothin' you can't take. You got him going, he'll be tired in a minute and that'll be your cue to finish him off!"

"Yeah, lots of luck," I dreamed.

I was hurting clean through to the bone and had had enough. I had him going all right, "going" right at me with only half of what he needed. It seemed he was in no way as tired as I was. I knew if anyone was going to be finished off, it would be me.

Ding! came the last round—Damn! I arose from my corner and before I reached the center a bone breaker met my jaws. He seemed to be reverberating and soaring and I was sinking with no other thoughts but for peace on earth, goodwill toward men. I couldn't get a lick in by punch or prayer. I thought of clinching my way through the balance of the round, but the referee kept us apart. I started waylaying in a flurry, swinging all over the place, hoping the bell would ring before I ran out of steam. Seemed like I swung for three weeks but no bell came to the rescue and when I was lucky enough to make contact, he belted me square in the face. I stopped my swinging altogether. I covered my head only to feel my stomach cave in under a gelding grant he gifted my gut. I was molded to madness and swore I'd kill him if he hit me again. I swung repeatedly and clinched wholeheartedly, but received an oblivious uppercut that put me in prayer. The crowd was yelling and I was hurting so bad I vowed to drop down on the next blow I received, regardless of where it might land.

I clinched again, got close to Gillum's ear, and whispered, "Let's make it look good to the people. Let's give 'em a good show." The inconsiderate grinning maniac reciprocated with an unbearable bash, combined with a nose-smashing straight right, and all I could do was to grab him and hug him in a clinch again, hanging on for dear life. He pushed me out of the clinch, immediately punching me again in the gut, then the jaw, hard on the nose again, and back to the gut. Jesus Christ!

I had forgotten about falling on the next blow and I thought of running the rest of the way. I took off skipping backward then sideways so fast, at one point I skipped up behind him and the referee pointed a warning finger at me not to hit him from behind. When he turned toward me, I pivoted ninety degrees and took off, circling around the ring. I didn't care how it looked. I was sore all over, tired, mad, and wanted out. I was desperate to leave the ring at least alive. Once again I was coming up in back of him and started to kick him, just for meanness, but the referee came between us and prevented it. I took off running, looking back to see how close he was following me, and found his red glove was there hiding the whole arena. Nighttime! On the floor! Nothing! A moment's peace until I came to at the four count and thought, "Get U-U-P!" What for? I remembered not to get up. I looked up and pretended to get up but the count was already ten. In fact, I had been lying there for a half minute. When I really came to, I woke up happy, realizing it was truly over and he wouldn't be hitting me anymore. Let him continue his career but not with the aid of my jaw bone.

Big, black, sweaty Gillum was standing above me gobbling up all the glory. It should've been me, but I hadn't done my homework or paid my dues. The only "ring" I ever wanted to see again was on a woman's finger. My fighting days were forever over; be they in sport, grudge, or courtship, I swore I would not, in the name of love, ever battle again. I'll look for a silver love rather than book for a golden glove. Thanks for the memories. Finished!

I was then given a medal for being runner-up in my category and I carried my defeated bottom home to spend my final day in St. Louis celebrating my sore jaws. I had been the only Algoa runner-up and the only one to get knocked out.

Back at Algoa, I ate oatmeal and soups, nursed my chin, jaws, and gums, convalescing with aches and pains for a week. I began settling down and taking my time every time I found good time to do my time.

One day after the flop fight Katherine called for our boogie band to perform for some visitors she'd brought out at Number 9 dormitory, where the piano was used by the white church services. It was late afternoon and most of the guys were at work. Slim Esters was one of the two guys who always was in on anything good so he came along with the band to Number 9 and helped set up. Slim was thirty-one years old, Po' Sam was around twenty-eight, nearest to Katherine's age, GG was twenty-six, Steff twenty-four, John and Hillary were both about twenty-two, and I was the youngest at nineteen. When Mrs. Cockrell came down she had only one visitor with her, a girl about nineteen. We sang and played a half hour when suddenly Katherine suggested it would be all right to dance if we wanted.

Slim, near to terminating his sentence and doing mostly as he pleased, immediately started dancing with the young white girl. Steff also danced while I was stuck playing in the band. It was the first time anybody had ever done any dancing on the Hill while we played and it was highly exciting to us. After Katherine had sat and watched a while she beckoned for me so Sam doubled on the piano. I was the first, only, and last to dance with her. It was also the first time I'd ever danced with a white woman or been that close with one. I believe she knew I was experiencing the most erotic pleasure ever in my life and felt the effects it raised in me.

As we gathered our instruments to leave, we noticed through the windows that around thirty white boys who were returning from a night class had gathered in front of Number 9, watching us dancing. They were furious with envy, showing moblike unrest and threatening to attack the lot of us. I looked immediately to

Katherine in hopes of protection and directions. I saw both anxiety and courage in Slim's eyes but feared for our safety.

The mob was blocking the only exit door of the dormitory. They hovered angrily, inching and wedging their way in as we huddled in the large room listening to Katherine demanding they proceed to their dormitory. She beckoned for the very tall Slim Esters to assist her in enforcing her instructions. Again in vain she warned the mob to allow us to return to Number 4 or each of them would receive disciplinary action. The angry mob resented her threats and pushed past Slim and her, rushing toward the band and me.

I split back into the vestibule leading to the Cockrells' living quarters and stumbled up the stairway and stood listening in the darkness. Shortly the mob voices diminished and a well-known voice sounded over the threatening white inmates. The voice was that of the assistant superintendent, who had arrived on the scene with three of the Hill administrators and quickly cleared the exit, dispersing the gang.

I returned to the recreation room and Katherine turned, asking, "Berry! Did you lock my door?" I answered, "Yes ma'am," and she began explaining to the assistant superintendent what had taken place. He interrupted her to advise us to return to Number 4 which was a silent, long, and memorable trip.

No disciplinary action was taken, but it was ordered that I remain within the confines of the dormitory until the racial tensions had subsided. Rumors about Katherine skyrocketed in volume and variety for weeks but brought little change in her determination to weather the storm. In fact, during that period she almost daily walked over to my dormitory and talked to Mr. Scott about the incident and the rumors. Still stalwart, she sometimes left a bag of cookies or similar goodies for me with Mr. Scott. Scott was nervous and determined thereafter to keep a distance between her and me for our own good. Additional rumors were spreading that she was not only having an affair with me, but with some of the staff, which infuriated her.

The truth of her virtuousness was never believed but she never ceased to be herself, conspicuously friendly with whomever she chose. Our lack of communication after the incident was broken by a note sent to me via Mr. Scott with the lyrics to a song, asking me to please put it to music, which I yet intend to do someday:

I can never have you, darling
Though I know our love is true
I can never have you, darling
But I'll go on loving you.

I had avoided trying for parole the first time I was eligible and took Slim Esters's advice to wait for the second period. Skip and James both had not waited and were both turned down on their first try. Then Skip got in deep trouble and they sent him to the main penitentiary in Jefferson City to finish his term. We couldn't leave together as we had come.

Slim's strategy worked for me and I was scheduled. It was then that hard time, as it was called, started. Preston at the laundry was truly determined to put a smear on my record and lengthen my stay on the Hill. I had to walk the line constantly, especially when outside the dormitory. The temptation that lurked with Katherine ceased as the Cockrells had taken residence off the Hill. Only once in a while did she return and visit.

Meanwhile, Slim Esters had dressed out and the boogie band fell apart when Sam went home. All of this now left me feeling alone and depressed. It was beginning to feel like I was in jail. I'd gotten used to the place like a senior in high school, and now all the other exciting students had graduated.

When the dress-out chart was delivered to Mr. Scott, it stated that my release date was October 18, 1947, my twenty-first birthday. I was ready to go but had to wait for two days to pass. The night before I left, I walked the floor whispering farewell to the guys just as those before me had done. It's a wonderful feeling, to be the fareweller instead of the farewellee!

At five cents a day, for all the days I had worked, my earnings totaled sixty-nine dollars right to the cent. The following morning the cash was given to me along with a train ticket from Jefferson City to St. Louis. I was carried away from the Hill at 10:30 A.M. on my birthday to the depot in Jefferson City and left standing there waiting for the train. Four hours and thirty-six minutes later I was back at 4319 Labadie, home. It was four fifteen and I was twenty-one years, nine hours, and sixteen minutes old. I was a grown man, and free at last!

C   H   A   P   T   E   R   F   I   V   E

Toddy

Y ou might wonder, if you are a female, what I wanted to do
first after leaving Algoa. If you are a male you likely know. I
was free. Can you realize what that means to a captive of
three years? Free, black, twenty-one, single, and unbelievably horny. I had little on my mind but to make money so I could
buy all the many things I'd dreamed of while incarcerated. But
foremost, I expressly intended to find someone I could share a
romance with. Sacred or sinful, I needed a mate badly to make
love to.

I walked into the house and said, "Hello, Mother." I could see
a couple of new wrinkles upon her brow and noticed more silver
threads had joined the gray hairs that I'd help turn in the years of
my mischief. The smile that she delivered was genuine but it lasted
only seconds. Mother broke into crying, bruised from the years of
injury I had brought upon her. Dad was holding back the mist in
his deeply concerned eyes. He came forward and gave me a Russian bear hug saying, "It's good you're back home, Charles." Our
relationship thereafter was so warm that for weeks we had no
arguments. Dad began letting me use the family sedan occasionally
for an evening out, as Henry before me had been allowed.

Henry had returned from the Philippines and was back working with Daddy. Lucy had abandoned the nourishment of the most beautiful voice this side of Marian Anderson's and was devoting her talent to hairdressing. Thelma brought me up to date on social life. I suppose she was proud of me. She told me I could get any women I wanted with the looks and physique I possessed. Paul was sailing through elementary school with dreams of a future with his playmate, Shirley. Little Martha was in the sixth grade and now she was demanding her time at the piano.

I started out right away doing carpentry work with Dad and Henry, who was now called "Hank," a nickname inherited from his Army buddies. Hank was the first to introduce the name "Chuck" for me. In no time, the entire family and neighborhood were addressing us by our nicknames.

With determination to possess some of the finer things in life, I dug in and worked long hours to acquire a little bank account. I was earning four dollars a day while Hank earned six dollars. Although we were doing the same work, he was keeping our time and the job paperwork, plus he had a family, which Dad looked upon as applicable to the difference in our pay. Come the spring of 1948, I had three hundred and sixty-nine dollars in my savings account and was well aware of the value and practice of saving. A dollar saved is a dollar made, Daddy used to repeat to us over our piggy banks. I began paying room and board again at home, as was the ritual once any of us were employed.

It was 275 stacked, packed, greenback dollars I decided to fork out as a down payment on a used 1941 Buick Roadmaster sedan. The shiny black Dynaflow was a later model than Dad's '39 Buick and Hank's '37 Pontiac, but not as clean. I took it everywhere but to bed. When the girls noticed me driving down the street, they would smile in response to my nods and that meant something to me. The police weren't as friendly, they gave me tickets for small violations. But I loved my big Buick in spite of citations and payments that were really hurting me to meet. I kept it spotless and parked it right behind Hank's car on the slope of the hill at 4319 Labadie Avenue.

That black Roadmaster was dear to me and provided luxuries far greater than any of the other wheels I'd had. It wasn't so much traveling that motivated me to better cars, it was the quality of settling down I anticipated. With the restrictions we had at home,

*I lured Mother into Don Photo Shop
while working with Dad.*

it was imperative to have a place to base for face-to-face. Many of the one-hour rooming houses I'd heard of around the neighborhood were right next door to a church member where they could see anybody going in or out. Besides the rooms being a costly two-dollar trip, even if you could persuade a girl to take the ride you had to worry about who you might meet traveling the same hallway. But in your car, you could enjoy any sort of spectacular performance without the likelihood of a heckler or someone crossing the stage during the climax of your show.

A rumor got out in high school, I remember, that one of my classmates passed his school teacher in such a hallway and the teacher never slowed down to return the student's greeting.

Tales were told in school of guys playing pranks on friends they would meet in rooming houses. Just to be a nuisance they would knock hard on the door of the friend's room and shout, "Police, open up," which would naturally close down all activity for some time if not the whole of the evening.

May Day was always a big thing for our family because it was when Mother and Daddy met and began courting. It was an annual festival held at Tandy Park that was patronized by the entire ethnic population of the city. Everybody strolled around with popcorn, ice cream, soda and candy, games, gadgets, and girls for the getting.

I drove to Tandy Park with an old schoolmate, Phillip Hubbert, a friend who missed by ten minutes going with Skip, James, and me for ten days of play in Kansas City and consequently missed the ten years of stay awarded us in Algoa.

With little hope of meeting a date, Phillip and I were strolling around with the Buick parked close by just in case. My mother's words, "An idle mind is the devil's workshop," came to my memory as we spotted two angels of which one seemed to be guardian of the other. Each angel was enjoying an ice cream cone and looked too leisurely to be bothered with flirtation. My approach to them opens the living story of Toddy that I vowed shall never come to a close.

"Hello, what's your name?" I asked. "Themetta," she answered between licks of ice cream. Frankly I was surprised to get an answer at all but asked again, seeking her last name, "Themetta Themetta?" as she licked away answering, "No, Themetta

Suggs." I became encouraged having her attention and got excited and seriously asked her, "Can we walk with you all?" When she did not verbally reject us, Phillip stepped up beside the younger girl, who announced she was Leola. With my best manners forward I sided with the guardian, Themetta. We chatted, learning that Leola was Themetta's fourteen-year-old niece. They lived a fair distance across town at the home of Leola's mother, Neppi, who was Themetta's sister.

We fraternized until around sunset when I asked if they would join us in a visit to a carnival that had opened in their area. They agreed and I introduced them to a shiny black Buick and to the carnival fair we went.

Once there, I didn't care what she wanted, I made it available. I freely spent the entire sixteen dollars I had, providing the games and rides Themetta chose and picking up the tab for Phillip and Leola after Phillip's three dollars expired. When we were leaving, I asked Themetta if she would like to ride around a while. She told me she had to see that Leola got home first, but afterwards she would have no objections to going along. I parked in O'Fallen Park, my school-day picnic grounds, and we necked like teenagers. No, I was worse. I couldn't stay away from her lips or from embracing her but I didn't dare suggest intimate relations. I wanted her for life. I even came up with a pet name, Toddy, which I've called her ever since.

The next time I visited Toddy, I begged Phillip to come along out of fear that she might change her mind if there were not a foursome. But Leola had driven Phillip mad with giggling non-sense and he swore he'd never return to visit with her again. I went alone, fearful of rejection, as was always my hangup. To my delight and surprise I found that Toddy had planned to leave Leola home. She related so frankly and sincerely to me that I began to level with her about my feelings. I confessed that I had become sincere in wanting a lasting relationship and "marriage." She told me she had a boyfriend and had contemplated marriage to him until a recent dispute. I was engrossed with her honesty, especially since she had known me so briefly. I asked her if she was against marriage for that experience. She replied that she wasn't.

I knew I was falling in love again after four years of loneliness. I felt the ol' love bug nibbling away at the memorable itch left by an earlier injury called "first love," Margie. Thoughts about Toddy through the day generated my ambition to work hard. Daily I phoned seeking another date but weekends were the only times practical due to her job. My family thought well of the prospect of my marriage, especially Mother; I think she hoped it would settle me down.

Toddy phoned me one evening to tell me that Neppi and her husband had some people over to play cards and she'd prefer getting away from it for a while. Less than an hour had passed when I'd picked her up, and we had no particular place to go. We soon found ourselves in Baden, Missouri, hugging and kissing, confessing to each other the feelings we each had for the other. We desired each other and the life of marriage. Overtaken by feelings, spirited by craving, I hoped to never betray her. We managed without words or even encouraging gestures, on the seatcovers under the stars of an autumn night, to make love for real.

I was still on parole and had to have permission to undergo anything that required licenses. So the following day I went downtown to my parole officer and told him I was planning to get married. Mr. Sotorias, the officer, had me bring Toddy to his office. I believe the law was that she had to be approved by the parole administrators before I could be allowed to marry. He granted permission and plans began. Thereafter, each weekend Toddy and I accounted our earnings collectively, setting aside some for living but most for the life we were to live.

The browning leaves of autumn '48 were falling fast away as the essentials of the wedding were being prepared. We decided the wedding location would be at her aunt's home at 3580 Lawton and announced it for October 28, 1948. And so it was. The "I do's" were vowed, the ring was placed, and I kissed my manhood into matrimony, hopefully forever. Leola as bridesmaid and my friend Clarence Richmond as best man appeared with Hank, Thelma, and the others in the wedding photo taken by Harry Davis.

Strangely, the difference of my first love crossed my mind during the marriage ceremonies. I felt Toddy was kinder, more sincere, and far more beautiful. I wished Margie could have been there to witness the deadlock of her chance to be Mrs. Berry.

Our honeymoon nest was the surrendered bedroom of a three-room apartment Toddy's Aunt Harriet provided for a fortnight.

Me and Mrs. Themetta Berry during that moment of surrender.

For ten dollars a week, she zzzed on the living-room divan. Our first home meal was navy beans. Toddy had not soaked the beans, and though cooked an hour, they poured on my supper plate like peanut soup. But I loved them, gnawing with jaws of love and swallowing grit with grace. That night was my first experience in confidence with a love affair, and I would have done anything Toddy desired of me.

Night after night we were into discovering different new desires and ways of satisfying each other. Fantasies that I had long dreamed of were realized, along with pleasures unfamiliar to her but enjoyed harmoniously. Fetishes, latent in my anticipations, were whispered softly in the warmth of close embraces and fulfilled in the fevered moments of devotion for each other. Time after time we adventured into the mysteries of passion, mind with mind and body with body, swearing that only death would cause us to part.

One month later, in November, Thelma let us move into the front waiting room of the beauty shop she had opened. I partitioned off the storefront's bay window, hung a door, and constructed a bedroom there. We lived there until January 5, 1949, when Uncle Ed (my mother's brother) rented us a bedroom and kitchenette in his rooming house at 4352 Delmar. We had a 1941 Buick, a refrigerator, and were on our way to riches. We were living like the best of the white folks until one evening we dressed in our "Sunday clothes" on our way to a movie. All the tenants were on the porch chatting as we noticed our parking space. There was no '41 Buick parked where we'd left it at the curb. I boasted about calling the police but knew it had been repossessed by the finance company. I had ignored two delinquent notices in order to maintain a rhythm of deposits I had started in our savings account. One of the tenants yelled that she thought we had ordered the tow truck that had come two hours before and towed our car away because the guy didn't say anything, just took it!

I made a withdrawal and redeemed the Buick. Later in the cold of that winter my Uncle Ed encouraged me to secure a job at the Fisher Body auto assembly plant, working on the evening shift. This almost tripled my income. Working nights I was earning sixty to eighty dollars a week, plus over thirty-five dollars working with Dad. Toddy was still working at a garment-cleaning establishment earning twenty dollars. The plant work was sweeping the floors around the assembly line while the carpenter work with Dad began with setting up the truck each morning with the materials for whatever job we were going on that day, then doing the jobs with Hank while Dad went other places, estimating and checking on future jobs. Toddy went to work on the bus, came home, and cooked. We would eat, and I would light out to my second job and get home past midnight.

Soon I was changed to the day shift at Fisher Body and had to abandon Dad's employment. The new schedule left over two hours daily to idle away before Toddy would get home from her work downtown. Soon I was wandering from the confines of our love nest, talking to females and neighboring tenants, playing records in the rathskeller Uncle Ed had in his basement, and fraternizing on the front porch. It led to one of the females giving amorous attention to my wandering idleness. Her temptation was awaiting my default and ate at my ethics like an itch.

It was not many times of temptation before I became disloyal to the dearest one I'd ever known. My regret started before the incident was even over. That night in bed with contentment in my wife's heart and guilt in mine, I surrendered and confessed the entire episode from the chatting in the rathskeller through the betrayal in the girl's bedroom. Toddy did not interrupt my confession as I struggled to complete it. When I had finished, she turned to me and said that it did not seem to be all my fault, that she did not want to share my love with another, but would not hold that against me because I was truthful about it. She was not just then in a mood to enjoy lovemaking but told me she would not hesitate to try and satisfy me if I needed her. Those sweet words drowned me in a pool of sorrow for causing a drop of sadness to befall her sweet heart. I was overtaken with intentions to thenceforth live the full life of loyalty that her love deserved.

I had been taught that a man's home was the first thing to be considered in life and owning it was the essence of success in his economy. Toddy and I both planned that we wouldn't touch our savings account for anything other than real estate. Consequently, a new car had to wait even after the transmission of my Buick Roadmaster went bad. We deliberately held out making payments and let the finance company repossess it again. Without the car we stayed in most of the time. Uncle Ed had parties down in the rathskeller on weekends, and since neither of us indulged in liquor, we did a lot of dancing as they drank. We went to the movies once a week and in general became introduced to the boredom hours of out-of-bed matrimony. I always thought I could never get enough of "it," and hadn't actually but surely didn't want Toddy to get bored with the nights of love that we never missed making. Plus I had learned that condoms were the only way to regulate family planning and Toddy had never been happy being even that much apart from that part of me. I was always so excited during those times that I didn't realize the difference. My determination to get ahead with a home and bank account helped me to manage to withdraw when we did wade nude in the nest.

Our bank account was handsome and had few withdrawals as Toddy and I lived low on the totem pole. A little light began to flicker when my friend Carl Collins told me of a job he was abandoning that had living quarters offered as part of the janitor's salary. Toddy thought it a good advantage in savings to take the janitor's job. We purchased a gas range matching our refrigerator and moved in to start fully keeping house. The owner, Mr. Weinder, saw how I'd renovated the janitor's basement quarters and employed me to subdivide one of the larger units on the second floor of the four-family flat. With Dad's tools, at night, I took the truck over to work on the big job that would clear over two hundred dollars. I completed the divisions, banked most of the earnings, and got back on wheels again in a 1933 Plymouth two-door coach; a sharp little ticker that gave me no problems, just ran like a clock.

Things were looking up again until one of the tenants, a single, unbiased Canadian woman, started stopping by to chat when coming in from her work. I'd been taught that white women were tricky as well as dangerous, but my thoughts about the risk of being with her diminished as she continued to talk with me in my quarters. I saw logic in what she was explaining about Canadian ideals of racial differences. How glorious it would be to not be snarled at or refused at a café when the food window for the colored people would close early.

She invited me to come into her place for tea one night. I hid it from her but I was scared close to diarrhea; yet I was too intrigued to resist despite the presence of Dad's warnings and stories I'd heard.

In great anxiety I followed her into her apartment. She latched the door and turned to me with a half smile, reaching for my hand and saying, "Don't be afraid, you have a right to be in here." I thought. That statement was part of one Dad had once said: "Black men have often dreamed their last dream where they thought they had a right to be." I had never been that close to a white woman since when I was eighteen, at Algoa.

She told me that she realized I was too anxious to relax and suggested I return another evening when I was more confident. Toddy was asleep when I went back downstairs and I looked up "confident" in the dictionary and found she was not referring to my physical attributes but was speaking of my mental attitude.

I did return, and on my own, with not only confidence but determination not to leave her dissatisfied with my visit. She seemed more eager than I'd expected which brought me to readiness. It was only after she had disrobed that I thought of Toddy being two floors below while I was carrying on like this over her head. What if she had a disease, I wondered, she did have a funny looking mole on her cheek, but it wasn't enough to hinder me from following her lure to love.

What I thought I'd feel as we were united was not what I experienced which brings me to mind of a poem I constructed in memory of her and some other rare occasions. I never named it so I'll now just call it "What's the Difference?"

What's the Difference?

I have given much love and received some
I have known many women through time
Who've taken me through many changes
And given in to many of mine.

Back when I was young and in high school
Shy from the girls to begin
But then Alma she taught me to please her
Which started it way back then

She was older than me and my first one
A child to his mother we were
I learned like a nurturing baby
The taste of a woman's bosom from her

The second was different in nature
Though Alma enjoyed me some more
It faded while yearning for Margie
Who bled my heart to the core

Months I had begged for her pleasures
Which Alma had showed me of her
But Margie's makeup was different
And I learned of how lesbians were

Then on to the road playing music
Singing and strumming guitar
In London I met a Parisian
And rode her home in my car

In Stockholm I dated a blue blood
From two different worlds we were
But love is like lickin' a lolly
And I learned about women from her

It's so hard to figure a woman
When you've not known them too long
You never can tell 'til you've tried them
And then you could still figure wrong

But from all the women I've been with
The beautiful thing that I cite
Is the pleasure I've found
In the yellow and brown
Is equal to that of the white.

    What I felt physically was not different from what I'd felt with companions I'd been with before, but the memory of making love to her is like no other before or since. Hearing sounds of endearment unlike any I'd heard embedded a taste of mental solidity, never to be forgotten.

That pleasure brought an end to my employment at those apartments. A fellow who had tried dating her before reported my visit to her apartment to the police. The very next day I was picked up by patrolmen and taken to the sergeant at the district police station. With the captain in his office, the sergeant positioned himself beside me with a baseball bat cocked on his shoulder as though my head was to be the baseball. I was told that if I lied just once, the sergeant would try for a home run. I knew he wouldn't likely hit me with the bat but I also knew that if I acted as if I believed he would, it would entertain the three officers there and lessen the heat of hate they felt for what they believed I had enjoyed.

One officer placed my head at a tilt, sort of like a football in position for punt, and the sergeant asked me right out, "Did ya fugger?" He was harelipped. My answer was, "No sir. A white woman? No sir!" I meant to appear scared out of my wits, knowing from past tight corners how white men enjoyed the superiority they could muster. The sergeant kept cocking the baseball bat, like he was ready for a lying drive, but I was still denying having relations with the woman. When I noticed one of them holding back his laughter at me, I relaxed internally but kept clowning. Then two of them broke into laughter, told me they were still going to keep me under surveillance, and released me.

Thinking about it afterward, I realized they really could have killed me and said anything to justify the slaying with no witness in my behalf. Daddy was right.

The episode brought my janitor job to an end and we moved from 5056 Delmar. We stayed with my sister Lucy until spring, then moved back to the homestead at 4319 Labadie. Thelma was back home after a long stay at the hospital. Hank had bought a home and was supporting his family. Lucy was still supporting herself and her beauty shop. I was working in and out with Dad, which he always allowed me to do until I landed a better-paying job.

I auditioned at white bars around this time and got jobs playing music also at private parties of friends and would sing alone with the guitar, earning four dollars a night. It helped me progress on my guitar playing and kept my piano keyed up for plunking. I joined the musician's union to be ready for any gig that might come up, though I worked "scab," earning under union wages, just to get to play. The competition among musicians at that time was critical since the older and popular AFM local members got the better jobs of the leavings left after the white local members had been employed.

I quickly learned that my four-string guitar was uncommon and I began searching around for a six stringer. When I would sit in with a band singing and the people would favor my performance, the band leader would step up and cut my bit short, thanking me and continuing his own show. I realized I had to have something to attract a club owner over the musicians they were used to. I decided to add little gimmicks I had observed here and there to my songs to try to sell my bit. One was making gestures that complemented the lyrics, such as squatting low to do a passage in a song that was sentimental and bluesy; another was to deliver facial expressions that pronounced the nature of the lyrics. I could tell from the response that it was going over.

I was also taking care of business at home because Toddy whispered to me one night when I came in that she'd had an examination that confirmed she was in the family way, the term Dad had taught us for pregnancy. We were going to have a baby. I was going to be a twenty-four-year-old father. Me?

As the first day of the summer of 1950 was crossing the Atlantic, Mother was advising Toddy, Lucy, and Shirley, the wife of my youngest brother, Paul, on baby care. All three were expecting that fall. The homestead was taxed with future dependents for deductions. Toddy was in the lead and I suggested that she had seen the last of her days of outside employment. In the search for a name for the baby, Toddy agreed to a suggestion of mine that we'd name the baby Ingrid since Bergman had long been my favorite movie star.

Savings were really accumulating in our joint account and we finally found a house we were able to buy. We chose a small three-room brick cottage with a bath and full basement at 3137 Whittier Street, only five blocks from 4319 Labadie. Four hundred fifty cold cash dollars at one counting was the sweaty down payment on the forty-five-hundred-dollar home. The white family of Dimottios who lived next door welcomed us with open arms, giving us a pot of spaghetti over the backyard fence the third day after we moved in. I remodeled the house, adding a half bath and bedroom in the basement, where we moved so we could rent out the upper three rooms for additional income.

We bought a new Muntz television set when TV first appeared on the market in St. Louis in 1950. Toddy and me and soon the three would enjoy Milton Berle, Jack Paar doing "Tonight," and all those little Kukla Fran and Ollies that I hated, thinking it was a real waste for such technology.

Toddy was hosting the biggest stomach I'd ever seen and on October 3, 1950, while I was working on a store-front bay window with Dad, a phone call was relayed to me from St. Mary's Infirmary that Toddy had just given birth to a girl who was named Darlin Ingrid Berry. Toddy told me she had been in tears on the way to the hospital wondering if she would survive her first delivery. She was rather slim and had once said to me that if there were complications that required a decision, she would want me to have them save the child instead of herself. There were no complications and the baby made a great difference at home with the additional atmosphere that infants bring. However I assured her that if ever, I mean ever, there came a decision of that nature that I had jurisdiction in, she would be the one saved and we would try again for a child. There would never be another Toddy if she was lost.

During the months that Ingrid was in infant care, I took on another job as janitor at WEW radio station. Joe Sherman, a renowned guitarist around St. Louis, played for the Sacred Heart Program there. In time he offered me his old electric guitar for thirty dollars, payable at five dollars a week.

I found it was much easier to finger the frets of an electric guitar, plus it could be heard anywhere in the area with an amplifier. It was my first really good-looking instrument to have and hold. From the inspiration of it, I began really searching at every chance I got for opportunities to play music.

During the summer of '51 I bought a secondhand reel-to-reel magnetic wire recorder from a friend who recorded me singing on it at his house. I think I would have stolen it if he hadn't sold it as I was completely fascinated by its reproduction qualities. It was that inspiration that started me to recording the first of my original improvisations, both poetical and melodical.

With the recorder, I started hanging around more with Ira Harris. I picked up a lot of new swing riffs and ideas from Ira's playing, which was similar to the style of Charlie Christian's. Ira showed me many licks and riffs on the guitar that came to be the foundation of the style that is said to be Chuck Berry's. Carl Hogan, the guitarist in Louis Jordan's Tympany Five, was another idol of mine. I buckled down and started taking seriously the task of learning to play the guitar. I studied a book of guitar chords by Nick Mannaloft and practiced daily. The chord book led to my getting a textbook explaining the basics of theory and harmony and the fundamental functions of notes, staff, and scale. It's amazing how much you can learn if your intentions are truly earnest.

On June 13, 1952, Tommy Stevens phoned me to ask if I could sing with his three-piece combo at Huff's Garden. It was to be our first time to play together since the All Men's Review yet we had seen each other at many intervals. My heart leaped as I answered, "When?" We squared away the address, agreed on the finances, and I showed up shouting that Saturday and every Saturday thereafter on through to December, earning six dollars a night. It was my first paid nightclub appearance.

The combo, a small group, consisted of Tommy on lead guitar, Pee Wee (can't remember his last name) was on alto sax, and I was on guitar singing the blues. Muddy Waters, Elmore James, and Joe Turner with his "Chains of Love" were the favorites of all the black disk jockeys' turntables while Nat Cole sang love songs and Harry Belafonte was popular also on the tropical scene. These were the types of songs that made up our selections, along with the backbone of our program, which was always the blues.

On November 1, 1952, at two o'clock in the morning, when I returned home from Huff's Garden, there was a message that my second daughter was being born. We named her Melody Exes. Melody was a welcome companion to Ingrid, who was barely two years old and would try to pick up and hold little Melody in her arms as she'd done with her toy doll. I was beginning to get a taste of how my father felt with six kids to come home to after work.

My work was divided into day and night with music. While Tommy Stevens didn't have the stage personality of some musicians I had encountered, he did have a congenial personality. He had no objection or reservations whatsoever about my presenting ideas and tactics that often went beyond his own showmanship, in fact he encouraged me. For example, I would suddenly break out with a hillbilly selection that had no business in the repertoire of a soul-music-loving audience and the simple audacity of playing such a foreign number was enough to trigger the program into becoming sensational entertainment.

We were making a little name for ourselves, enough to keep the club packed every Saturday night until that Thanksgiving, when the owner added on Friday nights. After the first two weeks of two nights straight we were drawing a full house. The owner agreed to our salaries being raised to eight dollars per man for each night. As Christmas approached, a rumor was out that a good band was at Huff's Garden and Tommy was telling us that we were being sought by larger nightclubs for jobs.

On December 30, a piano player named Johnnie Johnson phoned me, asking me to join his Sir John's Trio for a gig on the eve of the year of 1953. The nightclub he mentioned was four times as big as Huff's Garden, six times as plush, and ten times as popular. It had been renovated from a supermarket and named the Cosmopolitan Club, which is still located on the corner of 17th and Bond Street in East St. Louis, Illinois. It was on New Year's Eve of 1953 that my career took its first firm step. If I could have stored the drinks that were offered me that night, I think I could have set up everyone in the house twice. The owner of the Cosmo Club, Joe Lewis, asked Johnnie to have me come back the following week to start singing steady.

Johnnie Johnson was the leader and the pianist. Ebby Hardy was the drummer, and I replaced somebody to play guitar and sing. On holidays, Joe Lewis hired a bass to fill out the music more completely. By the Easter holidays we kept a steady packed house on weekends with a well-rounded repertoire programmed to the varied clientele.

The music played most around St. Louis was country-western, which was usually called hillbilly music, and swing. Curiosity provoked me to lay a lot of the country stuff on our predominantly black audience and some of the clubgoers started whispering, "Who is that black hillbilly at the Cosmo?" After they laughed at me a few times, they began requesting the hillbilly stuff and enjoyed trying to dance to it. If you ever want to see something that is far out, watch a crowd of colored folk, half high, wholeheartedly doing the hoedown barefooted.

Johnnie Johnson was reserved and jolly just like Tommy Stevens, and we didn't have any clash on stage when I would express myself and perform in excess of his own performance. In the beginning, when I would get applause for a gesture, I would look back at Johnnie and see him smiling in approval of what I'd spontaneously added to the song or the show. We made a name for ourselves there at the Cosmopolitan Club.

Toddy would get the biggest kick out of our rehearsals around the house, hearing me sing the country stuff. She cared less for country music, being a blues lover, and saw only the fictitious impressions I would insert in a tune to impress the audience with my hilarious hilly and basic billy delivery of the song. It could have been because of my country-western songs that the white spectators showed up in greater numbers as we continued playing at the Cosmo Club, bringing the fairly crowded showplace to a full house. Sometimes nearly forty percent of the clients were Caucasian, causing the event to be worthy of publicity across the river in St. Louis.

The state of Illinois in the beginning of the 1950s was a bit more liberal than Missouri in regards to relations between blacks and whites. A traveler might notice a considerable difference in the community just across the Mississippi in East St. Louis. For one thing, if a black and white couple were stopped by a squad car there they did not have to go to a police station and get a mandatory shot for venereal disease, as was the custom across the river in St. Louis. Nightclub people were known to flock across the river to the east side, where they could escape the bounds of Missouri's early-closing blue laws and continue their enjoyment.

Over half of the songs I was singing at the Cosmo Club were directly from the recordings of Nat "King" Cole and Muddy Waters. They are the major chords in the staff of music I have composed. Listening to my idol Nat Cole prompted me to sing sentimental songs with distinct diction. The songs of Muddy Waters impelled me to deliver the down-home blues in the language they came from, Negro dialect. When I played hillbilly songs, I stressed my diction so that it was harder and whiter. All

Manager and waitresses during Cosmo Club engagements.

in all it was my intention to hold both the black and the white clientele by voicing the different kinds of songs in their customary tongues.

Way back then, to me, a gig was played for the purpose of entertaining the patrons. So many times I have sat listening to a group knocking themselves out playing three-week-long songs that have the audience taking pit stops. I can never see why any group would not terminate a song that has boredom showing from the audience. But then some groups don't seem to consider that pleasing the patrons is their main objective. The varied audience at the Cosmo Club gave me an early start at judging the state of the people to be entertained.

Tommy Stevens had heard of our good draw and asked me to make a one-night appearance with his little combo back over in St. Louis at the Crank Club. He told me it was paying almost twice as much as my fee that weekend at the Cosmopolitan Club. Johnnie granted me the time off and I played the Crank that weekend with Tommy. But Johnnie had not mentioned to the owner that I wouldn't be there. He just substituted another guitarist in my

place, and as a result, Joe was furious. The guitarist didn't sing and the audience was quite used to hearing vocals. Consequently, Joe asked me for a contract, an item that Johnnie had been working without, and told me I could bring some other musicians in if Johnnie didn't go along with the change. When I mentioned this to Johnnie, he said that it would be no problem at all and that he would be happy with me in charge because he didn't care for the business end, dealing with the local union dues and all.

I added an *n* onto Berry in the AFM contract, naming my act the Chuck Berryn Combo, in an attempt to camouflage my worldly doings from the holy environment my father's name was associated with. Other than carrying a poster advertising the Chuck Berryn Combo back to the Cosmo Club area, there were no internal changes in our trio there so we kept cooking week after week. News spread fast about us and along with Toddy, my family started coming over once in a while, except Dad (no one would dare ask him). Toddy never let me forget to play a blues every two or three songs. She, a stone lover of down-home blues, would hum along until tears came in her eyes and then declare she wasn't crying.

I had become fluent enough picking the guitar to fill in full choruses without repeating licks. Johnny and I became so tight in feeling each other's direction that whenever I played a riff with any pause in it, he would answer it with the same melodic pattern and vice versa. We were especially entertaining at this time as we each knew many little quickies to each other's returns. I would slur my strings to make a passage that Johnnie could not produce with piano keys but the answer would be so close that he would get a tremendous ovation. His answer would sound similar to some that Jerry Lee Lewis's fingers later began to flay. Ebby was a show himself with his prominent snag tooth, dead center, always laughing with the audience at our gimmicks. But all in all we were slaves for the patrons, searching for whatever would elicit a favorable response. I feel that it wasn't my guitar playing, my dancing or gestures, my stage appearance or the programming of tunes alone that was responsible for the success I realized at the Cosmo, but all of these components combined and delivered with the objective of receiving the maximum applause. By and large the songs I played on my first recording were quite like what we were then delivering at the Cosmo Club.

Along about here, I also started making up new words to existing songs and adding extra verses to them as I was singing. It worked out pretty well and I began getting compliments on some of the improvisations, as they were said to be funny.

The carpenter work with Dad plus the gigs gave substance to my bank account and I bought a spanking-new, cherry-red '55 Ford Esquire station wagon, my first new vehicle. Toddy was a full-time housewife and bookkeeper to our little family that was soon to enjoy two additional rooms that were being built onto our little cottage. We bought a Zenith hi-fi console phonograph and radio and listened to Milton Berle, Elliot Ness, and Jack Paar of evenings. Things were going great; I even tried to color bust the lily-white AAA automobile club on Lindel Boulevard, but it was too heavy for that time. They simply had me postponed for two consecutive years while they claimed to be considering my application, then politely rejected it.

During this period, there were only two black disk jockeys in St. Louis, and the many small record companies had problems getting major white stations to spin records by black artists. There were great songs by black performers that were still seldom played on stations listened to by the white population. In some of the larger cities where black disk jockeys had gotten a foothold in a major radio station, many of the white kids were lending an ear and picking up on the black sounds, often against family traditions. Some of the kids in well-integrated cities heard black artists performing firsthand and would have to sneak to buy the songs they had heard and liked.

When I began playing additional gigs at neighboring cities around St. Louis, Toddy would go with me and I began to notice her being quite contented lounging off to the sides of the center of excitement or partying areas. She was always my greatest fan but would not share the glory that often comes with the support that she was also a part of. The girl behind the guy behind the gun that gets the glory, that's how she'd be interpreted by a rock lyricist, I suppose. Another thing I picked up about my Toddy was, being southern born, she helped considerably with theories regarding racial tactics, that some whites seem to still favor.

Trying all avenues at another club in St. Louis.

It seems to me that the white teenagers of the forties and fifties helped launch black artists nationally into the main line of popular music. Like in the sixties, when the white teenagers who became known as hippies brought the entire world into so many changes, these transistor-radio teenagers exercised great liberty in following their musical tastes. Some of these songs caused parents and radio authorities to declare they were unsuitable listening and initiate record-breaking sessions on their programs. But still the doctors, lawyers, and (well) police chiefs of today, who then were teens, bent an ear to a totally different music and decided to delight in what was destined to become known as rock 'n' roll. And so it was that Toddy, in putting up with lonely nights and days of me being away from home, was the greatest cause of my being able to reach the level of success that had and has come to me so far.

A Long Way from St. Louis

It was a hot Friday typical of summer in the Gateway City. It was only May, but in Missouri the month doesn't matter. When it decides to be hot it just does it. Dad, Hank, and I had been disassembling an old frame bungalow in the suburbs of St. Louis but I'd asked for this day off because I had an urge to hit the road again in the new station wagon.

Ralph Burris, my high-school classmate and long-time friend, had agreed to take off with me to visit his mother in Chicago. We arrived at sundown in the equally hot but windy city and drove directly to Ralph's mother's home to pay our respects, ate a well-prepared supper, then hit the streets to paint Chicago's Southside. Starting on 47th Street at Calumet, we hit most of the blues joints, bar after bar, spending time only in those that had live music.

I saw Howlin' Wolf and Elmore James for the first time on 47th Street, a tour I'll never lose memory of. I didn't want to leave the place where Elmore James was performing but Ralph had seen these artists before and insisted that we try other places. At the Palladium on Wabash Avenue we looked up and found the marquee glowing with MUDDY WATERS TONIGHT. Ralph gave me the lead as we ran up the stairs to the club, knowing I sang Muddy's songs and that he was my favorite blues singer. We paid our fifty-cents admission and scrimmaged forward to the bandstand, where in true living color I saw Muddy Waters.

He was playing "Mo Jo Working" at that moment and was closing the last set of the night. Once he'd finished, Ralph boldly called out from among the many people trying to get Muddy's autograph and created the opportunity for me to speak with my idol. It was the feeling I suppose one would get from having a word with the president or the pope. I quickly told him of my admiration for his compositions and asked him who I could see about making a record. Other fans of Muddy's were scuffling for a chance to just say hi to him, yet he chose to answer my question.

Those very famous words were, "Yeah, see Leonard Chess. Yeah, Chess Records over on Forty-seventh and Cottage." Muddy was the godfather of blues. He was perhaps the greatest inspiration in the launching of my career. I was a disciple in worship of a lord who had just granted me a lead that led to a never-ending love for music. It was truly the beginning as I continued to watch his most humble compliance in attempting to appease his enthused admirers. The way he communicated with those fans was recorded in my memory, and I've tried to respond in a similar way to fans of my own.

(Somewhere, somebody wrote in their column that on the occasion when I met Muddy he allowed me to play with his band. It has always hurt me when a writer replaces the truth with fictitious dramatic statements to increase interest in his story. I was a stranger to Muddy and in no way was I about to ask my godfather if I could sit in and play. He didn't know me from Adam on that eve and Satan himself could not have tempted me to contaminate the father's fruit of the blues, as pure as he picked it. Furthermore, I had wonders about my ability as a professional musician, singer, or anything else when in the presence of someone like the great Muddy Waters.)

I had planned to drive home to St. Louis that Sunday afternoon but, with anticipations of a chance at recording, I decided to stay over in Chicago until Monday. I couldn't believe I would be making connections with the Chess Record Company after being lucky enough to speak with Muddy, too.

Monday morning early I drove over to 4720 Cottage Grove Avenue to the Chess Record Company and watched from a store

Leonard Chess.

across the street for the first person to enter the door. After a lady entered, a man came in dressed in a business suit, so I ran across Cottage Grove to challenge my weekend dream. While I was posing just inside the office door, he looked up from scanning mail and said, "Hi, come on in," then left for a further office.

Before I started my well-rehearsed introduction, I saw a black girl receptionist (Adella, as I remember) and asked her if I could speak with Mr. Leonard Chess. I was getting more of the shivers as I glanced through the big window into the studio. She told me that the man I had followed in was himself Leonard Chess, and he reentered the outer office and beckoned me into his. He listened to my description of Muddy's advice and my plans and hopes, asking occasional questions regarding my expectations. Finally he asked if I had a tape of my band with me.

I had been taping at home on a seventy-nine-dollar, quarter-inch, reel-to-reel recorder that I'd purchased in contemplation of such an audition. I told him I was visiting from St. Louis, but could return with the tapes (which I hadn't truly made yet) whenever he could listen to them. He said he could hear them within a week and I left immediately for St. Louis. He had stood all the while I was talking to him with a look of amazement that he later told me was because of the businesslike way I'd talked to him.

After I traveled down from U.S. Highway 66, I contacted Johnnie Johnson and Ebby Hardy and began arranging rehearsals. Johnnie, Ebby, and I had been playing other people's music ever since we started at the Cosmo, but for this tape I did not want to cover other artist's tunes. Leonard Chess had explained that it would be better for me if I had original songs. I was very glad to hear this because I had created many extra verses for other people's songs and I was eager to do an entire creation of my own. The four that I wrote may have been influenced melodically by other songs, but, believe me, the lyrics were solely my own. Before the week had ended, I brought fresh recorded tapes to the ears of the Chess brothers in Chicago.

Chess was in the heart of the Southside of Chicago amid a cultural district I knew all too well. Leonard told me he had formerly had a bar in the neighborhood as well, which accounted for his easy relations with black people. When I carried the new tape up I immediately found out from a poster on the office wall that Muddy, Little Walter, Howlin' Wolf, and Bo Diddley were recording there. In fact Bo Diddley dropped by the studio that day.

Leonard listened to my tape and when he heard one hillbilly selection I'd included called "Ida May," played back on the one-mike, one-track home recorder, it struck him most as being commercial. He couldn't believe that a country tune (he called it a "hillbilly song") could be written and sung by a black guy. He said he wanted us to record that particular song, and he scheduled a recording session for May 21, 1955, promising me a contract at that time.

I went back to St. Louis to more carpenter work with Dad but also with a plan to cut a record with a company in Chicago. Each time I nailed a nail or sawed a board I was putting a part of a song together, preparing for the recording session to come. At the Cosmo Club I boasted of the records we were going to make soon and we took the lead in popularity over Ike Turner's band, our main rivals at the time in the East St. Louis music scene.

Muddy Waters was in the St. Louis area one night around this time and visited the Cosmopolitan Club. Enthralled to be so near one of my idols, I delegated myself to chaperone him around spots of entertainment in East St. Louis. Ike Turner was playing at the Manhattan Club and since he was my local rival for prestige I took Muddy there to show Ike how big I was and who I knew. When we got to the Manhattan Club, Muddy preceded Johnnie, Ebby, and myself up to the box office and announced, "I'm Muddy Waters." The cashier said, "A dollar fifty." Muddy just reached in his pocket and forked it out with no comment. That incident remains on my mind unto this very day. From that experience I swore never to announce myself in hopes of getting anything gratis, regardless of what height I might rise to in fame.

I took Muddy to my house that night, introduced him to Toddy, who was a devout lover of his music long before I came into her life with mine, and took a photo of him holding my guitar. May his music live forever, he will always be in first place at the academy of blues, my man, "McKinley Morganfield," Muddy Waters.

Finally the day came and I drove back to Chicago with my little band, on time, as I'd promised Leonard Chess. According to the way Dad did business, I was expecting Leonard to first take me into his office and execute the recording contracts. But instead he said he wanted to get "that tune" on tape right away. So we unloaded my seven-month-new red Ford station wagon and Phil Chess took the three of us into the studio and placed us around, telling us how we should set up for the session. I could see right away that Leonard was the brains of the company because he was busy making decisions and dictating to the five or six employees there. Phil ran around making friends and seeing that everybody was jockeyed into position for the flow of productions during the day.

I was familiar with moving in and away from the microphone to project or reduce the level of my voice but was not aware that in a studio that would be done by the engineer during the song. Having as much knowledge about recording as my homemade tapes afforded me was a big help, but I listened intently and learned much

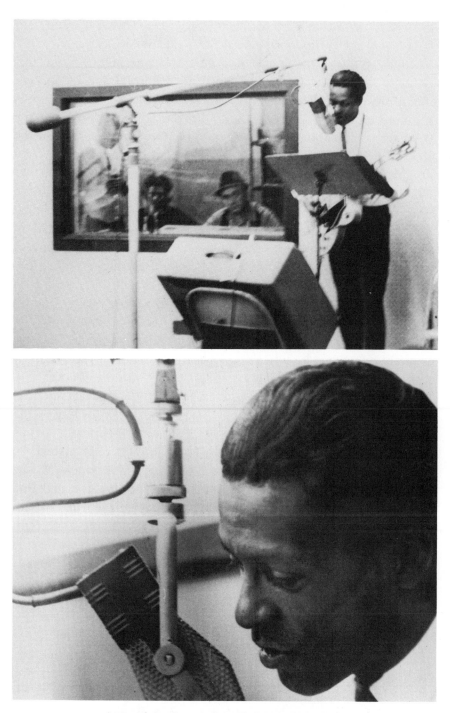

*At work in the studio. Phil Chess watches
from the control room.*

from the rehearsal of the tunes with Phil instructing us. I tried to act professional although I was as frightened and green as a cucumber most of the time.

The studio was about twenty feet wide and fifty feet long with one seven-foot baby-grand piano and about twelve microphones available. I had used only one for the tape I'd come to audition with and eight were used for our four-piece session. There was a stack of throw rugs, a giant slow-turning ceiling fan, and two long fluorescent lights over a linoleum tile floor. Leonard Chess was the engineer and operated the Ampex 403 quarter-inch monaural tape recorder. Through the three-by-four-foot studio control-room window we watched him, or sometimes his brother Phil, rolling the tape and instructing us with signs and hand waving to start or stop the music.

The first song we recorded was "Ida May." Leonard suggested that I should come up with a new name for the song, and on the spot I altered it to "Maybellene."

Leonard had arranged for a lyricist/musician, Willie Dixon, who'd written many of Muddy's tunes, to sit in on the session, playing a stand-up bass to fill out the sound of the music. Electric bass instruments were yet to come and Willie, stout as he was, was a sight to behold slapping his ax to the tempo of a country-western song he really seemed to have little confidence in.

Each musician had one mike, excepting the drummer, who had three. I had one for the guitar and one for my vocal, which I sat down to sing because a chair was there and I thought that was how it was supposed to be done. We struggled through the song, taking thirty-five tries before completing a track that proved satisfactory to Leonard. Several of the completions, in my opinion, were perfectly played. We all listened to the final playback and then went on to record the next song which was "Wee Wee Hours." By then it was midafternoon. Around eight-thirty that night we finished the recording session. "Maybellene," "Wee Wee Hours," "Thirty Days," and "You Can't Catch Me" were the songs completed. Leonard sent out for hamburgers and pop and we lingered an hour picnicking, an ordeal that became a ritual with Leonard bearing the tab.

It was nearly ten o'clock when we went into Leonard's office and sat down for the first time to execute the contract he'd promised. The recording contract he handed me seemed to be a standard form, having no company-name heading at the top. It was machine printed on one side of the single sheet of paper. The other paper he gave me was a publishing contract, a segment of the music business I was totally ignorant of. It was printed on a double sheet, but I didn't understand most of the terms and arrangements of publishing either. I did see the word *copyright* several times as I read through it and thus figured if it was connected with the United States government, it was legitimate and I was likely protected. I remembered when I was a child, Dad had talked about getting a patent for a perpetual-motion apparatus that he'd invented, telling us nobody could take your achievements from you when they're patented and copyrighted.

Anyway, I read it word for word. Some of the statements were beyond my knowledge of the record business, such as the "residuals from mechanical rights," the "writer and producer's percentages," and the "performance royalties and publisher fees," but I intentionally would frown at various sections to give the impression that a particular term (I actually knew nothing of) was rather unfavorable. From the white of my eyes I could detect Leonard watching my reaction closely all the while I was reading, which made me think I was being railroaded. In fact, the corner of my left eyeball was checking out his response to my reaction, yet still knowing full well I'd sign the darn thing anyway. I slowly read on, finally signing it at last. I took my single-page copy, shook hands, and bade happy farewells to what was now "my" record company, loaded up, and drove off into the night with Johnnie and Ebby to St. Louis.

As we drove home through the black night more songs were sprouting in my head. As easy as it seemed now that the session was over, another four were bound to come forth.

Back home I continued to enjoy the local action at the Cosmo Club. The immediate future looked stable enough to support the little family I'd started. Melody was approaching two years old, Ingrid was nearing four, and I had been married nigh six years, a veteran at paying monthly bills. Toddy and I were looking forward to Ingrid being enrolled in grade school that September. I was feeling no pain, playing three nights a week at the Cosmo Club and, except for the half day I took off to go to Poro College of

Cosmetology to study hairdressing, I was working with Dad during the day. Our bank account had risen to fourteen hundred dollars, with the Ford station wagon payments paid to date and the house installment note one month ahead.

Days and weeks passed with no word from anyone about the recording session. No mail or phone calls followed to reveal any results of the contract I had with the Chess Company. I sat and waited, wondering if all the time and effort was in some trash can or did it actually take a lifetime to organize these things.

Ike Turner was sizzling at the Manhattan Club in East St. Louis just a couple of blocks from the Cosmopolitan Club. By then Ike had recorded "I'm Tore Up," and it was just beginning to be heard making its air way back toward the ears of the home folks. People were asking when was our record coming out and we had nothing to answer. Albert King, another artist from the St. Louis area who sported a left-hand guitar, began climbing to the Ike and Chuck level.

Suddenly from the mouths of babes came remarks that they'd heard "Maybellene" on the radio and shortly after I picked it up while driving home from Dad's house in the station wagon. There is no way to explain how you feel when you first hear your first recording for the first time in your first new car. I told Toddy as soon as I reached home and we celebrated as you can imagine how!

Johnnie told me that while coming home from the Cosmopolitan Club one hot night he was tuning the radio for some blues and on station WGN in Chicago heard the unmistakable rhythmic bounce of "Maybellene" being played over and over. WGN was a big rock station, bringing a linked-up program by a New York disk jockey.

On July 19, a phone call came from Leonard Chess informing me to expect a visit from a Mr. Jack Hook, an affiliate of his, who was bringing a contract from the Gale Booking Agency for me to sign. I picked up this mediator at the St. Louis airport, brought him home, discussed the booking-agency contract, and signed it, keeping my copy. The exciting thing in the contract was that the Gale Booking Agency was to assure me of forty thousand dollars' worth of work each year for three years!

I was feeling so good about the way things were falling in place, I began wondering if I would die in a few weeks. I couldn't believe

Powdered pose I took myself for publicity shots, 1960.

I had the chance to earn such a sum in such a short period. The-metta and I stayed up until 4 A.M. reading over the contract for flaws and mistakes, but found none. Plus it had no obligation on my part that I felt I could not uphold. I would be earning the money if only I got to the concert, played, and sang. I knew I'd make it to them on time even if I had to hire a police escort.

So now we knew the session was processed and records made. Would they sell? What was next? When would we see them on the jukebox?

What had happened was that Leonard Chess had sent our re-cordings to one of his promotion affiliates, Alan Freed, a big disk jockey in New York whose program was on the network going to major cities of the U.S. It was sent to him as a test run to determine which of the four tunes got the best response. "Maybellene" took priority over not only the four Chuck Berry songs, but over all the records sent from other record companies for play that week. The phone lines from Alan Freed's radio audience were jammed with repeated requests for "another spin" of "Maybellene." Alan Freed was unknown to me at that time, but I was to become a distinct disciple. Leonard released "Maybellene" as a single, with "Wee Wee Hours" on the flip side.

I showed the Gale Agency contract to my folks, who wished me well. The fulfillment of the contract, traveling and performing, would put an end to the ritual of carpenter work with Dad. During the following days, up to the last day working with Dad, people would often mention that they'd heard a song and ask if I was the "Berry" who recorded it. Rapidly "Maybellene" rose to number one on the charts and there were many phone calls from Gale and Chess telling me what to expect in the coming weeks.

One such call from Leonard Chess culminated in an opportunity to go and play three thirty-minute shows with the trio on the fifth, sixth, and seventh of August 1955 at the Peacock Lounge in Atlanta, Georgia, for a total of five hundred dollars. I swallowed the opportunity, not letting on that I'd walk down to Georgia and play all week for half that bread. The Ford station wagon was loaded three days before we left and without tricks, treats, or trouble, I pulled my red wagon up in front of the Royal Peacock Lounge. The marquee on the front of the building blazed with names from the show, reading, the FOUR FELLOWS, MISS WIGGLES, and CHUCK BERRY. Seeing my name there reminded me that my mother had once predicted that "Maybe someday your name will be in lights."

We registered at Mr. B. B. Beaman's Savoy Hotel on Auburn Avenue, shaved, shivered, and shot over to the gig to find out when and what we were supposed to do. Evidently we were liked and enjoyed since they requested "Maybellene" six times one night, and we played it as many. When the club owner paid me the five hundred dollars, it reminded me of making the down payment on 3137 Whittier, our little home, which was the largest amount I'd handled up to then.

That was our first professional road gig and after it we returned to the Cosmo and twenty-one dollars a night. A farewell party for our little combo was held there on August 14, the eve of our departure for a week-long gig in Cleveland. The entire family, including my dad, was present. My brother Paul, without a drop in him (he doesn't drink either), made his debut singing "On Top of Old Smokey" along with me during the country-western segment of the program. It was the first time my dad had ever chosen to be in such unholy surroundings and to date, as far as I know, it was his last. Nevertheless his attitude while there would have never given light to his indifference. "When in Rome," Dad always told the children, "do as the Romans." He seemed to be happy for my prospects but I could sense he had reservations about my ability to handle the wicked world he envisioned me headed into.

Then it was on the road, going to Cleveland and Gleason's Bar in the little red wagon. The bar was a jazz hangout and I thought we didn't go over too well, particularly with "Maybellene." At Gleason's Bar I received telegrams from the Gale Agency telling us to continue on around the lake to Vermilion and Youngstown, Ohio; Lynn and Roxbury, Massachusetts; and to Linden, New Jersey, doing two shows in each city, with the exception of Youngstown, where three nights were booked. We did it in great spirit, learning as we went how to manage the traveling.

A big entry, near to four hundred pounds, a friend of Jack Hook's named Teddy Roag, came into my ventures on this swing. Teddy was organized by Jack Hook to arrange my schedules and assist my trio while traveling up the New England coast. The tour itself was a great education for me as to what a "concert" was, what a box office was actually for, and how to register into a hotel. I was unaccustomed to hotels, having never up to then experienced any out-of-town sleeping accommodations other than rooming houses. I also learned about percentages of gross-attendance income. My nightly fee then was 60 percent of the gross box-office intake with a minimum guarantee of $150. Teddy Roag, my acting manager, somehow always managed to see to it that the attendance was just at the brink of entering the 60 percent range, never into it.

I was a fair wizard at math in high school and could eyeball the dance houses to estimate attendance. Most nights I determined that there was enough attendance to carry into percentages, but

C H U C K

when I mentioned this once I was told I'd have to prove it, so I didn't question anymore. I couldn't think of any way to support my judgment or monitor the attendance. The figures that Roag would return with, after sometimes over an hour of counting the gross paid attendance, would reach me on a handwritten statement and would usually show us just a few dollars under the amount that would have started my overage payable. Teddy had a habit of snapping his fingers and saying, "Damn, we almost made it."

Before I came to realize Teddy's tactics, he had been for weeks advising me that I needed his expert management and that he was available for the job. I should have known the big beer-bellied bully did not like rock 'n' roll enough to be traveling along without any compensation but the prospect of the job he hoped to get. I'd heard of managers for Marian Anderson and Joe Louis and thought having one was the professional thing to do, so I agreed and accepted him, signing him as my manager while still wondering about his integrity. Almost immediately after I signed him he stopped showing up at most concerts except when we'd be playing near where he lived.

After a concert in Lynn, Massachusetts, in 1955, he handed me a hundred-dollar bill, but without the usual written statement, saying, "How's that?" That night the crowd had to number over twelve hundred and the admission was $1.50 so it must have grossed at least $1,500 excluding freebies. We should have earned near to $750 aside from the guarantee of $150, but I could not have proved it. I pondered dearly how to overcome being vulnerable to such swindles. Since I had no other way to know the attendance I had to trust the promoters and my manager, who all knew each other very well.

After we had worked our way through New England, and down through the Capitol area, I accepted a very important contract for one week at the Paramount Theater in New York. It was my debut as an artist in New York with my little three-piece group, and one of my first acts on arrival was to order three pairs of brown suede shoes totaling thirty dollars and three rayon suits totaling twenty-seven fifty each to make sure we looked sharp for New York. When we reached the city we picked up Teddy, who directed us to the Paramount and finalized the details there. The big marquee was glittering with names of stars. Headlining the show was Tony

Bennett, the most pleasant and gentlemanlike artist I have yet come to know in show biz, followed by Lillian Briggs, Nappy Brown, the Four Voices, Chuck Berry, and Red Prysock's Orchestra, including Big Al Sears.

Teddy, the biggest thing in the wagon, including Ebby's drums, took us to 52nd and Broadway to the Alvin Hotel and assisted us in registering for our rooms. Never had I viewed so many people rushing to and fro between so many skyscrapers. It was almost like another world. I phoned Jack Hook, Alan Freed, and Gene Goodman, who were New York business affiliates of Leonard Chess. Leonard had asked me to phone them to introduce me to his New York contacts and them to the guy who wrote "Maybellene."

Jack had a distributing shop in Manhattan where our number-one, and only one, record was being shipped out to dealers. He persuaded us to come immediately over to his storefront business on 8th Street, where I observed boxes and boxes of disks bearing the label of MAYBELLENE, CHESS, CHICAGO. They were triple stacked ceiling high covering one entire wall. We were stepping over opened boxes scattered about on the floor of the combination office-warehouse.

Between steps on the way to his desk in the back corner, I thought well of the amount of product carrying my identity on each item. Still it never entered my mind how much wealth such quantities should bring in sales. I didn't have any idea that Alan Freed was being compensated for giving special attention to "Maybellene" on his radio program by a gift from Leonard registering him part of the writer's credit to the song. In fact I didn't know then that a person also got compensation for writing as well as recording a song. My first royalty statement made me aware that some person named Russ Fratto and the Alan Freed I had phoned were also part composers of the song. When I later mentioned to Leonard Chess the strange names added to the writer's royalties, he claimed that the song would get more attention with big names involved. With me being unknown, this made sense to me, especially since he failed to mention that there was a split in the royalties as well.

The next stop was show time. We wiggled through the concrete jungle, arriving at the Paramount at high noon of the day we were to open. We had seen Nat Cole and Dizzy Gillespie chatting on the

*The sheet music for "Maybellene," or "Mabellene," as it
was originally misspelled.*

corner of 8th and Broadway while in traffic. I wanted so much to
touch Nat or shake his hand, but the midmorning lull on the streets
of Manhattan was like the downtown rush-hour traffic in St. Louis.
As many of my fans since have done, I shouted out his name and
caught his eye but was then too excited to utter another following
word.

At the stage-door entrance of the Paramount, the security man
assumed who we were from reading our big red plyboard "Maybellene" sign atop the fire-red station wagon. As we stood like
cattle from Missouri, he yelled, "Chuck Berry 7-H." I thought he
said "7-A" and we met Lillian Briggs face to face when we had to

vacate her dressing room, which we had occupied by mistake. I hadn't even known prior to then that a dressing room was provided for accommodating a performer. It was neat to have a free room, and private at that, to lounge around in. It was a far cry from dressing in a car. When we unpacked our rayon show clothes, we discovered they had wrinkled so badly that they appeared to be seersucker suits. But we found that they even provided a smoothing iron and seamstress service if you were a heavy tipper in need of the luxury.

Watching how the other stars were handling various situations I was learning lessons I desperately needed in order to keep pace with the level that both fans and peers thought I had achieved. I hardly knew anything and was being congratulated and asked advice for everything. Some of the advice I gave was merely horse sense from the "Show Me" state. I wasn't about to appear to be the dumb, small-town, full-grown, lucky idiot of show business.

We had five shows a day to perform, starting at one o'clock in the afternoon and continuing until one o'clock in the morning, with a one-hour movie between each show. Most shows held over seven thousand kids screaming through the live performances each of the seven days of that week. Never before had I confronted more than a thousand people watching me perform, and I had never seen the inside of a theater as enormous as the Brooklyn Paramount. My hometown's answer to the Paramount was the St. Louis Fox Theater, but the time had not yet come when a black person could patronize the big Fox in St. Louis. While I'm thinking of the racial policies of the Fox at that time, I remember farther back when my mother used to take me all the way to the back of the city streetcars to sit down. It's a funny thing though; then it was fun passing all those pale faces who you could look at but they would never move their heads an inch to notice you staring at them. It was quite noticeable to me that such practices were not prevalent when we reached New York.

The day of the first show we dressed and waited. They had us booked as the opening act, and while Johnnie and Ebby seemed quite relaxed I was scared out of my wits. The show was about to start, and I was the newest act on the show with the hottest tune on the charts. Finally the half hour was shouted, meaning the stage show would start in thirty minutes. I was pushed onto the wing of

The Paramount Theater in 1955.

*The crowd outside the Apollo in Harlem, New York,
the last week of August 1955.*

the stage by Jack Hook for readiness to go on. I heard loud amplification and Alan Freed's voice proclaiming, "And now that 'Maybellene' man, Chuck Berry!" The curtains rose and over seven thousand people, focusing fourteen thousand eyeballs on a carpenter from Missouri, cheered as we trotted out on stage.

I'll never forget that when Jack pushed me out I broke into a sweat but broke wind as well. Saved by the roar of ovation, the bitter fright in me was diluted with the sweet applauding, but I really didn't know whether to start or wait until they stopped clapping and screaming. Three weeks I stood there waiting as the thirty or forty seconds clicked by; then I struck out with "Maybellene" and the roar of cheers rose again to over the volume of our delivery. It was actually the same feeling I felt in my high-school auditorium singing in the All Men's Review some sweet sixteen years prior; the welcoming cheer wiped the doubt clear of any fear of being there. The quality, tonation, nature, and volume of the sounds from the people told me like never before that it was a positive response, and I performed with gestures and expressions as if I had been the trainer of Milton Berle, Sammy Davis, Jr., Bob Hope, and Louis Armstrong. Immediately I was wondering how I could keep the enthusiasm up after "Maybellene" was completed. "Wee Wee Hours" was a blues and the audience seemed to be solid white.

It seemed they should have wanted me to do the latter song first but I never disputed this when reading the rundown. I waited four weeks between songs, until the crowd had really subsided, then softly led into the intro to "Wee Wee Hours," which surprisingly brought a similar yet more soulful cheer. Then I was finished until the next show, which was three hours away. That was it, I did my bit and sang my hit.

As we came offstage from our seven-minute performance, we realized that the drive to New York, the lousy hotel, the wrinkled rayon suits, and the frightening multicult audience were all worth the reception we got plus meeting all the big stars that, until then, we'd only heard on radio or records. And so the morning and the evening were the first day of Paramount Show Biz.

The following performances of the week might have been a recording of the first. Each time, the same volume and quality of response greeted each of my songs. I even thought the same people returned for each show. I've been asked many times how I felt at such moments. Well, I doubt that many Caucasian persons would come into a situation that would cause them to know the feeling a black person experiences after being reared under old-time southern traditions and then finally being welcomed by an entirely unbiased and friendly audience, applauding without apparent regard for racial difference.

Whatever has bestowed longevity on my career, be it learning, luck, or ad-libbing, I owe it to the ignorance of any talent I knew I had at the time of these first appearances. I was merely playing it by ear and taking in every move made around me. Many of the actions were not of the nature I had been trained to follow, but I found them fruitful to survival.

The Paramount engagement terminated, leaving me feeling I might be able, as it was turning out, to carry on for a little while in the big business, around all these big stars. I'd talked to many of them about the hooks and crooks of show business, and I was learning what services a manager usually renders and how and why one is useful to an artist. The 10 percent of all income I was paying Teddy Roag was not in the least being earned, as he was continuously out of reach when I needed him, so at our next meeting I called his attention to that fact and got some remark about his needing other income to survive.

Our next engagement was at the Apollo Theater in Harlem, New York, for a week. They ran a ninety-minute stage show six times each day, seven days a week. Each show had a thirty-minute interval of cartoons, ads, and previews; then the next show would start. All day for twelve hours, people, artists and their gofers and visitors, would run up and down the stairs to backstage dressing rooms. It seemed everybody was greeting, cursing, meeting, or fussing about anything that could diminish the strain brought on by the frequency of the twelve hours of shows being produced. Peddlers, managers, lawyers, admirers, relatives, hookers, and beatniks would pass among the artists, but all seemed to mix with each other. There seemed to be more girls backstage than out front. Half of them were offering you anything you could want from muttsi balls to matrimony. It struck me that it was a far cry from the attention of girls that I experienced back in high school. At the Paramount they didn't allow the girls to wander backstage, but the Apollo security was of no use and as loose as a bucket of juice (which was also flowing freely). White folks mingled and conversed as black as colored folks, if you know what I mean. They (blacks and whites) jived between each other. All were artists, playing foolish, having fights, and making love as if the rest of the world had no racial problems whatsoever.

There was a soul-food restaurant across the street from the stage door where Johnnie, Ebby, and I had our meals. There and then I first began hearing the term "black" being used in reference to and replacing the terms "Negro" and "colored person." But in the familiar environment back home in Missouri, the latter terms were still being used, although when joking among ourselves and in rudeness from some of the white populace, "nigger" was still in the lead, as popular as ever. It took me a while to swallow the term "black" in reference to race, but it came to be as normal as anything else.

The Apollo engagement was a whole new ball game. I noticed there was only one white artist in the show and hardly any in the audience. It quickly became obvious that the Apollo audience was harder to satisfy than the Paramount's. If you played anything other than your hits or some hit they all knew, you were in deep trouble, most likely booed if not personally insulted in typical Apollo style. It would be better if you knew what you were doing there, and I wasn't quite sure I did. One thing for sure, I was going to stand the test and face the folks; after all, it wouldn't be the first time I was booed while performing. I hadn't forgotten that once I sang my own favorite hillbilly number in a soul club and got booed by a belligerent crowd for the audacity.

We all know booing is the expression of contempt or disapproval, but there are some levels of the expressions that one side of society may never see. Take the most elegant of productions, say a symphony. There a person will cough or, as a sign of multiple dissatisfaction, you will hear scattered little cracking noises throughout the audience that definitely would not occur during an appreciated performance. With another class of people one might hear an obviously faked clearing of a throat or the general restlessness and stirring of the audience during the performance. Then there are the average people who pay, wishing to see their purchased product. In a polite way they may openly announce their desire to hear your hit or something they know better than what's being delivered. Or they might start moving around, visiting the john and murmuring out of discontent with the performance at the moment.

Finally there's a crowd that intends to get what they paid for and makes it known if they don't. One might witness the standing protester who revengefully exaggerates his discontent, blatantly shouting his views of the performing artist's unpopular choice. The crowd collectively may stomp and roar so loudly that an alert producer will pull the act off and replace it with a more favored one.

Some of the hecklers at the Apollo did protest outright, standing up during a soft ballad and yelling, "Sing some 'um we know, fool! Don't nobody wanna hear that crap." The heckler would get applause when many thought likewise, while the singer could only sing on in embarrassment, bearing the insult. Bobby Charles, a friendly country boy from Louisiana, was the only white on the bill. He had a mild country-western hit that could have been mistaken for rhythm and blues. When he came on for the first time, that's when the show hit the fan. He couldn't have received more boos if he'd sung "Ol' Black Joe" in Yiddish or "White Christmas" in Slovak. In a standing disparagement that lasted throughout his performance (and the producers let him continue), the audience riddled his selection with heckling howls.

Once, when I hustled in from the soul-food place, late for the show, I heard my name announced as I ran through the stage door. I skipped right onto the stage, hooked my guitar in, walked up to the mike and a guy stood up in the third row and yelled before I could start my song. I knew I was in the right business when I heard him say, "You need you some shoes, Chuck." (I had my bed slippers on from relaxing between shows.) Ignoring him and the laugh he received, I belted out, chanting, " . . . Maybellene, why can't you be true." I would have much rather been doing Beethoven's Fifth Symphony with the other-type audience, receiving only a throat clearing or a sneeze for my unpreparedness.

We made it through the seven days, bringing the show to a close with Ebby drinking beer, Johnnie sipping wine, and me bearing the responsibility of learning how to be show people in the awful empire of New York City. On our last day at the Apollo the three

tailored yellow suits with green collars we had ordered before starting at the Paramount were finally delivered, C.O.D., leaving no time for a final fitting let alone wearing them in a show. We were learning fast the New York ways of business.

On the last night, the show ended at 1:45 A.M. and Teddy Roag showed up as usual to collect our salary. Afterward in a ham-and-egg joint he hit me with the biggest problem up to then, asking me for an additional 5 percent for his managing fee. Besides the three full weeks of theaters that were directly succeeding the Apollo plus a forty-two-engagement one-nighter tour after that, which he also would not be on, I was determined to follow my resolution not to have a manager, simply because I saw little use for the service they provided compared to fees paid. I told Teddy I would be thinking about it up to our next business transaction, and soon after that I fired him, using the fact that he had illegally cashed a check made out to me as reason.

I was too overwhelmed with the rise of my status in show biz to tell the Chess people of my concern about due compensation for performances. The greatest loss I'd had up to then came not from making a mistake but from the mistake of not making sure I hadn't. Fine print in contracts had been talked about by my father, who said one must read carefully to comprehend all obligations, "both to and of the other party." But enthusiasm is one of the more pleasurable emotions that I fell victim to during my youth, and as a result I accepted and signed some of my contracts without entirely understanding some portions. Items I was entitled to were shifted to others, who evidently were shifting back favors in return to the Chess Record Company's benefit. Had I known the music business better, or for that matter, at all, I would have known I was not receiving due fairness. Then there's another saying my mother dwelt on, "Don't let the same dog bite you twice" and, believing it also, I learned from my mistakes. Woe be unto him whose wrongs are revealed.

Such dealings, favor for favor and sometimes extra holler for extra dollar, were to become known as "payola." Sharing "Maybellene" with Freed and Fratto made me most acutely aware of this practice. I just recovered the full rights to "Maybellene" in 1986, some thirty years later. That loss was two-thirds of the total, or twice as much as the royalties that I received from "Maybellene" for years. I was told that registering their names was a compliment of the record business that was generally practiced to promote a song that would likely not be a success without the push. With the first royalty check I received being right at ten thousand dollars, over twice as much money as the cost of the home I'd purchased a few years prior, I wasn't about to question the trends of the trade. Yet, blind as I was, I wondered.

Back in the studio, things were so harmonious and friendly that there did not seem to be any room for distrusting the integrity of the Chess brothers with the paperwork that followed a recording session. I was just learning about much of the paperwork because

back then I had no idea how big the business of writing and publishing was in itself. I had thought publishing was only promoting
or advertising a product. But as time went by I learned that a
publisher held the fate and direction of a tune and had a great
equity in its sale. Nevertheless, I continued to write my songs,
knowing at least of copyrights and recording royalties.

Southern Hospitaboo

F orgive me for using my own word, *hospitaboo,* which is
meant to represent *hospitality* with *taboo* or in other words
how do you do but don't-you-dare. I feel that the greatest
hospitality on the entire globe is found in the Southland of
the United States. There is no other place, at least that I've been,
where friendliness and consideration for others are perpetuated
more. But be that as it may, when it comes to matters of race the
type of hospitality practiced by most southern people seems to fit
the compound word I've improvised.

Remember that my view, the only true view I can see with, is
through the black eyes that I have. As I toured far from St. Louis,
I saw and I wondered, then reasoned and felt, then realized and
believed. But I don't know any truths about racial matters but
what I have seen.

Two buses were parked at the stage door of the Apollo when we
closed the two-week engagement on September 16, 1955. Teddy
Roag had given me a list of cities that the Gale Booking Agency
had lined up for me as part of a tour that included Arthur Prysock;
the Four Fellows; the Spaniels; the Cleftones; a comedian, Clay
Tyson; Queenie Owens; an upside-down dancer known as Miss
Wiggles; my group; and Buddy Johnson and his orchestra, featur-

ing Ella Johnson. We all felt pretty much at home since all of the acts were black and there weren't likely to be any internal racial problems.

My heart sang when I viewed the list because I had been to only a couple of the cities listed. The instructions informed us that a bus ride plus hotel reservations would be provided, which left me only to ride, get dressed, sing, and peep then eat, meet fans, hide and sleep. It was for sure going to be exciting to be on the road with all of these recording stars who, just a month before, I had only heard sing on radio and records. Now I was going to be practically living with them.

At 3:30 A.M. the buses rolled across the George Washington Bridge and down the New Jersey Turnpike. Buddy's eighteen-piece orchestra, the roadies, the valets, and the equipment occupied the second bus and I was with the rest of the artists on the leading bus. I saw things going on among them that I had never known about a month before. I saw my first live gambling, a bold and blazing crap game in the aisle of the bus that carried on until dawn. When I woke up at the announcement of a breakfast stop, only three were left in the game and maybe twenty thousand dollars had changed hands in the aisle.

On we rode, snacking, arguing, singing, and still sleeping half the day until we reached the auditorium in Youngstown, Ohio, where the tour was to begin. We went directly to a hotel where I learned fast to rush to be first checking in to get the better rooms of those reserved collectively. At eight o'clock that evening the Buddy Johnson Show opened the Nu Elms Ballroom in Youngstown.

Many of the places we played on that first tour did not have enough dressing rooms or toilets for such a large show. Things were just getting started with rock 'n' roll and a lot of places weren't prepared for shows on a grand scale. This ballroom was one such and we all had to share the few dressing rooms. The fans were not restricted from freely coming backstage, visiting the artists, and whatnot. Whatnots were real nice then, since the management knew not what would be going on backstage. I thought the older artists knew all the fans who would come backstage and chat with them so I would leave the room when chats became whisperingly soft.

All first shows are bummers as far as everybody getting tight with the orchestra and getting coordinated with the time schedule of the show itself. Considering all, the Youngstown date went well with a near full house in attendance. After the final act of the show that night, everybody who knew the ropes let their hair down and the good times rolled in the hotel rooms.

I found that the custom of travel was to lay over on a night after we had traveled a long way that day. The following noon took us south to the Municipal Auditorium in Charleston, West Virginia; then we traveled on to the Skating Rink in Kyle, Virginia, and to the City Auditorium in Raleigh, North Carolina, where we began to bump into bits of biased behavior. The danger deferred any desire for drumming up any dilly-dally down in Dixie. Up to then I had never spent much time in the southern states, though I had constantly heard of things that occurred there from my father. Now I was traveling through the Heart of Dixie, where heeding his advice would behoove me to behave better than a Baptist bishop.

We played the Recreation Center in Kingston, North Carolina, on September 20, followed by Columbia, South Carolina, then the Duval Armory in Jacksonville, Florida. That is where southern habit hit home. My memory of how it went down remains vivid. We had to stay in a private boardinghouse and dined collectively on soul food. The conditions were good, I might add, except that they were the only legal accommodations available.

Once we got to the Duval Armory that evening, the conditions radically changed. "You boys this" and "You boys that" was the language used until an elderly stagehand started to address one of the band members with his customary term. It wasn't a nice or necessary name for a neatly dressed black guy, but then the addressee was hip to the old man's concept. After the obvious re-addressing of the slip-lipped word to "ni-boy," the trombone player replied, "Yahzza, we need da platform over 'ere."

Just before they were to open the doors for the spectators, four of the maintenance guys came out and roped off the armory with white window cord. They looped and tied it to each seat down the center aisle, making it an off-limits zone that neither coloreds nor whites could tread. They didn't, we didn't, no one else didn't during the entire show although the armory was jam-packed with standing room sold as well. That six-foot-wide aisle, holding the

A sequence of publicity shots taken
long before "My Ding-A-Ling" came out.

choicest views in the place, stayed clear as a whistle.

At the close of the show, twice as many young whites as blacks rushed toward the stage, climbed on, and began socializing with us. After mumbling to ourselves the whole evening about the conditions we performed under, we overwelcomed them, extending hugs and some kisses. We knew the authorities were blazing angry with them for rushing on stage and at us for welcoming them, but they could only stand there and watch young public opinion exercise its reaction to the boundaries they were up against. Almost as if it was rehearsed they hugged, kissed, greeted, or shook a hand and filed off to the exits untouched by the helpless, amazed security.

I'd been hearing of this sort of racial problem for years from my father, except his stories were more severe. The difference that I could conceive between his stories and my observation showed that some progress had taken place in race relations.

On to Mobile, where the same attitudes prevailed. We were determined, at least I was, to bring those southerners to accept us for what we thought we were: northern artistic performers and not Yankee black lord-knows-what. When my turn came, I skipped on stage and belted out my song, "Maybellene." I put everything I

had into it: a hillbilly stomp, the chicken peck, and even ad-libbed some southern country dialect.

Contrary to what I expected, I received far greater applause from the white side of the ropes than the black side, where I noticed only a chuckle or two. Okay, I thought, with my mind on getting next to my brethren and sisteren. There was truth showing up in what Leonard Chess had told me about ''Wee Wee Hours,'' which was on the B side, selling mostly in the rhythm-and-blues market. On the other hand, ''Maybellene'' had hit in the pop charts, identifying the popular or the white market. When songs were so posted in the trade charts it seemed to serve as a guide to help disk jockeys and merchants direct their respective businesses. Thanks to the trade magazines, by the time any new recording reached the broadcasting or merchandising market, it had already been ''Anglopinionated,'' my own word for being ''white worthy'' of broadcasting.

Determined to retaliate, I bowed longer to the bored black side than I lingered on the left, let my fingers crawl into the introduction, and poured out the pleading guitar passage of ''Wee Wee Hours,'' hoping to pierce the perfect passion of my people. It seemed to be going homeward as I continued to pour on the profound pleadings. I began hearing the "uhmms" and "awws" as I approached the kissing climax and how beautifully the black side began to moan. I knew I was getting next to them. It was just like we were all then boarding da' ol' ribba-boat, about to float into a land of flawless freedom.

The palms of black and white were burning as the producer signaled me to exit. My act was scheduled for only two songs and my ad-libbing during "Wee Wee Hours" had carried me overtime, which was frowned at in such a regulated show. But I was thrilled and dragged my feet walking off stage as the applause simmered.

That night when the concert ended, it seemed the whole police force had surrounded our bus. Over a dozen patrolmen were lined up forming a path for the show people to walk through. The isolation ignited ill feelings in the fans as well as the artists, who vented their feelings by ridiculing the conditions in disguised voices. My father's stories came to mind as I watched the officers taking the abuse and I thought, do in Rome as the Romans do. Fear that the police would reciprocate led me to board the bus. As it turned out, nothing happened except bragging on the bus as we continued the tour westward.

On the show buses, while traveling to engagements, I would pass the idle time away writing lyrics that would be put to melody during dressing-room jam sessions or merely in lonely afternoon hotel rooms with the guitar as a guide. Many of my songs were born during these solitudes when plunking on the guitar and coming across an inspiring passage that brought about a theory for lyrics to be added. Once in a while I would hear a song that I liked so well that I would write my own lyrics to the admired melody and then rearrange the melody in order to bring it to originality. This sort of birth mostly wound up rejected and abandoned due to the loss of the feeling in the original tune that inspired me in the first place. However some of the stack of lyrics awaiting work would be reviewed some time later and tailored to fit a melody, maybe coming from somewhere in space, and worked out into a finished product.

One song had its birth when the tour first brought me to New Orleans, a place I'd longed to visit ever since hearing Muddy Waters's lyrics, "Going down in Louisiana, way down behind the sun." That inspiration, combined with little bits of Dad's stories

and the thrill of seeing my black name posted all over town in one of the cities they brought the slaves through, turned into the song "Johnny B. Goode."

We reached New Orleans at noon and again stayed at a well-to-do schoolteacher's hotel in the Negro district, but this time the hotel was right downtown among the general population. Normally in a city that is new to me, I like to wander alone incognito to get a real concept of the people. One reason I would go alone was that not one of the guys on the tour would go back to the back window of a segregated café as I would to eat. But that was the only way I could get to talk to people and seek their true feelings.

That evening before show time I followed the guys who'd been there before to the French Quarter. It was like no other place I'd seen. We passed a place that was right up my alley of entertainment but the fellows I was with only glanced at it. I lagged back and made a flip-flop to the beer joint through whose doors could be seen strip dancers. No! I discovered in the smiling but rejecting expression of each doorman of every strip joint. With great dignity and perfect timing, each would draw the door closed as I strolled past, reopening it beyond my sight. Unlike Georgia, Alabama, and Mississippi, where they frowned at you even for strolling in to get a pack of cigarettes, I noted in New Orleans that segregation was practiced in a more polite manner, with some strategy.

That night our show was superb. I was getting into the swing of delivering my act perfectly and everyone was becoming tight with Buddy's orchestra. There was ease in the fraternizing between artists and patrons after the concert, but my mind was still on Rampart Street. Alone, I went back to the row of strip joints, this time with a little strategy of my own. With the exception of when the door would close because a black male happened to pass in front of the bars, I enjoyed a half dozen full shows wearing a cowboy hat and gloves, standing in doorways and using my field glasses from across the street.

From there to Houston, Corpus Christi, Austin, and then Waco, the tour plowed on. As we worked the road show through Texas, it was obvious that race relations were far less incompatible. The deeper we played into the heart of Texas the bigger it seemed the hearts of Texans opened to us. Outside difficulties died away while internal problems seemed to be rising.

In the Walker Auditorium, in Waco, it was a drag insofar as publicity for the tour but a big thrill to Johnnie, Ebby, and myself when we substituted for the big Buddy Johnson Orchestra. The concert was delayed because Buddy's bus was being detained and searched by the local police for drugs. After a while the patrons became restless and initiated a rhythmic clapping. The local promoter suggested that live music be played in the interim. Our trio was the only musical group on the tour other than the orchestra, so they asked us to "do something" to hold down the restless crowd. Johnnie, Ebby, and I agreed and rushed to the stage. Without the usual big orchestra sound we managed to hold the attention of about nine thousand spectators with the two little hits and some unrecorded songs. Forty minutes I sang, from Nat Cole's sweet songs to school-day ding-dongs, analyzing each last tune in prospect of the next best to deliver. The spectators gave us a tremendous ovation for our contribution as the rescued orchestra set up behind us. The promoter said, "Thanks, Chuck."

When I came off this tour, I phoned Leonard to tell him that the Gale Agency had me booked another four weeks straight in theaters. His reply was to urge me to get into the studio as soon as possible to record enough songs for an album.

We went back to Chicago December 20, 1955, for the requested recording session, where big Willie Dixon again joined us on his upright bass fiddle. I had written three new songs in preparation for the session: "No Money Down," which Leonard liked best of all, "Down Bound Train," and "Together We Will Always Be," which I hoped to start on Nat "King" Cole's trail with. It was a little more relaxed doing this second recording session although Johnnie and Ebby brought some beer in with them. Leonard and Phil had us jam for two additional instrumental tracks which they recorded and said they would be for fill-ins of albums. It turned out later on an album that they named both songs themselves. That passed me off.

It was always good to finish a session regardless of the stops for lunch and the pauses for the guys to have a beer break. I was well aware of the patience it required to come to a satisfactory cut from my own trials and errors in trying to do a perfect tune on my homemade tape recording machine.

We never had the time nor did I even know I had a right to participate in the editing of the freshly recorded songs because we were on the road nearly constantly, supporting the popularity the tunes were creating for us. I thought all the perfection had to be rendered in the running roll of the taping while the songs were being recorded.

When we would finish a recording session and listen to the playbacks in succession, I would think a certain song should be the A side of the next single and leave the studio expecting to hear it come out next. But Leonard always followed his own judgment and mastered the tune he, or whoever he confided in, thought was the most marketable selection for the time. I tried to outsmart him after I caught on to his tactics and came to the studio with just four songs that I liked, thinking he would have to go with one of the four for an A side. (He would usually have a B side left in the "can" from the last session.) Once I came in with four sweet ballads and went out having done four boogies of which one was

"Guitar Boogie." Leonard never took anybody's suggestion on what would sell best, but he was good at predicting it as far as I could tell.

I don't think Leonard ever knew I caught on to one of his tactics, which was that whenever he was about to do something that was not in your favor, he would inevitably precede the scheme with an unexpected good deed. I figured this out after one time when before a recording session, he took the whole band out to a big breakfast and then offered me his nine-day-old Cadillac Eldorado to run down to the Southside of Chicago for a couple hours to see Toddy's ill sister. When I returned he had my band jamming with a guy he was auditioning and this session later turned out to be an album by the guy without any compensation for my fellows. He then issued me a handsome royalty check as he shoved an unrelated songwriter's agreement toward me to sign quickly as he was leaving for an urgent appointment. Six months later I realized what took place at the signing, which took twenty-eight years to redeem.

Although the Chess studios had fairly good equipment, they let many blunders pass on the master tapes for release on the finished product, for example the tailing notes that dribble away into space from the end of "Little Queenie," which agonizingly reverberate in my ear still today. Even some of the DJs who liked the song then would fade the ending out, as it should have been edited in the original master. But we were all young then and tender (well, tender anyway) and so was rock 'n' roll, and we cared more about the intentions than the preventions.

The nation's capital at the Howard Theater was our next engagement for a seven-day week, to be followed by a week each at the Royal Theater in Baltimore and back to the Apollo Theater in New York. By now, Johnnie, Ebby, and I had the road routine down pat. The hotel rooms allocated to the artists were usually all on the same floor and the traffic in the corridors was a show in itself. As was the custom, the performers and band stayed together, this time just across the street from the Howard's stage door at Cecelia's Hotel. But the higher-paid acts secured accommodations at the more elegant residential home of Mom Bueford, a nonrestricted lodging establishment facing the front of the theater. Because I didn't make the cattle run for the more economical rooms at Cecelia's, I had to check in at Mom Bueford's too.

My high-school yearnings for a girlfriend were far in the shadows now. Not only was there an abundance of chance for intimate relations but an ampleness of choice. The Howard had a mixed audience of about half white and half black of which a certain half had the whole of my attention. Not without Dad's warnings present in the routing of my behavior, I began to stretch out beyond my hopes of reaching. Oh, virtuous reader, remember as I did then, that I was still solidly married and had vowed to let not temptation taunt me into betraying promises again. I tried, believe me I just tried.

Knowing I was reserved in my behavior on the tour, a singer (still very well known) invited me into his dressing room to witness what he thought I was missing by evading close companionship. At the designated time I walked in to see, for the first time in my life, a lady, unaware perhaps that I had entered, paying personal homage to his magnitude. The view is vivid in my memory today. The lady was truly one of great beauty, at least from the rear view that I had of her long golden locks of hair. I bumped into two other viewers smiling in envy as I turned to leave. I waited down the hall to see the woman's face as she exited. She passed me glowing with more beauty than I could conceive as I wondered why she, of such beauty, should have to pay such homage to her idol.

Another debut, during a night at the Howard Theater engagement, happened as the Cleftones singing group scored a playmate from the audience who appeared overwhelmed by the spirit induced from the rock 'n' roll songs. The next morning one of the Cleftones summoned me to show and boast about the girl, who they'd seen me speaking with the evening prior. At their room, I was shown her lying sprawled on her back upon a bed undignifiedly exposed and obviously drunk as a skunk. The male singing group, in their early twenties, were boasting that they'd all enjoyed the fruits of her femininity and could not resist offering a sample to someone else, namely me.

I must admit I have never denied mine eyes the beauty of femininity in the buff by turning my head therefrom. I thanked the guys, entered the room, bade them farewell, and shook the girl to awaken her. She awoke and stared at me momentarily, then her eyes drifted fast into tears. She turned to her side in sorrow saying, "I must have drunk too much—can you tell me where my clothes are? Are they gone? Aren't you Chuck Berry?"

All four questions got a yes, but already, my opinion was no! Her attitude awaking seemed to have much more dignity than did her appearance sleeping. She could have been a lady, though young and inexperienced in the vulnerabilities that alcohol can place one within. She likely lost her leverage in the lush of liquor. As I sat chatting with her, watching her dress from the bare while trying to explain to me that she was not that kind of girl, a confession from her and a lesson from me was the impression I left with her.

Only lacking the moment of sheer ecstasy, I felt I knew the real person better than the fellows as she had soberly revealed her intimacies while nobly appealing to my sentiment. Imagining she should be well into her forties by now, I truly would cherish seeing that person once again just to observe how, after that experience, she must have changed.

Watching the other artists on the tour I began to wonder why they allowed themselves to waste money as I had observed so many times. I was sure that some of my colleagues didn't realize the value of the money we were being paid for the service we were rendering. They consumed too much in trifling purchases, gambling, and gifts to flatter girls, ordering foods that were outrageously priced only to impress a companion who tomorrow would not be remembered. When I once questioned a certain high-earning artist about his real estate, he assured me he was comfortable in the elegant condo he was contemplating buying. At the time, I was in fear that "Maybellene" would catch pneumonia and die off the charts. The nearness of the not too distant past kept me frugal.

I didn't see my "manager" Teddy Roag until the last show night at the Apollo, when in he came to collect his commission. He informed me that our trio had a flight the next morning departing from Idlewild Airport at 10:30 A.M. I informed him that I didn't fly. Didn't fly into New York and wasn't flying out, that in fact I didn't FLY! I was ready to ditch him anyway and became arrogant and shouted that my father was a big-foot Baptist by faith and stood on a true foundation. I'd once driven from St. Louis to New York City in seventeen hours and it never crossed my mind when I signed the contract for the Chicago engagement that we couldn't drive it overnight. Neither Johnnie, Ebby, nor I had ever flown before. But it would be a breach of contract if I didn't fly. Either fly or blow my career. Chances are one in a thousand that airplanes crash. But what if that one is one thousand? I said damn—went to the hotel, went to sleep, got up, went to the airport, and flew to Chicago. I swore that if I arrived safe at the Regal Theater I'd never sign another contract without reading every line of it thoroughly. That situation was a major lesson to me. I didn't observe the dates and times on the contract as well as I did the ticket of that fat-bellied, four-engine, propeller-driven Stratocruiser.

From the Regal it was back home to get the first realization of what it was like to have some popularity, receiving congratulations from acquaintances declaring, "I heard you on the radio." "Wee Wee Hours" and "Maybellene" were being heard at every other jukebox and rising in the charts of *Billboard* and *Cash Box*.

After I fired my manager, I began transacting my affairs as I saw fit and continued to feel my way through the business as best I could alone. I began flying to some of the distant concerts and routing my bookings by mail or phone. I think I developed a keen

sense for feeling my way around in the music business, but many times I came out losing from bidding too low, when trying to estimate the worth of my performance. Rather than face embarrassment by bidding ridiculously high, I watched expressions and the contracts of other artists lying around in the booking agency. Based on the last job I would have worked, I would raise the fee a little, but cautiously, so as not to overbid. Many bidders would respond to my asking price with a broad smile, which I sensed meant a fee set too low. They always had the upper hand, asking me what I wanted for playing a place I didn't know the capacity of.

Later, near Christmas of 1955, I heard Clyde McPhatter doing an interview in which he was asked what it was like playing in his hometown. His reply was, "You can't even draw flies eating watermelon around your hometown." But at home that Christmas eve, we turned over two hundred people away at the Blue Flame Club, where just months prior we had played for musicians' scale of forty-two dollars flat fee.

Our first drive of 1956 was to Buffalo, New York, for a week at Mandy's Lounge. Johnnie, Ebby, and I stayed at the Vendome Hotel, next door to the club. Playing a week-long engagement at a nightclub was a new experience in meeting people in a different atmosphere. An intoxicating one. I had never, even in the city of New York, been so warmly accepted in such a close-knit working and social environment as I was there.

About twenty of the three hundred nightly patrons were black people, but I only learned that most of them were black because they acknowledged it. To see those who were apparently black dancing among and with the whites reminded me of the rope of restriction in the Atlanta auditorium. Why is it so, Dad told me once, that black hands could knead the dough of the bread that white tongues savored, yet blacks could not be favored to feast at white tables. Here there were some who appeared white to me but declared and enjoyed being black, although they looked whiter than most whites. The white people there mixed with the blacks who were black as well as those who appeared white, leaving no black blacks or white whites feeling uncomfortable. I never learned if Mandy himself was black or white, but where I was born and raised it would have been an issue of great befuddlement. Once I learned that there were places in the United States with such harmony in racial rapport I started keeping a mental tabulation of them.

More than once the racial rhapsody was broken by confusion. From the black-and-white eight-by-ten lobby photo sent out preceding concerts it was not always evident that a performer was a descendant of a native field hand of days gone by. Photos of black faces only required less exposure to appear as bright as white faces. I suppose I was booked in the South many times as a white singer. For one such concert I was booked in Knoxville as a single with a local backup band. I flew in, picked up a Hertz car, and proceeded to the gig. I parked the car at the rear of the building and knocked on the stage door. It was around 6 P.M. and the dance was to begin at 8 P.M. The door opened and some big guy asked what did I want? I said, "I am playing here tonight and I came early so I could rehearse with the band."

The guy broke into laughter and told me that Chuck Berry was playing there tonight and the show was sold out. I was sensing he had a little racial attitude about his air, so I cautiously proclaimed that I was Chuck and promptly produced the contract for the engagement that night. He observed it a couple of seconds and told me to wait a minute, closed the door in my face, and left me standing outside.

About fifteen minutes passed and then another man opened the door and presented himself along with three other males and four females. The bossy-looking guy spoke, telling me that he was sorry and that they had booked a hillbilly band for Chuck's backup. He went on, "It's a country dance and we had no idea that 'Maybellene' was recorded by a niggra man." They had sold out the place but couldn't permit a black person to perform, as it was against a city ordinance. They all stood there looking befuddled while the guy explained and excused me, whereupon I left the premises, drove around awhile, came back at dance time and parked, paid but puzzled, at the back-alley entrance. As I sat in the dark of the Hertz car, it was annoying to observe the passing patrons talking of how much they anticipated hearing "Maybellene" sung live that evening. I faded away fast after hearing my song played by the band they had hired to replace me.

Later the promoter of the date wrote the Gale Agency in New York, who had booked the job, arguing that from the lobby shots enclosed with the contracts they thought Chuck Berry was white. The Gale Agency retained the deposit, and I learned through that experience that in such cases of default I would be paid regardless, so I coined it fortune without fame.

On February 1, 1956, I was booked at home in St. Louis, at the "lily-white" Casa Loma Ballroom, which did not admit black people. I wanted to impress the home audience so I added Leroy Davis, a tenor saxist, and Albert Moseby, a magnificent bassist.

BERRY   1 3 7

Omitting the barricaded distance between the stage and ballroom floor and the temporary partitioned corridor to the dressing rooms, the Casa Loma Ballroom treated us nicely and jitterbugged to our music. Having been away from home for a while, I was cautiously looking around to see if there'd been any social changes at home, but Mandy's was far away.

The five pieces went over so well that I carried the addition with me on the next trip on the road. The fun of traveling increased, but so did the problems. Johnnie and Ebby were vividly showing increasing deficiencies in their performances due to their drinking. Johnnie would become quiet and clumsy when intoxicated, while Ebby would get loud and silly. This annoyed me to the point where I began to try to set drinking rules for them. I tried to reason with my band that if they were drinking to bring pleasure to themselves it was a fact that they would not feel the wanted effects as much when the mind and senses were dulled from the liquor. And if it was meant to dull agony or sorrow, the fact of the feeling would return once intoxication subsided, plus a hangover. They didn't understand. This drinking pattern continued throughout a tour that worked us on out to a dozen cities in California. My restriction against drinking in the station wagon was followed—Ebby and the bass player who rode in the rear seats would hold the jug of wine outside of the window and swallow. When I would protest, Ebby would confidently reply, "Not in the car, boss—just as you said," and take another swallow.

In San Jose I bought a homemade motor home, converted from a 1937 Syracuse, New York, city bus. It had space for four to sleep, a cooker, closets, and an illegal toilet with a highway deposit, all for eight hundred dollars. Before we could use it we had to have a $708 motor put in it and order a radiator for the engine. We stocked it with bologna and crackers and headed for our last engagement in San Francisco at the Auditorium in Fillmore.

The kids at the Fillmore were the freest living of any I'd worked before. It seemed that all the senior citizens were in Sacramento, all the parents were in Fresno, and San Francisco was oriented to natives and beatniks. In fact, all I saw were eyes that were half closed or too wide open with whatever. The entire audience was lying around the floor smoking, some sitting, some almost sleeping, but all hearing the sounds we were sending out. When I went to the john, the men's I must add, I saw two guys staggering out of the girls' john. Between and during some shows, I walked up on busy lovers in the lounge located backstage. It was mainly a seat for the groups waiting around to go on, but often a layout for the groupies waiting around to get off. I must admit I couldn't resist doubling back through at a slower pace and was pleased to find the young couple seemed delighted by my presence. Near to thirty years old, beyond my view in the mirror, it was my first time to actually see the act.

With memories of our San Francisco debut, we headed back to St. Louis in the new bus. Then on April 16, 1956, we drove in to the Chess studios again from Kinosha and cut five more original compositions that I had written in between all the excitement that would take my attention away from creating. They were "Roll Over Beethoven," "Too Much Monkey Business," "Brown Eyed Handsome Man," "Havana Moon," and "Drifting Heart."

Along about now, I was beginning to hear feedback from the disk jockeys and newspapers quoting my age, which was thirty. The kids were beginning to approach me with the respectful greeting of "Mr. Berry." Such greetings came as a surprise to me since I had not thought about how it looked for an adult to be playing teenage music. Whatever would sell was what I thought I should concentrate on, so from "Maybellene" on I mainly improvised my lyrics toward the young adult and some even for the teeny boppers, as they called the tots then.

The thing that surprised the artists, the producers, the media, and the record merchants was the number of adults that participated in the craze that the music was creating. That vast age bracket made it easy to fill larger-capacity houses and reap greater box-office revenues. Our shows grew in size and to my own surprise became broader minded in casting both black and white artists. In the southlands, we still had to split up when it came to dining and residential accommodations, but the stages were integrated and the traveling buses rolled in rapport.

A major decision that I reached after my first couple years of touring was to stop carrying the two other musicians of my trio with me to performances. My contacts at the Gale Booking Agency explained that they could book me more easily as a single, which would also clear more revenue for me. Plus, they enlightened me that most local bands were playing a lot of my hits on their gigs anyway. I didn't consider myself any better than any other musician out there. In fact, half the time I knew I wasn't as good. I asked them about the responsibility for securing a backup band and about the pay. They informed me that the respective promoters would be responsible for the backup bands' cost, character, and traveling. The first thing I thought of was no more botheration of drinking or being late on the gig. Since I had started flying on airplanes I could work in Miami one night and Seattle the next.

The advice soon turned into arrangements and I acquired the capability of flying cross-country if necessary to make consecutive engagements. The agency drew up my contracts with the provisions for the promoters to supply amplifiers for my use as well as a backup group. It seemed to be logical. I could brief the different guys about the progression of my songs, those they didn't know, during rehearsals.

Most of my concern was like that of a nonsmoker having a close relation with a heavy smoker. It infuriated me to smell liquor on the breath of anyone, and Johnnie and Ebby by then were drinking like bigmouth bass.

I continued to put together bands for tours occasionally, but from then on I mostly toured solo. Without the drinking hassles and traveling responsibility of my own group, writing and managing myself was a feasible objective along with raising a family and trying to run all my businesses as I was. Years had passed with my health walking the chalk line and my wealth running a close second. I was a family man and still rockin', moving on down the road, arriving and rehearsing that evening, playing the gig and checking into a hotel that night, hoping to reach the family the following morning from off the first flight out of wherever. A man shouldn't have to live like that but I loved it and I'm still doing it. Now that I'm a little more mature at age sixty I truly feel that I have been blessed.

The Creation of My Recordings

I have been asked many times, "Where did you get the idea to write that song, Chuck?" Off hand, I wouldn't know, but I always refer to the story within the song, which usually recalls my inspiration. Or sometimes the melodic lines bring me in sync with the time and place where the tune got its origin. The embarrassing thing is that sometimes when I have been asked about a song's origin I have made up a reason that is dramatic enough to get by the question. But the origins have varied under different circumstances or with different interviewers. In the pages that follow I'll recall whatever I can about a few of my songs *true* origins. They appear in the order, according to my records and memory, that I recorded them.

Writing a song can be a peculiar task. So much time can pass during the intervals I would be putting a song together that each time I'd get back to it, the tune or story it was following would likely take an entirely different route.

The kind of music I liked then, thereafter, right now and forever, is the kind I heard when I was a teenager. So the guitar styles of Carl Hogen, T-Bone Walker, Charlie Christian, and Elmore James, not to leave out many of my peers who I've heard on the road, must be the total of what is called Chuck Berry's style. So far as

*Me with Little Walter, a Chicago disc jockey,
and Roy Hamilton in 1955.*

the Chuck Berry guitar intro that identifies many of my songs, it is only back to the future of what came in the past. As you know, and I believe it must be true, "there is nothing new under the sun." So don't blame me for being first, just let it last.

To quote the lyrics the genius Ray Charles sang, "Sometimes I get sideways and stay up all night with a tune . . . I like what I am doing and sho' hope it don't end too soon." The nature and backbone of my beat is boogie and the muscle of my music is melodies that are simple. Call it what you may: jive, jazz, jump, swing, soul, rhythm, rock, or even punk, it's still boogie so far as I'm connected with it. When I can't connect to it, I have no right to dispute its title. When it's boogie, but with an alien title, the connection is still boogie and my kind of music.

What about slow songs, love songs, or blues? I like! In fact, I love love songs when loving my love, just as I dig blues when I'm blue. The thing about a love song is that one is not likely to be able to compose a real good one if one is not endowed with that magnificent feeling during the process of writing it. So far in my career, I have felt or lived what I've written and have yet to mix dollars with desire—or better still, commerce with passion. I've been in love much more than twice, but in no period did I have the least desire to expose these beautiful intimacies in a song. Those artists that improvise or register their lovely feelings in lyrics may be blessed with the formula for expressing love, but I am cursed with only the fantasies and feelings thereof. I have composed so few songs about love, if any really were, but instead have had fairly good success with songs of novelties and feelings of fun and frolic in the lyrics of my compositions.

So here are the stories of how and why a few of my earlier compositions came about. The entire catalogue of all my songs will be in a *Chuck Berry Songbook* that will follow this one with much data of when, where, and who were involved in the recordings plus information on every concert I ever played.

"Maybellene" was my effort to sing country-western, which I had always liked. The Cosmo clubgoers didn't know any of the words to those songs, which gave me a chance to improvise and add comical lines to the lyrics. "Mountain Dew," "Jambalaya," and "Ida Red" were the favorites of the Cosmo audience, mainly because of the honky-tonk gestures I inserted while singing the songs.

"Maybellene" was written from the inspiration that grew out of the country song "Ida Red." I'd heard it sung long before when I was a teenager and thought it was rhythmic and amusing to hear. I'd sung it in the yard gatherings and parties around home when I was first learning to strum the guitar in my high-school days. Later in life, at the Cosmo Club, I added my bit to the song and still enjoyed a good response so I coined it a good one to sing.

Later when I learned, upon entering a recording contract, that original songs written by a person were copyrighted and had various rewards for the composer, I welcomed the legal arrangement of the music business. I enjoyed creating songs of my own and was pleased to learn I could have some return from the effort. When I wrote "Maybellene" I had originally titled it "Ida May," but when I took the song to Chess Records I was advised to change its title. That was simple because the rhythmic swing of the three syllables fit with many other names. The music progression itself is close to the feeling that I received when hearing the song "Ida Red," but the story in "Maybellene" is completely different.

The body of the story of "Maybellene" was composed from memories of high school and trying to get girls to ride in my 1934 V-8 Ford. I even put seat-covers in it to accommodate the girls that the football players would take riding in it while I was in class. Just to somehow explain the origin of the lyrics of "Maybellene," it could have been written from a true experience, recalling my high-school days thus:

As I was watching from the windowsill,
I saw pretty girls in my dream De Ville
Riding with the guys, up and down the road
Nothin' I wanted more'n be in that Ford
Sittin' in class while they takin' rides
Guys in the middle, girls on both sides

    Oh Pretty girl, why can't it be true
    Oh Pretty girl, that it's me with you
    You let football players do things I want to do.

Girls in my dream car, door to door
My Ford bogged down wouldn't hold no more
Ring goes the last school bell of the day
Hurrying outside, see 'em pullin' away
Backseat full even sittin' on the hood
I knew that was doing my motor good

    Oh Pretty girl, why can't it be true
    Oh Pretty girl, that it's me with you
    You let football players do things I want to do.

The guys come back after all that fun
Walking with the pretty girls, one by one
My heart hangin' heavy like a ton a lead
Feelin' so down I can't raise my head
Just like swallowin' up a medicine pill
Watching them girls from the windowsill

These lines were written just to provide an example of the true depiction of an event. This differs from the improvised writing of a song, which does not necessarily, if ever, coincide with a true story but mostly just goes along the pattern or close to the train of events. I have never, in my life, met or even known of any woman named "Maybellene." The name actually was first brought to my knowledge from a storybook, when I was in the third grade, of animals who bore names. Along with Tom the cat and Donald the duck, there was Maybellene the cow. Not offending anybody, I thought, I named my girl character after a cow. In fact, the girl was to be two-timing, so it would have been worse if I had used a popular name.

When I wrote "Maybellene" I had never been in a funeral or parade which would have been the only opportunity I could have had to ride in a Cadillac, though I had sat in a new one on occasion.

Cadillacs don't like Fords rolling side by side because they hide half their beauty so I cause the Caddy to pull "up to a hundred and four, my Ford got hot and wouldn't do no more/Created clouds detected rain/Elated motor to the passing lane/Heat gone down—highway sound/Caddy and the Ford bound dead downtown." And so many times have guys' girls done unfavorable things that you wonder "why can't 'cha be true . . . doin' the thing you used to do?"

The lyrics really explain the story. In fact, it was so popular that after five of the song's twenty-five years, I added another verse as I sing it on stage:

> I peeped in the mirror at the top of the hill
> 'Twas just like swallowing a medicine pill
> First thing I saw was that Cadillac grille
> Doing a hundred and ten dropping off that hill
> An uphill curve and downhill stretch,
> Me and that Cadillac was neck and neck

"Wee Wee Hours" was based on the memorable tears that Joe Turner's "Wee Baby Blue" brought from me when I was a teenager, so much in love with Margie. Blues are simple anyway and only seem to need the lyrics of a lonely confession to be put to

CHUCK

music. It took the memory of one of the evenings that I didn't get to see Margie at her window to put the words together and the tune is anybody's cry for companionship. With the exception of a couple of ten-minute repair changes, I think it took all of an hour to complete the writing of "Wee Wee Hours."

"You Can't Catch Me" was embodied from an experience I had when returning from New York City along the New Jersey Turnpike. The New Jersey Turnpike itself is long enough, but the song was well on its way in theory as I rolled off the west end of the Pennsylvania Turnpike. It was at night and Toddy and I in our Buick had been overtaken by some dudes with crew cuts (flat tops) who pulled up alongside and passed us, waving. Their car was not as late a model as mine, but must have definitely been in better shape or souped up. Naturally, I sped up and trailed them a while, losing ground intentionally for the kill. Any hot-rodder knows the way you lag back a little and the fore-running car can't possibly tell when you began your surge to overtake. I had really gotten a good jump on acceleration before he realized I was still in the race and though he tried to barrel up I crawled past him and at that particular time I was happy that my car was smoking like a choo choo train but in his path.

There were two cars abreast barreling after me so I gave it my best shot and stayed in the lead until one of the vehicles turned a bright red cherry. It was a New Jersey state patrol car that had suddenly, out of nowhere, come alongside me.

It was then that I improvised the prayer (in the lyric) wishing I could have "let out my wings" and just disappear and "become airborne." The other guys had quit the race and dropped back over a mile it seemed but it made me feel better when they were about to cruise by and the officer stopped, went out, and waved them down to give them a ticket as well.

The balance of the lyrics were improvised excepting the tail end of the chorus, "cool breeze." In a novel I read some time ago, there was an explanation of how a saying got started. A native on a safari in the deserts of Africa was standing in the blistering heat, behind one of the camels, and suddenly the camel broke wind. The native only remarked that at least it was cool, and the phrase was carried throughout the trip: "A cool breeze from a camel's ass." My mom used to have me mimic that line for company so I'm passing it on in my book.

"Thirty Days" was a song that I had a bit of experience in putting together from memories of the Algoa period. It wasn't quite as funny then as the lyric of the song makes it seem but nevertheless that experience helped in the writing.

Sometime in my past, I had seen a movie that had a comical scene in an all-black court room where an accused young guy was sentenced to a year in the state penitentiary for grand theft. Upon hearing his sentence, he confessed to the judge that he had been desperate and in the light of his despair was not himself. The judge then compromised, changing his sentence to six months in the county workhouse but the defendant responded with a plea for mercy because he was ill.

The judge then leaned forward with growing impatience and granted the young man further leniency, reducing his sentence to one month in the city jail. The man, bowing in tears, then begged for further leniencies because he was married with four children and to serve a month would put their survival in danger. He then looked sternly at the judge, and asked him to take into consideration that he was the man who had introduced the judge to his wife. The judge then pounced out of his seat and shouted, "Life, you rascal you!"

Where the above may be doubted worthy of such elaboration, it shows that I have found no happiness in any association that has been linked with regulations and custom. In other words, conformity is not the fragrance found in my fantasies. So I was stimulated by the judge story and found something similar in category yet different in aspect for a creation of my own. Hope you've heard it, if so, liked it.

"Together We Will Always Be" took a good while to write because I had hoped to produce something similar to the selections that my favorite love crooner, Nat "King" Cole, sang. Nat shared the throne of fame with a peer known as "Ol' Blue-Eyes" Sinatra and they were each better than the other in singing love songs that would lure one to fall for an admirer one was leaning toward. Unfortunately, after recording it, I tried to find and collect all the copies on the market after it was released. No way did I feel it could compare with the songs of the geniuses who inspired it.

"No Money Down" was a song that Leonard Chess liked. I had bought over a dozen automobiles in less than a dozen years and "No Money Down" got its origin from the salesman's pitch that I usually got when buying my first few cars. They inevitably would lure you in with signs like the song's title and once you drove onto the used-car lot, all the cars there would automatically go up to a price equal to the value of themselves plus your car which would cause your car to be traded in for free. But the curve of the pitch is, whatever you want, they got it; and if they don't they'll get it; even if they don't they'll find its twin and fake it, showing you in the meanwhile that you don't need it. Just you sign for it and then we'll talk about it.

"Down Bound Train" surely was cultivated from my background of religious teachings. It took little to bring the thoughts of a sinner worrying over his destiny and coordinate the circumstance in a dramatic display of contrast to the average person's life-style. I could say my father, in many ways, really wrote the foundation for "Down Bound Train" in his constant preaching of the horrors of hell once you've missed the blessings of salvation and heaven. So let it be known that I'm not alone to reap what I've sown in fire and brimstone because of my own bad traits that I've shown. Nevertheless each time I hear it now, it gives me a chill to think that I still could fail to fulfill the behavior that will let me fit the bill in trying to kill any thrill of riding that train.

"Roll Over Beethoven" was written based on the feelings I had when my sister would monopolize the piano at home during our youthful school years. In fact most of the words were aimed at Lucy instead of the Maestro Ludwig Van Beethoven. Thelma also took piano lessons in classical music but Lucy was the culprit that delayed rock 'n' roll music twenty years. Telling Mother in an attempt to get support for my kind of music did no good, but writing a letter and mailing it to a local DJ might have, as stated in the opening of the song.

What sounds like, "Way lay in the . . ." is really "Early in the morning, I'm giving you a warning." Out of my sometimes unbelievably imaginative mind, the rest of the self-explanatory lyrics came forth.

"Too Much Monkey Business" was meant to describe most of the kinds of hassles a person encounters in everyday life. When I got into writing on this theory, I realized I needed over a hundred verses to portray the major areas that bug people the most. I was even making up words then like "botheration" to emphasize the nuisances that bothered people. I tried to use (or make up) words that wouldn't be hard to decipher by anyone from the fifth grade on. I hadn't received any kickback about using "motorvating" in "Maybellene," so why not compete with Noah Webster again? Anyway, the first verse was directed toward a family supporter paying bills, while the filling station attendant, the seduced, the student, and the veteran all declare their problems in the lyrics.

"Brown Eyed Handsome Man" came to mind when I was touring California for the first time. After leaving St. Louis with six inches of snow lying under sub-freezing temperatures, I found green grass under clear blue skies with eighty-degree breezes loitering along the evening sunset.

What I didn't see, at least in the areas I was booked in, was too many blue eyes. The auditoriums were predominantly filled with Hispanics and "us." But then I did see unbelievable harmony among the mix, which got the idea of the song started. I saw, during the length of the tour, quite a few situations concerning the life of the Mexican people. For example, a Caucasian officer was picking up a fairly handsome male loiterer near the auditorium when some woman came up shouting for the policeman to let him go. He promptly did so, laughingly saluting the feminine rescuer.

The verse in the song is situated a bit differently but was derived from that incident. The verse about Venus De Milo (believe it or not) came from thoughts out of a book I had come upon entitled *Venus in Furs* and the last verse from a fictional condition always appreciated in a baseball game.

"**Havana Moon**" took its origin from Nat Cole's "Calypso Blues" song which I used to do at the Cosmo Club when the Latin tempos were soaring in popularity. The Havana location of the song's setting was from my introduction to the Cuban population in and around Harlem, New York, when playing the Brooklyn

Paramount and the Apollo. Being influenced by the Spanish language spoken fluently in both New York and Los Angeles, I was eager to try to learn some.

It is the differences in people that I think gives me a tremendous imagination to create a story for developing a lyric. Moreover, I believe everything seen or heard will ink a memory that helps a person improvise. For example, I had read, seen, or heard in some respect all the situations in the Havana story. Certainly missing the boat and surely missing the girl had been experienced many times by me. I should declare myself the "Founding Father of Missing-the-boat," at least while in high school. I wanted like a hog but was seen as a boar, feeling like a hunk of pork in an orthodox deli.

"Drifting Heart" was another attempt to write a ballad. Nat Cole had me so wrapped up in his tunes during my high-school days that I am yet today waiting until all the singers catch a year-long case of laryngitis so I can put out a couple of ballads and get away with it. I was always moved more deeply by sentimental music than faster tunes; in fact, omitting boogie woogie and rock 'n' roll (in that order too!), blues could hold my attention a while but no other music really moves me generally. The lyrics to "Drifting Heart" hung over in my memory of nineteen-year-old Margie when I was a shy seventeen and though I was thirty-one when I composed it, it was from the heart.

"School Days" was born from the memories of my own experience in high school. The lyrics depict the way it was in my time. I had no idea what was going on in the classes during the time I composed it, much less what's happening today. The phrases came to me spontaneously, and rhyming took up most of the time that was spent on the song. I remember leaving it twice to go get coffee and while out having some major lines come to me that would enhance the story in the song, causing me to rush back to my room to get them down. Recording the song with breaks in the rhythm was intended to emphasize the jumps and changes I found in classes in high school compared to the one room and one teacher I had in elementary school. That's 90 percent of the song; I suppose the remainder could have been talent.

"Deep Feeling" was done on a steel console that I was learning on, in fact it was only two weeks old, costing a never-you-mind

$585 but it sounded so sweet. There is little to tell of the song other than that it was the way I felt that came out from under the steel bar I was pushing along the strings of the whining instrument. I shall try again one day in 1999 when they'll have the steel guitar so computed that you can lay it against your heart and it will play to the feeling your heart is tuned to. Since this song was recorded, I have grown to cherish its melody from so many requests for it on gigs. Without carrying the steel guitar regularly, I can't deliver it in most cases.

"Oh Baby Doll" was created from scratch in that I was intending to come up with another form of the feeling that "School Days" had brought about. Instead of being in the school semester, it was to relate the feeling of leaving the term and parting from classmates at summer vacation. Sort of a sequence, it was, of the period that would follow from school days into the summer. Some things have no date factor, such as the behavior of kids in class when the teacher is momentarily absent and the yearning to be free at times of captivity. Whereas other things referred to in the song like the "transistor radio" and "balling-the-jack" pertain to the time.

"Reelin' and Rockin' " During a visit to Chicago at sixteen with my boyhood friend Ralph Burris, one of the nightclubs we were too young to be admitted to was on 55th and South Parkway under the name of "The Rum Boogie." This particular night, the great singer Joe Turner was featured and the place was packed. Ralph and I went around to the side of the building and climbed up to a high ventilation window and peeked in. Molded in my memory is the sight of Big Joe Turner rared back singing the song that Bill Haley covered for the then so-called white market, "Rock Around the Clock." If ever I was inspired as a teenager, I was then. What I then heard and felt, I tried to reprovoke in the song I then entitled, "Reelin' and Rockin'."

I say "then" because later I rewrote it and named it "Rockin' and Reelin' " with updated, meaning a little more suggestive, lyrics leaning toward the permissiveness of the changing times. It was such a versatile song that you could install any set of words you wanted in it, and during the time it first came out, I heard others singing different lyrics (that were shady) at clubs I'd visit here and there after work. They were knocking out the audience, sounding more entertaining than my own version. Why not me, I thought.

"Rock and Roll Music" Now this song is my sole doing and I take responsibility for every sold copy. I was heavy into rock 'n' roll even then and had to create something that hit the spot without question. I wanted the lyrics to define every aspect of its being and so worded it to do so. How do you like it?

"Thirteen Question Method" This song was held on the shelf for months before it was released. From the work we put into it I thought it would be an A-side yet it wound up released for the first time hidden away on a side track in a foreign album. I was trying to depict the course of a shy guy taking a shot at trying to date a girl having no experience of how to go about it. Though thirteen is considered unlucky to some, his thirteenth question was the one that would bring him to the brink of bliss, should he manage to reach that rank.

"Sweet Little Sixteen" began from an incident in the Ottawa Coliseum, the night I first saw Paul Anka, just a child then, running through the corridors with a song he'd written and wanted somebody to consider recording. Everybody was recording songs named after some girl then, including some of my own tunes. His was "Diana." At the same time there was a small German doll that was trying to catch up with different artists on the show that Paul was also pursuing but evidently she and Paul were failing to make contact. Later I was coming through the exits in the opposite direction and came upon the little doll again still in flight and in search of autographs, not in the least bothered that the show was progressing toward the end. She was mainly interested in getting autographs in her fat little Mickey Mouse wallet that she held like the torch on the Statue of Liberty. Other kids were searching as well but the pretty little tot seemed to mold in my memory more than any other. She was actually around seven or eight but the gross of the others were in their mid-teens. I was one year past thirty at the time, seeing them all as mere kids but somehow I could understand how they must have felt in their ambition to collect the signatures. I presumed that years later the kid running around collecting autographs would come out ahead with recorded evidence of having met the various artists. The essence of the story is portrayed in the song for I was once sixteen and had the "grown-up blues."

"Guitar Boogie" was another selection intended to be a B-side or album filler. I wondered how the title would pass legitimately (having learned that no two identical titles could be registered) when I had heard four different guitar players playing their guitar boogies. I guess some did and some didn't get by, anyway mine did get by but not so high.

"It Don't Take But a Few Minutes" A certain Jewish girl from University City followed my concerts whenever I played in the hometown area. After becoming a fan and favorite, she suddenly showed up one weekend at a concert in Jackson, Mississippi, and sent me a note backstage inviting me to where she was staying at the Stonewall Hotel. She closed the note with endearments offering me the best of entertainment. The hotel she mentioned was in the heart of downtown Jackson, and the year was 1957, and the social climate was not just hot but the humanity was sticky. I wanted to go for the southern up-to-date experience but the forecast was too cloudy and the white man was still holding the reins. At that time, most of the public water fountains and restrooms were still in racial dispute.

When I phoned the hotel and requested (with handle and full name) to speak with her, the hotel operator asked me who I was and whether I worked for her. I left word, because the next morning she was waiting with a veiled black hat on, in the hallway of the colored hotel I was staying at, smiling as I was summoned.

The song was written originally in reference to how she popped up in the most weird places, unconcerned of the circumstances and conditions that prevailed. The first writing of what went down in her behavior was too bizarre to record and I wound up with lyrics about travel and conditions. With all the strange things that have happened around my life, I find it takes little effort to conjure a story worth somebody hearing. So far as rhyming the words, my love for poetry lays the obvious in my lap for lyrics.

"Johnny B. Goode" Leonard Chess took an instant liking to this song and stayed in the studio coaching us the whole time we were cutting it. I'd guess my mother has as much right to be declared the source of "Johnny B. Goode" as any other contender in that she was the one who repeatedly commented that I would be a millionaire someday. She constantly proclaimed she knew I would become lucky in my life and urged me on to get an education (which I fumbled around with until I was grown) to aid me in maintaining that fortune that I would likely come into.

With Johnnie Johnson and Ebby Hardy,
the original "Sir John's Trio."

"Johnny" in the song is more or less myself although I wrote it intending it to be a song for Johnnie Johnson. I altered the predictions that my mother made of me and created a story that paralleled. It seems easy, now that it's been around so long, that it took only a period of about two weeks of periodic application to put the lyrics together when I worked on "Drifting Heart" almost four months and it sold scarcely twenty copies.

It is obvious that a story that brings a subject from out of the boondocks to fame and fortune is more dramatic than one out of midtown to somewhere crosstown. "Rags to riches" even sounds more attractive than "fortune to fame." It was with this in mind that I wrote of a boy with an ambition to become a guitar player, who came from the least of luxury to be seen by many, practicing until the listener believes he has all but made it to the top as the chorus prompts him like his mother's encouraging voice, "Go Johnny Go."

The gateway from freedom, I was led to understand, was somewhere "close to New Orleans" where most Africans were sorted through and sold. I had driven through New Orleans on tour and I'd been told my great grandfather lived "way back up in the

Johnnie Johnson, sitting in with the Buddy Johnson Band in Atlanta. He's playing without sheet music, watching for progression changes.

woods among the evergreens" in a log cabin. I revived the era with a story about a "colored boy name Johnny B. Goode." My first thought was to make his life follow as my own had come along, but I thought it would seem biased to white fans to say "colored boy" and changed it to "country boy."

As it turned out, my name was in lights and it is a fact that "Johnny B. Goode" is most instrumental in causing it to B. I have many times said and now again say "Thanks" though I could never voice it loud enough to equal the appreciation that so many people have claimed to have enjoyed from something that I created. I imagine most black people naturally realize but I feel safe in stating that NO white person can conceive the feeling of obtaining Caucasian respect in the wake of a world of dark denial, simply because it is impossible to view the dark side when faced with brilliance. "Johnny B. Goode" was created as all other things and brought out of a modern dark age. With encouragement he chose to practice, shading himself along the roadside but seen by the brilliance of his guitar playing. Chances are you have talent. But will the name and the light come to you? No! You have to "Go!"

"Around and Around" sprouted from a jam session during a rehearsal before a concert. Sometimes I didn't jam before a concert but these guys were on-the-ball musicians and we almost had a concert before the concert started that evening. For nearly two hours we jammed, playing standard sweet songs to gut-bucket, rock and boogie. One of the riffs we struck upon never left my memory and I waxed in the tune with words about a dance hall that stayed open a little overtime. Rocking 'til the early morning had been used so 'til the moon went down was the same time of day. Let it be known that at the actual experience, the police didn't knock.

"Carol" was written for and about the daughter of a companion of Clyde McPhatter whom I had met at the Paramount Theater in Manhattan and became attracted to. Her child was four years old then but as time went by, circumstances with her mother, quite similar to the story in the song, brought her to finish high school under Francine's guidance, living at Berry Park. Discussing her teenage environment with Francine was much help in putting "Carol" together. Details from my schooling like meat-loaf and potatoes costing only 5 cents and a notebook with paper for 12 cents were far outdated. Whereas some guy stealing another boy's girl was a thing that hadn't changed any. Boys still will be boys, especially when it comes to girls.

"Sweet Little Rock and Roller" Naturally it was around Christmas when I wrote this one, pumped by Leonard to bring something in for teenagers that could be a Christmas song. Just like John Lennon said on the Mike Douglas show once, "Well, I don't just

IN PERSON ALAN FREED WITH ROCK AND ROLL STARS
CHUCK BERRY LAVERN BAKER CLYDE McPHATTER
FRANKIE LYMON & TEENAGERS THE MOONGLOWS SCREAMIN' JAY HAWKINS
JODIE SANDS JOE TURNER LEWIS LYMON TEEN CHORDS EVERLY BROS
THE ORIGINAL CADILLACS JOHNNIE AND JOE TEDDY RANDAZZO PAUL ANKA
NEW SHOCKS AND THRILLS "BEGINNING OF THE END"

sit down and say I'm going to write a song about a bug today."
He's right, it just doesn't happen that way. But I have set out to
write of a certain predicament or situation and once into thoughtful
processing, the state of affairs seems to flow and establish a story,
sometimes real enough to believe. Such was the progression of this
tune. Once I started into the Christmas spirit of a kid liking rock
'n' roll, other ideas fell into order.

"**Anthony Boy**" was directed toward Italians at the request of
Phil Chess who encouraged me to give "Mama Mia" a little something to rock on. A close companion of his was the recipient of the

CHUCK

glory it would have generated had it been a hit. He helped me with the dialect which fitted the behavior of the shy guy that the story depicted.

"Jo Jo Gunne" This song was prepared in fact and phrase from a rather naughty but funny toast I had heard back in the Algoa days. I'm not going to harp on the original lines of what I learned then but the humor of it remains potent for a laugh and that's what entertainment is all about. I still think the way I heard it is funnier but then I was nearing twenty-one when it reached me. Even an adult would shy away from the naked truth when approached by a lie neatly dressed.

"Memphis," also known as "Memphis Tennessee" and "Long Distance Telephone," was recorded in my first office building at 4221 West Easton Avenue in St. Louis on a $145 homemade studio in the heat of a muggy July afternoon with a $79 reel-to-reel Sears, Roebuck recorder that had provisions for sound-on-sound recording. I played the guitar and the bass track, and I added the ticky-tick drums that trot along in the background which sound so good to me. I worked over a month on revising the lyric before I took the tape up to Leonard Chess to listen to. He was again pressed for a release since my concerts (driving on the road then) kept me from the recording studio for long periods.

The story of "Memphis" got its roots from a very old and quiet bluesy selection by Muddy Waters played when I was in my teens that went "Long distance operator, give me (something . . . something), I want to talk to my baby, she's (something else)." Sorry I don't remember any more now but I did then and spirited my rendition of that feeling into my song of Memphis. My wife had relatives there who we were visiting semiannually but other than a couple of concerts there, I had never had any basis for choosing Memphis for the location of the story.

The situation in the story was intended to have a wide scope of interest to the general public rather than a rare or particular incidental occurrence that would entreat the memory of only a few. Such a portrayal of popular or general situations and conditions in lyrics has always been my greatest objective in writing.

For a long while, "Memphis" was the song covered most by other groups, until the sleeper, "Johnny B. Goode," caught on to take precedence. The rest may well be history.

"Little Queenie" In this song I leaned toward a story for the teen market which had gone so well for me. While writing it, I re-lived the feelings of the character presented. If you notice, in the lyrics the first party is standing by watching a pretty girl at some dance while music is playing. That was typical of me in high school, to stand around thinking instead of acting during occasions when I'd have the opportunity to get next to a girl by dancing. The slow, and most times no, acting is prevalent in the second verse—"There she is again standing over by the record machine"—show-ing the guy is still standing hoping for a miracle to occur to bring the girl within his grasp. It's just like me even today to wait around 'til it's too late to latch on to the chance to meet a person I favor. To a certain extent, I would think listeners live or relive the lyrics of a song that they come to like as they hear it over and over. Such was the kind of product I was aiming for in most of my lyrics rather than a story that depicted a singular episode or incident that could only happen in the life of a few people.

So that was how some of my songs came into being. To have included in this chapter each and every song I have written would detract from the continuity of the autobiography so I have just given you a taste.

Francine

A fter seeing me at the Syria Mosque in Pittsburgh, Pennsylvania, as part of the 1956 Show of Stars tour starring Fats Domino (who at the time was said to be earning ten thousand dollars a week), the owner of the Rock and Roll Club, on Sixth Street, booked me for a week of performances. On my second night there, June 19, I decided to abandon sitting in the dressing room and instead fraternize with the customers. During the first fifteen minutes, a trim, short-haired blonde walked up and asked me to sign two autographs. The distinct quality of her voice and diction struck me as the most eloquent I'd heard. I chose to chat a moment, then she returned to her companions. The following night at intermission she came again to my chosen sitting place, greeted me, and invited me to meet her mother and friend, Dan. We exchanged addresses and I learned she spent time at Carnegie Tech in Pittsburgh, where she also worked.

Her talk sounded so interesting that I made up a tale that later rebounded with confusion about my age. I had mentioned that I didn't have a bio and she prepared one for me based on our conversations and sent it to me. Later, I sent it to Leonard Chess, who'd been pushing me to submit one. Leonard sent the same information to the Gale Agency for publicity use and the lazy lies that I lined out at the bar that night in hopes of impressing a girl were out and on the way to outer space. Yeah! I've regretted it each time I read it quoted or whenever some disk jockey in San Jose would pump me for details of the roots that I had falsely acknowledged.

I was intrigued with her and my interest in her rose to supremacy. After that second meeting I suggested she join me for lunch at the coffee shop in the Hotel Roosevelt the following afternoon, where I became determined to maintain the momentum of the acquaintance. We realized we had bridged two worlds and united a path that could well lead to passion. There had never been another woman, including my wife, who had shown such interest in my career and public image. Where my wife had taken me totally in the conception of companionship, this young, rapid-but-distinctly-speaking girl was taking me by storm, pouring out the possibilities that could snowball my destination into a long, sunny career. I thought that her acquaintance was good to have, better to develop, and best to keep, and I was trying.

Her name was Francine, a highly ambitious, twenty-year-old girl who meant to find in life all that she thought was capable of being found in it. At times when she wasn't looking I would stare at her and wonder "Why me," why would I be so fortunate to meet such a person?

After the sufficient lunch with this sophisticated lady I drove her to a little town called Turtle Creek, where she lived with her parents. Thereafter, through the course of our correspondence, she spoke with me about a corporation that I should form and operate under. I in turn conferred with her about the possibility of her coming to St. Louis to live while assisting me in launching the project. She decided it would be something to look forward to and she anticipated joining me in business.

When my acquaintance with Francine was around a year old, she turned twenty-one, moved to New York, and found a job. During my trips through New York we came to favor her moving to St. Louis and working for me to keep my real-estate and song-writing records straight. Themetta was loaded with managing the home and raising our two children, who then were in elementary school. Relating these conditions to Francine, she saw my career headed for a catastrophe, realizing I couldn't possibly tour, write, record, manage, and keep my books and family life intact at the same time. She agreed to come to St. Louis for sure. Themetta was delighted about it since it would give her more time to see to the needs of the children.

Meanwhile, I had been booked on a three-day engagement in Honolulu, Hawaii. Subsequently I had to phone Francine of my expected absence on the day she would be arriving in St. Louis to start working for me. However, I'd arranged for her to stay at a hotel in a white neighborhood not too far from my home and had left funds and instructions for her.

When I got back to St. Louis, Francine had arrived as promised, on November 24, 1957, and found her way to the Northwestern Hotel. I went there promptly and requested to speak with her and was denied the privilege. They allowed me to reserve the room but told me they did not cater to colored people as residents or visitors. However, they did allow me to phone the room. When she came down, they also refused to let me visit with her in the lobby, and Francine immediately decided to move to a hotel that would. She didn't know the conditions of racial relations in St. Louis, having been reared in Pennsylvania, but I did. I had to take her to the Poro Hotel, the only colored hotel I knew that was adequate for her life-style. Soon after that she settled in a small apartment owned by a black Christian woman who welcomed her with open arms.

Highly ambitious Francine couldn't wait for my business to get under way and meanwhile found work in downtown St. Louis and supported herself until the office was established in the storefront of a duplex building I'd purchased.

It was very important to maintain constant attention at the box office on concerts booked with a percentage of the attendance as a part of the fee. I learned of many shortcuts and unwarranted deductions from my portion of the take that the promoters would calculate to their benefit. Some of these were fictitious door guards, free tickets to the press and disk jockeys, and not counting in late recoveries of advance tickets. Knowing I would be leaving for the next concert presently, many amounts were promised to be mailed but never reached my post box. I came to the conclusion that when business was so good that it became tempting for others to be dishonest so often, I needed Francine to watch it.

The first concert she worked was locally in the city where she handled the tickets at the door on Christmas night 1957 at the Dugout Club on Olive Street. It was then and thereafter I began calling her Fran.

I persuaded Francine to come along on a short tour of California, where most of the dates were percentage deals. I had grown weary of challenging the eternal discrepancies that arose in calculating the percentages and deductions of local dance taxes. I discovered that with Francine doing it, the promoter was less argumentative and more prone to take it like a man. Plus, they found she was alert and businesslike and clever to boot. But let her tell it.

The best place to begin telling a story is obviously at the very beginning. However, I can't begin at the beginning because when I try to think of how it began there isn't any starting point. He was there and I was there and the conversation was of records—the record industry, that is—music, musicians, fan clubs, nightclubs, and so on. We became deeply involved in conversation about a fan club as well as about other business aspects of his future and I suddenly realized that I wanted to be this man's secretary/business partner/manager/confidante. Did he have a secretary? No. Did he ever give any thought to having a secretary? Offhand, no. Did he need a secretary? But definitely, if nothing more than to answer his fan mail. And, so I became Chuck Berry's private secretary. Sounds simple, but from that moment on my whole life completely changed, and it's wonderful to say it changed for the best.

As soon as I moved to St. Louis we immediately started to remodel the building we purchased for our music company and fan club headquarters. The music company was established and incorporated December 1, 1957, under the title of *Chuck Berry Music, Inc.*; the fan club automatically formed itself when Mr. B announced the national headquarters address on a Saturday night Dick Clark TV show. Since Mr. B had a few pieces of property here in the city we joined this force and incorporated it also, December 1, 1957, titling it *Thee Investment Inc.* After all the legal technicalities were completed and we officially registered the businesses with the

CHUCK BERRY

city and state of Missouri we opened our front door February 4, 1958, at 4221 West Easton Avenue (now Dr. Martin Luther King Drive).

December 1957 and January 1958 were two hectic months as we were incorporating the companies, remodeling the building, buying office furniture, and installing telephones. The usual run-of-the-mill entanglements one involves oneself with when starting a new business fell into a delightful picture.

After the announcement of the fan club headquarters (which was too far in advance to accommodate the mail outburst) the fan mail poured in to the office continuously. Within three days after his announcement Mr. B received over twenty-five hundred letters and cards, all requesting pictures and everyone wanted to join the fan club. This was only the beginning.

It seems I'm putting so much emphasis on the fan club when most people would think the music and investment companies are the more important. This may be true, but I was ready for them. The mail that boomed into the office caught me off guard as I didn't know Mr. B was announcing the address on that particular Dick Clark show and I was completely unprepared. This was just one of the many, many tricks Mr. B pulled out of his hat and bestowed upon my brow. In the years to come I soon learned how to keep calm under any circumstances and how to have complete control over my nerves at all times—especially around the viewing public. This was my most valuable ability and I had to keep it above all others.

Everything went along well for us, and when he was home we were terribly busy. The phones rang constantly, business from out of town, in town, and the uncountable number of calls from his fans. Until Mr. B could make up his mind as to how he wanted me to answer the phone he drove me to distraction. Sometimes I think he would leave the office and deliberately forget something just to have an excuse to call me back and listen to the sound of my voice. Then I would hear: "No, Fran, too much emphasis on Berry, sort of keep your voice at one pitch, like this, 'Chuck Berry Music,' like that, now try it." Naturally, you don't tell your boss the other phone is ringing off the hook, nor do you cut him off short. You simply say: "Yes, sir, how's this: 'Chuck Berry Music,'" and he replies, "Much better, Fran, but it still needs improvement."

Mr. B decided he wanted the names and addresses of his fans typed on long sheets of paper. These sheets would be in alphabetical order by state, then each state broken down by cities. After you have the state and city in order you then inserted the name and address of the fan and phone number if available. By this time the fan mail had reached to a point of

CHUCK

sixty-five hundred, so the typing of this particular project called for another typist. Mr. B called in his niece to help me and so I met Carol, who soon was to have a song written for her. How we worked. Came in at about nine in the A.M. and at six or seven that evening we were still typing. Once we started this project we couldn't wait until we reached Wyoming, the very last state to be registered.

Mr. B was most helpful during this typing era. I often wonder if it would have been better to have him locked in his cave. When he was in his section of the building his charming vocal cords would ring out, "Fran, out of cigarettes. Fran, my pen? Fran, stop typing, I can't hear this," whatever it was. But the real blows came when he would be in his office recording one of his songs and we had to turn the phones off, stop typing completely, and watch the door so no one entered. The office was not soundproof, and the slightest sound we made would come out on the tape. Mr. B had his tape recorders in his office and would record directly from there, and carry these tapes to Chess Records.

When Mr. B worked percentage dates out of town I usually accompanied him, as these were the most important dates. As I remember how we traveled from city to city on a two-week engagement I wonder how Mr. B was able to stand such a strain. He was a human dynamo. We would get into the city at 3 or 4 A.M. It always took an hour or longer to register everyone in the hotel; then we would get something to eat. By the time we said good-night we had four or perhaps five hours

TV interview. Maybe Mr. B and the band were to make an appearance at a benefit, sometimes a disk jockey had a luncheon for him, and then there were the usual wonderful fans waiting in the hotel lobby to surround Mr. B for a picture and autograph. When Mr. B had finished his interviews for the day, had his dinner, and was just about to relax, it was time to go to the auditorium, or nightclub or wherever he was playing for the night for another four hours of work.

Being Mr. B's secretary is a twenty-four-hour-a-day job. When he is on the road I must confine myself to the office or my home so that any hour of the day or night he can reach me by phone. The telephone has played, perhaps, the biggest role in our lives. Quite a bit of money has been saved from one call from him to me over this or that pending deal and also many a contract has been signed via his voice dictating to my typing fingers. He is on one phone, I'm on the other, and the agency is in the middle. When I quote him, he demands the quote be exactly his quote, word for word, comma for comma. Or no quote at all. Mr. B is a very conscientious man, his feelings go deep, he is warm and tender when he is speaking to you or about you. Never, since I have known him, has he spoken harmfully of anyone. In times of anger he becomes withdrawn and keeps to himself. He never raises his voice under any circumstances in anger—only raises his voice in rock 'n' roll. The only times I hear him shout is when he is singing in an exceptionally large auditorium and the P.A. system isn't too hot. He has taught me control—control of myself and others, especially in situations that involve me. He has taught me to be a pathfinder; I knew he was one when I first met him. We always seem to find a way together. If we disagree, we argue intelligently and reach a mutual understanding. We help each other by projecting ideas together. We iron out the difficulties in the business together. My opinion is weighed and balanced the same as his. We are equal. When he is about to undertake a new project or a new interest he confers with me and asks my opinion. Mr. B knows I am honest; we talk freely and we discuss matters to the fullest. We leave nothing out of the conversation and we keep probing until we think we have covered every detail. He is mainly interested in "Can you handle such a project?" And my answer to him is always the same, "If you have faith and confidence in me for this as you have in the past I can handle anything we undertake." Every employer must have confidence in his secretary. I like to think I gave him that confidence in the first place. So, we win a few, and we lose a few; we work very well together.

We originally opened the place we called Club Bandstand for teenagers. Its name came from Dick Clark's "American Bandstand" TV show where Mr. B had gained so much popularity. We started by having fan club meetings there and then we had dances. And as time came to pass we acquired a liquor

Performing at Club Bandstand when off the road during 1959.

The bar at Club Bandstand. I'm at the far right
and Fran is behind the bar.

license and had to relocate the teenagers. So the meetings were held at the Easton office and the adults took over the nightclub, which was fast becoming one of St. Louis's better night spots. We had a band every night and floor shows on weekends. This is where the fun began. For many a year I had been a secretary. Learned the tricks on how to get around embarrassing situations, how to keep calm when all the contracts are missing, how the boss likes this and that. Through the years with Mr. B I was not "just a secretary" but I was his partner and a stockholder in his corporations. Now enter Club Bandstand (March 1958). I just automatically assumed full responsibility where the bulk of the money was: behind the bar, hence, I became a barmaid. Since Mr. B and I are not drinkers we both had to learn together how to mix a drink. I bought a book, how to mix 1,001 drinks. In the day we were boss and secretary and at night we were ticket-taker and barmaid. Talk about leading three lives, we led six. I ended up moving my office into the club, as it became quite confusing when the liquor order arrived at the office and the fan mail arrived at the nightclub. When the sandwich man arrived I'd

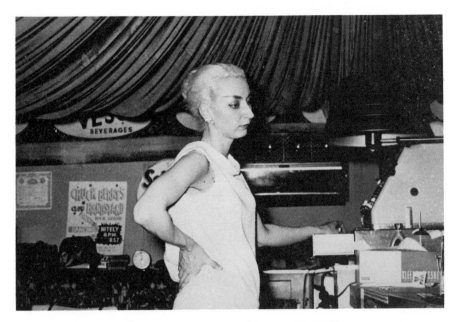

Fran as manager and barmaid, 1959.

be at the Easton office, and when the exhaustion set in from my constant running back and forth from office to nightclub—well, we had to move something.

All the phones had to be transferred as well as the Easton address. As we still carried on the corporation businesses eventually everyone came to know the new address and also that I was there in the day as well as the night. Naturally I had to have most of my clothes moved into the club. I was still a quiet secretary in the daytime, only at night was I behind the bar. The only real problem I had was with the people who insisted on carrying on a business conversation at 11 P.M. or midnight when I was the busiest. Not to mention Mr. B asking me to "leave that bar a minute and come over here and take a few notes." Is it any wonder I became a split personality? First I'm standing there mixing a Manhattan and within a second I'm at the typewriter confirming an engagement in Tennessee. But the office boomed and so did the club. We both worked twice as hard and time suddenly became very valuable in our lives. We had to clock meetings to the very second; anyone who was ten minutes late for an appointment had to wait until the next opportunity to make another appointment or he would find himself in conversation with Mr. B trying to get his music published while the band was blasting "The St. Louis Blues Cha Cha" in his ear, and the once-upon-a-time-secretary was opening a half dozen bottles of Bud.

Club Bandstand began moving right along, showing more and more progress as the weeks flew by us. The music company business was ever increasing, the investment company continued to prove worthwhile. Mr. B told me once that having Club Bandstand was like having a party every night; it seemed that way to me, too.

Quite a few years back Mr. B had invested in some property about forty miles out in the country from St. Louis west en route toward Kansas City. For about two years we made countless trips out to the property to look it over. I don't know what I expected to see on my first visit; I do know I didn't expect to see what I saw. There it was before me. Thirty acres of dirt. Yellow mud. A make-it-as-you-go-along project. There was one shelter on the property and that was an old bus (we call it *Maybellene*) he had purchased in 1956 for transporting his band on a California tour. When you came close to it, the mammoth letters on the sides blinded you with CHUCK BERRY ORCHESTRA—way out there in no-man's land. We got out of the car, and as Mr. B measured different sections of the land I trailed behind taking notes and jotting everything down. That was the first pair of shoes to become initiated in the mud club of '57. If I knew in advance of my going out to the "country estate, excuse me, the future country estate" I would be prepared, but I never did. Mr. B would come into the office and say, "Get your notebook and pencil, I'll need you to take a few notes, come on." Since this happened so often I finally wised up and stashed some old penny loafers in his car.

As 1958 got further behind us we could look back and see the progress we had made on the once barren thirty acres. This was our future Berry Park.

I don't think I shall ever forget the day I saw Mr. B clear some of the land for a road. There he was: white shirt, tie, blue jeans, and boots, on top of his tractor while they were digging and building. I pitched in and helped Mr. B clean the old bus for the construction workers to use. We thought this would be a nice place for them to eat, as the grasshoppers invited themselves to every open sandwich. Needless to say this turned into an all-day job. Mr. B found some old clippings from when he first recorded "Maybellene" and naturally that brought on a discussion of one thing or another. We found a checkerboard and some checkers so that gave us a chance to try out our talent. Then there were all sorts of interesting bottles, books, advertisements from previous dates, tracks of field mice, and hundreds of dead mosquitoes, grasshoppers, and flies. The next time I was called upon to clean the bus for the workers it was a less dirty job. This time I just had human elements: cigarettes, cigarettes, and cigarettes.

Among Mr. B's many talents we find a would-be architect. The plans for Berry Park, all specifications, dimensions, and everything that goes along with drawing blueprints came from Mr. B solely. Mr. B would do the measuring of the land, allowing so many feet and inches for equipment, machinery, and all other elements that go into building a structure. After Mr. B had the measurements jotted down he would hurry back to the office and start to draw. Mr. B proved to be a true engineer, complete with slide rule, drawing board, and colored pencils. My office was turned into an engineer's study. Many were the days and nights I watched Mr. B laboring over his drawing board. For hours and hours he would diligently lean over the board—pencil in hand, cigarette in mouth—and never raise his head. After he would complete his drawing, he would present his masterpiece to his hired architect, at which time the architect would blueprint it. I moved to Berry Park August 12, 1960. My final move. The Berry Park dream became the Berry Park reality.

Everything seems to be moving so swiftly around me I can't waste a precious moment thinking about what is happening. We have worked hard for what we have and so often I think we have pushed ourselves too much. But we still have a great deal ahead of us and the harder and faster we work the more time we will have to enjoy our future—our "golden" years, I

think you call it. Keeping our interest in what we plan to share is beginning to play an important role in our lives. Mr. B and I are constantly talking about next week, next month, and of course, next year.

Francine handed me the above story after one of my long absences on a tour, and it may well have been the spark that lit the flame that fired me into starting this book, or, more accurately, its original, which was lost in fire.

My appreciation of Fran's attributes owes much to her mother, Marie Prager, who I pray will read these lines. This most wonderful lady reared Francine none but chaste and indoctrinated her with a fear of ignorance and insecurity, something too many women of today seem to lack.

Francine was never overenthused about traveling through the South, and once I sent for her to handle a count on a percentage engagement. I was to pick her up at the New Orleans airport. While I was waiting for her plane to arrive, two police officers walked up and began begging me for autographs. I seldom have refused to stop to sign an autograph, especially for an adult. So I did, and since they were so friendly, I decided to play a little "scare-trick" on Fran since she was in her feared Southland, against her better judgment.

I set it up so it would appear that the two policemen were there to arrest her as she deplaned. I was hidden around a corner watching. Fran, to my surprise, was either petrified or in disbelief, because she never showed the least fright as she approached them or frustration during the announcement of her arrest. Too "cool" was she, I thought, until she saw me step out from behind the cigarette machine. Then she screamed in apparent relief, collapsed in the policeman's arms momentarily, and began beating on his chest in retaliation for the joke. That night, long after the joke had faded from my mind, she got me back by deliberately reporting an extremely low count of the concert percentage earned. I reacted furiously, thinking the promoter had definitely cheated since I knew there had been a large attendance.

Another memorable occasion with Francine took place in Paris on the Left Bank of the Seine in November of 1964 as we stopped the Hertz car to watch the sun setting amid the girders of the Eiffel Tower. We had nothing to do as we just rode around listening to "voulez vous." Francine told me she never wanted to part from the job of looking after my business. Back in the United States, they were at high noon but on the Left Bank we were in Paris. The traffic had disappeared up on the rue above us leaving only the rippling water whispering through the City of Paradise. She continued saying to me,

Charles, you seem like a rocket to me. You have soared off so high and shining so bright in a heaven that I can only dream of what it would be like to try and follow you. While I am like a candle, merely flickering in the window of admiration that I see you from. Your brilliance has become so bright that I wonder if my flicker will still be seen upon your return if you should. But I will be there still if you should need me. You soar where many people see you and cheer you on your journey, yet you return to my window where I flicker in the shadows of your career. How, through the glare and brilliance that surrounds your life, can you see my twinkling light among all

the bright stars around you? It is my thought, Charles, seeing you among the many bright stars that surround you, that some day you will go away as you deserve, and join another star as brilliant as yourself. My little flame shall remain awaiting and hoping, that if it should ever be seen again in your moments of tranquillity, you would know I was still there where you had to leave me behind.

I have never forgotten how the amber setting sun sank beyond her blue eyes that evening. I was wrapped up in emotion that yet today lingers as I wonder how much it has enveloped me. On the little Hertz mini rent-a-car, I captured a pleasant memory.

CHAPTER TEN

Berry Park Country Club

M y Uncle Edward, who was always sort of a sport, told me about thirty acres of cleared farmland adjacent to a summer retreat he'd bought for his out-of-town peace. I purchased the lot for eight thousand dollars on April 22, 1957, marking the beginning of the realization of a long held dream to live at a place like the Glencrest Country Club, where Dad took me to help him work when I was just a child. That was the move that developed into the creation of the area now known as Berry Park.

I'd imagined it to be a place where people both black and white could mix together harmoniously. I was thinking of a place like Six Flags, but maybe only ''One Flag'' in my case, to accommodate families for fun and entertainment. The rides, I knew, would be real expensive, but things like fishing and hunting, swimming and dancing and picnicking would be economically practical for me to offer. So I leaned toward constructing the Park, as I wanted it to be called, in those areas of recreational conveniences.

Like Rock Hudson in the movie *Giant,* I walked around the plot with great anticipation of developing my own mini Disneyland. By June 29, another two-acre strip was added to satisfy a discrepancy in the acreage on the sales contract. I was fairly learned in simple real-estate purchasing and saved paying commissions many times

by buying directly from owners. Hiring contractors was nothing new to me either after watching my father manage his carpentry business for years. I was wise to contractors cutting corners by using a weak mix of concrete to save costly sacks of cement or such cuts as using inferior-quality wood in rafters and joists, which are never seen after they are covered with flooring or walls. During breaks in managing Club Bandstand, Fran drove out the forty miles suggesting changes in the course of the developments.

I took the 1937 Syracuse city bus that I had converted into a trailer out to the acreage to camp in as I administered the construction of our clubhouse and a seventy-six-foot guitar-shaped swimming pool that I'd drawn up the plans for. I hooked the bus up to electricity and sometimes would sleep in it overnight.

The one-acre front lake was the first thing to be contracted, then the concrete swimming pool at twenty-one thousand dollars and next the twenty-six-thousand-dollar concrete-walled nightclub building. (Sorry! There was a lot of talk going around then about hydrogen bombs.) During the months of heavy music touring, I was sinking a lot of my savings into Berry Park. Before the winter set in, two small four-room frame bungalows were completed, for an office and living quarters for Fran. We anticipated the time was coming when the "colorful" Club Bandstand's racial forwardness would be held back on Grand Boulevard, the great white way. It was a must to start anew in a business that had a chance to prosper while I was earning money.

Many times Francine had been stopped for questioning, such as, "What are you doing?" (referring to "in that neighborhood."). Francine, not accustomed to such a ghettoic style of society, offered an answer: "Attending to my business." Officer: "What is your business?" Answer: "A secretary." "Where?" "Around the corner." "For who?" "CB Music Incorporated!" "Is that Chuck Berry Company?" "No, it's a corporation." "Where do you live?" "Here" (she was in front of her living quarters) "where the car is parked." "In his place?" "No, he does not own or rent it. May I enter it now?" "Whose car is that?" Answer: "It is registered in the corporate name." "Oh, you're that one, the one that runs the nightclub he's got . . ." Over and over such harassment happened until she moved from the city.

Bluebirds, butterflies, and katydids were the only type of company that interrupted the tranquillity on Route 3, Buckner Road, once she settled at the Park, three miles south of the city of Wentzville.

I set up a checking account that Fran could draw from and furnish the developers with necessary items. She had to set up housekeeping and check on the workers when I was on the road. I well remember the early meeting of one of the contractors that caused me to be away from home all night for the first time while not on tour. But as improvements multiplied, the nights away began to also, during the construction of the Park. The first time Fran fixed a TV dinner, I learned that cooking was one of the things she must have truly despised, although she kept an immaculate kitchen, which sometimes by itself helps to encourage an appetite.

As the swimming-pool contractors were finishing, the autumn nights were finding us rejoicing as the Park was forming into shape. The concession stand between the twin houses was next in completion. The pool was next with a dozen neighbors waiting to jump in when it was being filled.

All the attention that building the Park required of me caused me to begin flying to my concerts at the latest safe hour and splitting at the earliest flight out. I was flying all over the place, making money, and banking as much as I could, thinking any week the bottom would fall out of the chariot and I would be sliding on my assets until it burned out any chance of sitting on top of the world. I would be thinking, How can people be so good to me, to pay me over six hundred dollars to do something I am thrilled to do anyway?

Irving Feld, a Washington, D.C., promoter, put together a thirty-one artist show with two traveling buses and labeled it "The Biggest Show of Stars," headlining Fats Domino, myself, Bill Doggett, Clyde McPhatter, La Vern Baker, the Moonglows, and the Schoolboys. We rolled out to perform seventy-two one-nighters in a span of ninety-two hot nights starting in New York City, February 1957. The artists traveled in from their various homes to rendezvous for the opening show at the famous Apollo Theater. There were eleven acts, of which five were white; again I want to mention that such was then called a mixed show. The mixing of races mattered little in the New England states, where all the artists could stay in the same hotel and dine together. But in the South, separation of the races was required by law.

When the tour reached St. Louis, I left the bus and picked up my sky-blue Fleetwood Cadillac and drove, following the show buses from city to city, through New England to Montreal then westward, weaving in and out of Canada across to Seattle and on down the West Coast to San Diego. It went through Texas into Dixie, where black people's country tears of thee were not so sweetly landing liberty and so did sing. It was not us watching our step so much as it was our white stepbrothers watching our every step.

It was becoming clearer to me, upon returning to many of these southern cities, that the tension was mounting between the black and white people. But still the differences seemed to be hidden when gathered for sports or music. As racially divided audiences were showing up to find mixed and open seating in the auditoriums, and with the security somewhat relaxed, the white fans

*With Fats Domino in 1966, when I wore
velvet-collar jean suits.*

visited backstage like we all were blue. Probably because of my
rearing I noticed the friendliness of the white females more than
that of the white males, going beyond normal musical appreciation
to wanting to personally meet and associate with the singers, something I never expected to occur, according to the outlook of my
high-school days.

Usually a concert wouldn't terminate until after one o'clock in
the morning. If my next job was less than a hundred miles away, I
would start out that night and drive ahead, using what I always
thought was the hyped-up energy instilled from the audience just
after a performance. The time that passed while driving late at
night often flowed with thoughts of things to write songs about and
it also was perfect for simmering down from the glory that ema-
nated from the show.

The contractors were building from my blueprints, which left me
free to travel weeks at a time. Then I would come back to or
through St. Louis and draw up another set of prints that would last
until I returned again. I had two hundred forty one-nighter concerts in 1957, with two versions of The Biggest Show of Stars,
promoted by Irving Feld (who, I heard, also promoted the Ringling
Brothers Circus) from February to March and September to No-

Onstage during the filming of "The T.A.M.I. Show."

vember, and Alan Freed's Summer Festival in July. When Feld booked he booked two and three months at a time. Once the show of thirty-one acts and the backup orchestra of thirty-seven were traveling on two DC 9 chartered aircraft, straight across southern Canada from Quebec to Vancouver, British Columbia, and down the coast to San Francisco, where we picked up the road busing again. I would write Themetta and Fran of all the strange places and they in turn would write me about the progress of the Park.

Sometimes Fran would send me dimensions or a decision to make for the contractors, mailing it two or three cities ahead of the tour to ensure receipt. I would draw the plot or return the decision that kept things going until I returned. All in all 1957 was a very busy year in music and construction of the Park. If the money hadn't been coming in I couldn't have taken on such a vast estate and kept it going as I have.

In May 1958, Dick Clark booked me in the Little Theater in New York after many, many performances at his "American Bandstand" for broadcasting on the TV show. At my first "American Bandstand" appearance, I ran into trouble because I thought it was ridiculous to lip sync the words to "Sweet Little Sixteen." The song was written in honor of first, the teenage girl, and second, the "American Bandstand" show that Dick Clark hosted. I was being stubborn in ignorance of the cost of live singing over lip syncing. Rock 'n' roll on television was in its early days with budgets low, and lip syncing rather than live vocalizing helped cut expenses. In Dick Clark's book *Rock, Roll and Remember,* he quotes me as saying on this occasion "Ain't going do any dancing." It's hardly likely anyone whose mother taught school would be trained to speak in such a fashion. Another point in the same section contains a description of Leonard Chess using profanity and lewd terms while speaking with me long distance, after Dick called him asking him to persuade me to lip sync. Leonard explained the reasons for lip syncing, but he never used profanity while doing business with me at any time in our affiliation.

In Dick's book the confusion that arose about lip syncing my performance is described as if I was not only unaware of sync, but incapable of even trying it. I was being asked to try something for the first time in front of a nationwide television audience! The point is: the writer dramatized his assumption instead of stating a fact. To me, regardless of boredom or stimulation, the truth should always perform. (I'm truly writing this book, I hope you're enjoying it.)

When Clark came back to me from his office, after being the last to speak with Leonard, he was very businesslike and said firmly, "Thank you, and good day," and spun into the studio. The negroid dialect and profanity in his book never transpired. As a matter of fact I'll yet have my first time to hear Dick Clark use such language as was written of his opinion of me. I doubt that he loves me, but I'm certain he does not hate me. My inexperience in lip syncing that day is what got me canceled off the show. I quickly learned to lip sync and, as Dick's book states, he allowed me to be a guest on "American Bandstand" at least a dozen times thereafter.

The fact that Dick's "American Bandstand" show did not then have black persons participating in the dancing was surely not his

With Dick Clark, joking about how he couldn't pay me.

own decision, but a policy in the production of the show. However I did hope that Dick Clark was not aware of what was being said among the black populace in America about the apparent restriction. I would have been just stubborn or bold enough then to mention the restriction, assuming he would have cared.

Dick has matured immensely since the old days but his features have not done likewise. He recently provided me ninety minutes on nationwide TV as part of his "In Concert" show, and he made me one of the stars in his "Twenty-fifth Anniversary" show that is still being talked about. So I suppose the wounds of ages are closed forever now, but he still just will not grow old with me. I must ask his darling wife Bobbie how he does that.

In May 1958, I also performed in Atlanta, at the Whiskey Club. I thought the club would have a typical southern atmosphere with restrictions regarding race relations but found the people were there just to have fun under any conditions. There were a half dozen go-go girls on side stages dancing. The star dressing room was provided with bath facilities, but the dancers had to walk through the crowded club, congested with customers and tables, to use the public restrooms located at the back. Some got friendly and sometimes asked me to use my facilities, including the shower. One particularly friendly dancer once had used it and I was practicing some stroke of the guitar as she came out. I asked her if she could hear me in there. In bewilderment she answered, "Yes." I smiled and replied, "I could hear you too." She smiled and skipped away backstage.

On the last night of the gig, after the show two of the dancers invited me to visit a club in the suburbs of Atlanta. I followed them in my car. Shortly after we arrived, a heated argument arose between two guys at the bar and swiftly turned into a brawl about three yards from our table. The fellow against the bar drew a pistol, and the other guy dared him, "Go ahead and pull the trigger." The dude with the gun immediately pulled it and the tempter was pushed back five feet by the bullet, falling on our table crying, "He shot me! He did. Somebody call an ambulance, will you?"

It was the first time I'd witnessed a shooting but while I froze stunned, the two girls I was with simply nodded their disgust at such behavior and said, "Come on and let's get out of here, Chuck, you don't need this kind of publicity." I was pulling the two of them by the time we reached the exit door, where I released their hands, parted, and in haste drove back to the hotel.

A half hour later I answered my room door for the same two girls who asked me if I would meet with them at the police station in the morning as a witness to the shooting of their injured friend. I nodded, they left; I packed and checked out, drove to the airport, slept in the car, and caught the first flight out. Go-go girls put a stop to my accepting invitations to go.

In 1958 I spent five days in Culver City, California, working at the Hal Roach Studio doing the movie *Go Johnny Go,* a story about a guy named Johnny Melody who was being promoted by Alan Freed to become a rock star. My greatest thrill while there was seeing all the big movie cameras and technical equipment I had only seen in photos. There were lots of people walking around doing nothing, it seemed, but surely on the payroll. My dad would have never paid them. (I don't remember much from the filming of *Rock, Rock, Rock,* the first movie I appeared in, where I only sang. In *Go Johnny Go* I had a speaking part.)

The making of *Go Johnny Go* came around a short tour I was

doing through southern California where the movie studios paid for hotel accommodations and food for the cast. I thought that was terrific because I nearly always acquired residence at the cheapest little motel near the airport, which also aided in making the morning flight to the next concert. Sometimes I was invited to a party after the concert and would be out too late to check in anywhere so I would drive on to the local airport and park my Hertz car directly in front of the terminal door entrance, curl up in the back seat, and dream of a king bed with queen covering.

I'd sleep there wearing sunshades, leaving my plane ticket and Hertz folder visible from the dashboard, with my name casually but intentionally exposed for the airport patrolmen to see, hoping they'd give me a hustle and accept an album in return for any violation. Once though, I was awakened by an officer, with his thumb cocked, shouting, "Move it." That experience later brought title to one of my songs.

It was during the filming of *Go Johnny Go,* in which Alan Freed played the part of himself as a New York disk jockey, that I realized what a heavy drinker Alan was. It seemed at first he could hold his take as well as Johnnie Johnson could, without it affecting his ability to perform his professional obligations. But just since I had known him, I could notice the physical deterioration of his body under the quantity of alcohol I assumed he was consuming. This has been said to be the reason that soon brought the habit and him to rest.

Once, before a Montreal concert and long before his ailment became critical, he invited me into his dressing room and fell on me, taking us both to the floor. I don't think he ever knew that I didn't drink, for he was constantly offering me a nip. I remember him being really stoned at the Montreal engagement, a condition he was in increasingly. This caused him to be interrupted by stage managers for reasons I call "baby handling" because of his inability to carry out his obligations regarding announcements on his shows or on the business end of the paperwork and tour proceedings.

I was about the same age as Alan, and although I didn't participate in his dressing-room drinking parties, I was always invited because he liked the interest I took in him and the stories he told during the gatherings. I joined the parties mainly because he was

Publicity shot with Sandy Stewart and Alan Freed in Go, Johnny, Go.

to me an employer and it was advantageous to have close ties with your employer. Plus back then it was in no way popular for a black person to be invited to an all-white get-together, so I hung around for the experience and information I could get about the music business.

There, at one of the loose-speaking drink gatherings, a bit of information was exposed that induced Alan to tell me that he intended to give me back the one-third writer's-credit rip-off from

Chess's false registration of "Maybellene." This was a promise that lingered on through his death and probated estate. It was sometime in the late seventies that I finally got litigation going that brought me rightful full ownership of the copyright.

One time Alan was discussing something personal with someone, and as I happened to walk by the conversation was terminated. That created a suspicion that lived thereafter between Alan and myself and quelled the warm relation I had with him.

July 11, 1958, I purchased a large eleven-room dwelling on the northern half of a private street, 13 Windermere Place, for thirty thousand dollars. It was more elaborate than anything Toddy and I'd ever dreamed of living in. On July 15, I moved what soon would be my family of three children. We decided Fran could occupy our vacated cottage on Whittier when she wasn't at Berry Park, where she could reside in peace next to our good ol' Italian-born neighbors, Mr. and Mrs. Dimottio.

Toddy was happy to be in a big house on a private street at last, she was so busy with the two kids in school and on the way with another. Things were looking up, I'd say, until she looked down and saw our new baby was another girl. She did so want a son that time but at 7:25 P.M., November 10, 1959, the little lady Aloha Isa Lei Berry was born. Now I was sho nuff a family man responsible for four ladies.

We did ten days at the memorable Brooklyn Fox Theater for Alan Freed in August 1958 and had a few days off at home before we went into the studio again. Chess Records had moved to new facilities at 2120 South Michigan that accommodated a larger staff and a more modern recording studio, and Leonard offered me a better rate on my contract with the company. His office was elaborate and he had others doing what once he enjoyed doing himself, for he was seldom there anymore. His interest was leaning toward a radio station. It seemed the sessions were becoming cold and foreign but we managed to have our tunes run down enough to be ready to tape.

What the Hail! Hail! Rock 'n' Roll, I thought, well, this is the way life is, sometimes looking up and sometimes down. I got Johnnie Johnson and Jasper Thomas, who was my main drummer along about then, and wheeled in to the Chess studios, where we ran through a bunch of cover tunes and galloped over a few lyrics I had scribbled on the long Show of Stars tours. At this time I let many distractions hinder me from really writing as I had in the beginning of my career, until my attention to women practically prevented me from giving any time to improvisations at all. Although Leonard and I both knew the recording session was inferior to the past ones, he congratulated me on coming up with something that kept the burner glowing with different sounds.

On one memorable occasion after a recording session, Leonard Chess told me with a sheepish smile to go straight to room 116 at the Persian Hotel on 63rd Street. I had been staying at the Persian all week but Leonard emphasized that there was a surprise for me in that particular room.

As free with his luxuries as I'd grown to know Leonard to be, I still didn't know what to expect: a party celebrating the success of our hit, a car sitting out front replacing our ever-crowded station wagon, or a quick two hundred dollars to pocket for a spontaneous gig. When I knocked on the door to room 116, the most attractive blonde I'd ever seen in person answered. She walked straight to the bed, sat back, and asked where I'd been, she'd been waiting for me. She mentioned that Leonard had sent her to be my company that evening. She said her name was Jan White and claimed to be studying modeling at the University of Chicago.

I thought she was too pretty to be a hooker but wondered why she was offering herself just to please another person. A conversation followed regarding photos and I was granted the freedom to take several cute snapshots while she lay back on the bed with closed eyes, puckered lips, cocked head, and resisting not. She obtained my attention in the latter dimension and need I mention subdued my suspense with long pauses of vigorous movements between murmurs of passion followed by fatigue and slumber. The undrawn window drapes let the dawning over Lake Michigan enter my memory of an unforgettable experience.

I flew off Christmas day, 1958, to New York City to join the ol' road show gang for Alan Freed's Christmas Jubilee, eleven days at the Loews Theater. The festive holidays were spent with Jackie Wilson, Bo Diddley, the Everly Brothers, Frankie Avalon, Jo Ann Campbell, Eddie Cochran, King Curtis, the Flamingos, the Crests,

Henry William Berry, Sr., 1958,
overseeing the building of Berry Park.

the Cadillacs, Dion and the Belmonts, Johnnie Ray, and others. I
would do my bit and get off stage so I could mingle with the
spectators and thus did not insist on closing the show even when
I had the right to, with the hottest hit. With that programming, I
could meet whoever I would and sometimes complete a relationship during the span of the show. This was the blackest white show
I'd been on so far, but the relations and companionship were beautiful.

Next I flew to L.A., where I met Bobby Darin, Jo Ann Campbell, and George Hamilton IV to start my first ever Australian tour.
We made a connecting flight and flew all night watching Pan Am's
four propellers spit fire across the Pacific Ocean, reaching Honolulu at daybreak. We checked in at the Surf Rider Hotel where,
upon entering my room, I found that Jo Ann Campbell, who was
about as big as a minute, had been allotted a room joining mine.
To my amazement (or should I say pleasure) while I was unpacking
I discovered her prancing nude through the connecting door left
open by the bellman. How she didn't notice the door being partly

ajar I'll never know. Why I didn't close it, I'll never tell, but it took me a good hour to unpack, tripping to and fro to my suitcase and the cracked door watching her completing her bath.

Bobby Darin had started what looked like an affair with Jo Ann before we'd even started out for Australia. On the long flight, he flirted while I had to listen to the background of George Hamilton the first, second, and third. Between shows, when the promoter took us around to see the sights, I noticed that Mack the Knife cared little to associate with me. When we reached Melbourne, Jo seemed to be friendlier than I'd expected but Bobby did not encourage me to believe that he was a peer of mine.

It was early 1960 when we closed down Club Bandstand. My aim had been to draw a biracial clientele like that I had seen around New England. It lasted a year.

In August 1960 we opened Berry Park to the public. There came an average of two hundred customers per day swimming, picnicking, dancing, and staying at a motellike "lodge" built shortly after the traffic of visitors began to flow. I had a stone placed to commemorate the founding of Berry Park and immediately was made aware that what I'd placed looked like a tombstone. The inscription reads:

WELCOME TO
BERRY PARK
FOUNDED AUG. 15, 1957
BY THE FAMILY
FOR THE PEOPLE

MARTHA BELL BANKS   HENRY W. BERRY, SR.
THELMA   HANK   LUCY   CHUCK   PAUL   BENNIE
THEMETTA SUGGS BERRY
FRANCINE GILLIUM

Those were the happy days, running a good thriving business after the hassles at Club Bandstand. My father and sister Martha helped Fran with desirable customers. Dad was constantly bringing wives of the good deacons of Antioch to see the progress of Berry Park, namely the queen of them all, Miss Julia Davis, my grade-school music teacher. It was always said by the deaconess of the church, "Oh, what a fine boy he is, I knew he would do well.'' Dad said they were still saying it, but not as often, while I was in the joint.

Then I started back out on the road, flying here to there, renting a Hertz car to travel from airport to gig to hotel back to the airport to lift off for another city to another auditorium hopefully to meet someone special to talk to and if lucky have dinner with after the show. Of course there were times when I was grateful enough to be blessed with a breakfast companion, but the shows went on.

CHAPTER ELEVEN

The French and Indian Ward

J une 2, 1958, on my way home after playing Topeka, Kansas, and loaded with the week's pay, I had a flat tire right on the viaduct over Interstate 70 in St. Charles, Missouri. A lady of French origin was in the car with me, Joan Mathis, whom I'd met at a Christmas eve concert the previous year at the Dugout Club in St. Louis. She had traveled along with me to visit people she knew in the area and see the Topeka concert. While I was changing the tire, we were approached by a state patrol officer, Don Medley, who stepped out of his car, walked up and faced me, clicked his heels, saluted, and ordered me to produce my operator's license. When I did he saluted again and ordered me to stand aside while he searched the peach-colored Cadillac, which I must admit was attractive. He made no remarks regarding the brunette in the front seat but proceeded to find nineteen hundred dollars in cash and a revolver that I had purchased in Texas during a layover between concerts. I kept it with me while I was traveling with large sums of cash, wrapped in a bag beneath the driver's seat.

Officer Medley clicked his heels again, saluted, and announced, "You are under arrest under section something code so-and-so!" He handcuffed me, then turned toward my companion and asked who she was. She informed him and was politely handcuffed and

Joan Mathis, the French connecting "ward," visiting Berry Park.

assisted into his patrol car. I got in, too, and we both were driven to the county jail.

When the dust had settled, I was taken into a room, stripped of all possessions, and seated in a soft chair with hard looks from several officials. Questions came from everywhere, but when my interrogation was over I was charged with possession of a concealed weapon. I believe they hoped also to charge me with violating the Mann Act.

Being a property owner I was eligible to and so signed a bond allowing me to be released. The money was held under some code number, the gun was confiscated, and Joan, I believe, was escorted home while I took a taxi back to fix the flat tire and go home.

That night Joan phoned for me at Francine's house and explained to her what went down at the interrogation. She related that she had insistently stated that she had not been molested although some officer encouraged her to declare that such was my intention. The legalities resulted in my appearing before Magistrate

Webster Karrenbrock on June 20, 1958, for a hearing on the .25 automatic and some minor fines for auto registration totaling thirty dollars. Nothing was said about the Mann Act charges. Thereafter the state of affairs regarding Joan, the money, and the gun seemed to lie abandoned.

Meanwhile things got warmer on the road and the mal-publicity seemed to increase the number of concerts I was asked to play. It became even hotter on August 27, 1959, in Meridian, Mississippi, during a concert.

I deplaned from a short flight off Southern Airlines and stepped down on native Dixie soil. Nine handsome young southern gentlemen were lined beneath the wing of the DC 3, elegantly welcoming me to Mississippi. I felt like the stately son of Stonewall Jackson, but it lasted only four minutes. When I rejected the limo the nine fraternity brothers had reserved and independently rented a Mark 1 Lincoln sedan from Hertz, the mood depreciated considerably. I followed them to an old army barracks renovated into a USO quarters, where my performance was to be held. There were several uninhabited barracks buildings adjoining its assembly building. The promoter, one of the nine gentlemen, took me to the stage and showed me around, then took me on a visit out to his home to meet his folks.

Later, after a rehearsal, the nine guys along with a half dozen girls they'd summoned, sat around and drank beer and chatted with me, obviously struggling to prove that I was not in the Mississippi that some people disdained it to be. Nine o'clock came and the concert got under way. The tuxedos became sweaty and evening gowns crumpled, hairdos drooped as mascara was running but fun and joy could not have been more abundant anyplace in America than in Meridian that night as the dance progressed.

When I had closed the show with my major hits, several fellows and girls stumbled onto the stage begging for more selections. One of the girls threw her arms around me and hung a soul-searching kiss that I let hang a second too long. She was too beautiful not to be some-rich-body's daughter, and the smack was the turning point of the cheerful attitudes. Her close hug muted my guitar strings, bringing the dancers to notice what stopped the music. The white student backup band stopped immediately, as did the humbug and chatter of all the dancers.

Immediately I stepped down off the low stage, with guitar in one hand and my small amp in the other, and started for the door. A tall fraternity brother in a tuxedo came before me with six or seven other brothers on either side and shouted, "Chuck, did you try to date my sister?" I said, "No of course not!" A bigger guy beside the accuser yelled, "He did, George, he's a Yankee like the rest of 'em." Several other brothers then joined in to support the accusation. More words were exchanged, a crowd began to gather, and the Mississippi mud hit the fan.

Ross, the fraternity brother who had taken me to his home, took the initiative and shouted appeasements to the angry students huddled close to me. It was then that I noticed a big switchblade knife opening in the hand of the larger brother standing closest to me. I swallowed several songs, raised the pitch of my voice and lowered its volume to appear as little belligerent as I could. I pattered out some pitifully puny phrases trying to get the big guy with that ugly knife to retreat a bit. Ross began holding back the angry few fraternity brothers up front, especially the one who held the knife, and advising them against unnecessary trouble.

"I'm a Mississippian, Ross, and this nigger asked my sister for a date!" explained George, who stood beside the guy holding the switchblade. Ross, really shouting in anger, overtook the two guys, grabbed my hand, and led me toward the side door, telling me to leave the guitar and amp and get across the lawn to one of the old barracks and wait for him. I did with great speed.

After reaching the barracks safely, I observed three police squad cars only two hundred feet away along the front of the dance building. The patrons of the dance were searching around in the likeness of a mob. Over three dozen fraternity paddles appeared, waving over the shrubbery surrounding the barracks building. I was concentrating on my father's advice and contemplating trying to make the nineteen miles to the Georgia border, letting my guitar and amp paddle their own canoe.

For five minutes I watched the ambitious crowd roving around until suddenly behind me two male silhouettes appeared in the doorless doorway. I crouched to make a track record for the other end of the long empty building but it was Ross and a police officer, feeling their way in the darkness and whispering my name. I joined them. They claimed they had arranged an exit for me and quickly

C H U C K

escorted me into a squad car sandwiched between two others and we sailed under sirens on to the city and into the jailhouse. My amp and guitar arrived just before I did in the sheriff's car at 1:50 A.M. When I was settled in the sheriff's office, Ross apologized for the fellows and the inconvenience, then bade me farewell, assuring me that I would be okay and not to worry.

After deleting my pockets of personal items, the sergeant suggested that the entire seven hundred dollars they had relieved me of would cover the fine for peace disturbance that I was being charged for. Fortunately they overlooked eight hundred-dollar bills in my rear pocket. They decided I should stay there through the night since a few infuriated fraternity brothers had followed the police cars to the jail to monitor my fate. I took a couple of Polaroid pictures of my bare-chested cellmates, slept on the jail bench, had a breakfast of bologna and cracker dust, then, as planned, was escorted with my belongings to the Meridian airport to meet my flight to Atlanta.

The plane was ready to take off, but the door was reopened when the screaming siren and flashing red lights pulled up under the wing. When a black man with an attaché case stepped out of a police car to climb aboard, the stone-eyed stewardess stood still in the doorway as if it couldn't be this she was held up for. Knowing she was acutely aggravated at her added passenger, I greeted her a facile good morning in fluent French, but no fellowship came forth in return. Posing as a politician from Paris for the entire flight, I enjoyed that beautiful southern hospitality from the other stewardess. I passed by my name in the headlines on the newsstand as I approached the Hertz counter, where I verified my reservations the previous night and continued my southern tour of rock concerts.

December 1, 1959, ninety-six days later, I was playing a concert in El Paso and I took my band over to Juarez, Mexico, where we spent some hours stopping at different strip joints, watching the girls, and browsing around with anyone we met. At the close of the afternoon we wound up in a cantina talking music and stuff with a couple of women. One of them, Janice, was the spitting image of a teenage photo of my mother's younger sister, Aunt Alice, with an olive complexion, pie face, and stout, high cheekbones, unlike her typical American black girlfriend, Beatrice, who'd lost my attention during the introduction. Janice seemed settle-minded while Beatrice yacked on continuously. The band guys coaxed them into coming along to the concert. Janice was saying little but agreeing to everything by nodding her head. The red Ford station wagon accommodated the plan and the party was on for the evening, with the drummer picking up the liquor and settling in the dressing room of the coliseum awaiting show time.

I was enthused about the setup. The quietness of Janice, who now I'd learned was not of African heritage but an Apache Indian, was appealing. She showed interest in what was going on around the stage and production end on the show. I asked her how old she was and while she shrugged her shoulders, Beatrice spoke up, declaring Janice was twenty-one years old. I could, from her familiar features, tell that the black girl wasn't twenty-one, but to me Janice's looks didn't betray Beatrice's claim. She was 130 pounds at five feet nine inches and acted much more mature than Beatrice, who was provoking a courtship with the drummer.

During the concert the drummer's anticipations ran into a brick wall that had strong arms and sturdy legs and appeared, from the authoritative demands he asserted, to be Beatrice's husband. In a typical "Lord help her" scene, he hustled Beatrice out the door. Later Janice told me that she was on her own, having just arrived in El Paso a few months prior from Yuma, Arizona.

There was a slogan among guys going with girls during my high-school days that advised a ritual of three Fs; put more decently this meant locate 'em, love 'em, and leave 'em. I was long out of high school when I finally became a passing pupil in the first one, then managed to reach a passing grade in the second, but have yet to adopt the philosophy of the third. I allowed the band members to take along a girl to the next town if they wanted to go. The fact was that I had fancied doing likewise myself and could hardly set up a rule for them that I, myself, did not care to practice. I could see Janice in Indian attire in my imagination, and I thought she would be a drawing attraction as a hostess at Club Bandstand. We discussed the idea, which she readily accepted, so I phoned Fran and asked her to prepare a place for Janice to stay while so engaged.

We next played Santa Fe, New Mexico, then up to a concert in Denver where we checked into the Drexel Hotel. While on the

road, Johnnie and I always had separate rooms while Jasper and Leroy shared a room and split the cost. I was picking up on the come-on Janice was giving me and I let her stay over in my own room. It was no easy thing to lay off of her when she proceeded to undress right before me and climb into my bed, but without the challenge that usually confronts a guy, I managed to postpone the joys, thinking we'd have a chance on the road later.

That afternoon when I awakened her, she boldly paraded into the bathroom in the buff and stayed twenty minutes, reappearing dressed and looking sad and unwanted as a homeless brown-eyed poodle. The day and evening passed slowly, and the courage I depended on was fast growing weaker, for I have always been subject to the sight of the female anatomy reaching my retina and taxing my tolerance.

> Maybe I should have let her go, but at the time, I
>   wanted to know
> Just what illusions she would fulfill, in following me of
>   her own free will.
> I do not deny that it made me sad, knowingly missing
>   what I could have had.
> Her love, whose origin, within her heart, was too
>   immature to fail to depart.

Christmas was drawing nigh and Fran had booked Redd Foxx at the club. We decided this was a good time to launch the Apache hostess in her native attire so Fran started processing Janice's social security, FICA, etc., files, under her full name, Janice Escalante, and dressed her in a brilliant native costume with feathers.

My curiosity became a successful reality in her reception at Club Bandstand. Her quietness and reserve, along with her humble characteristics, were welcomed by the clientele. I had a chance to become proud of my idea and Janice in her costume during my two-week stay in St. Louis before heading back out on the road. She would break a slight smile only at those she knew very well. I took a liking to her beyond that of employer and began returning gestures of admiration when the smiles were for me.

Just days after I went back out on the road, Fran phoned to inform me that Janice had not shown up for work since I had left.

The next information she received was a phone call from the district police saying that an employee of Chuck Berry's had been arrested and was requesting to speak with him from the station. Fran explained my absence and the following day told me that some detectives wanted to speak to me concerning a teenager I had brought from El Paso, Texas. I was accustomed to being hassled by the authorities for noise and crowd congestion at the club so I braced myself upon returning home for more hassles.

The night of December 21, 1959, two black plainclothesmen came down the stairs of the club and stood at the landing watching the show. One beckoned for me and explained that the sergeant at the local police station wanted to chat with me. Once I was at the police station the sergeant asked me, "Do you know Janice Escalante?" I said I did. "Did you bring her from Yuma, Arizona?" I said, "No, from El Paso." The sergeant tossed his pencil on the desk with a what-the-hell look and continued, "Do you want to make a phone call?" I did and seconds later sat quietly in a cell awaiting bond on charges of white slavery.

Forty-five minutes later the bail was made and I was back at the club for closing time. Everyone was leaving in a gay mood, congratulating us on the good show. I was hearing the sergeant telling me I could get ten years if convicted of violating the Mann Act.

Shortly after, an indictment was handed down by the grand jury. The St. Louis news media had a ball, playing all eighteen holes with our one club. A lot of people, including Toddy, Fran, and me, thought the local newspapers practically tried to crucify Club Bandstand, but the Holy Night came and the Redd Foxx show went on as scheduled with his hecklers being laid down like wheat timber in a hurricane of stormy laughter.

I was advised to get a criminal attorney, and I hired Merle Silverstein of the Rosenblum, Goldenhersh & Silverstein law firm. Stanley Rosenblum had been handling my real-estate affairs and Robert Goldenhersh my tax returns and corporation affairs, and their criminal cases were handled by Merle Silverstein. I thought of my mother's advice, "Don't put all your eggs in one basket," but failed to heed it.

On January 25, 1960, another indictment was handed down for violation of the Mann Act concerning my arrest with Joan Mathis back in June 1958. Nationwide the newspapers were reporting the

progress of the indictments. Interviews while I did concerts on the road suddenly rose to an all-time high while appearances sank to a leery low. There were only three jobs that February, a leukemia benefit gig in the Memphis auditorium, the Apollo Theater again at reduced fees, and a New England date scrubbed together by the booking agency. There were none in March.

The shingles were now about to hit the fan. When my attorney informed me they were having the trials of both the French lady and the Indian woman (and that's precisely how they termed them) together in the same court, my future was mud.

March 13, 1960, the Indian day in court came, the gingerbread preliminaries over, and my attorney started his opening argument. Before he was halfway through it, I had to go to the bathroom and just spit when I saw him trembling. Right away I wished I'd taken up a role in law rather than put down a rock in music. When the prosecuting attorney opened and trembled too, I relaxed a little but thought, what is this, a high-school play? These guys have my life in their hands and their legs aren't even stable. I decided to take a happy-go-lucky view of it all, since it was only my entire future they would argue.

Arguments commenced with Judge Moore looking disgusted. He was eighty-some years old, and, I assumed, just awaiting my guilt. It seemed he only intervened when the prosecutor would get in a jam and need assistance, never during the defense except to over-rule. For example, when a Denver hotel owner who was a witness for the government had been asked by the federal district attorney, "What type of hotel was it that Berry registered the Indian girl in?" The Denver witness answered, "Just a regular small hotel." Interrupting the D.A., Judge Moore interjected, "He asked you what kind of hotel! Was it a white or a colored hotel?" The witness again answered, "Well, Your Honor, in Denver we don't observe any differences between our citizens there!" The honorable Judge Moore shouted, "I didn't ask you what kind of people you ob-serve, just answer my question." The man evidently was not a racist and gave the judge a hectic round of answers.

No birth certificate could be found for Janice in Yuma, Arizona, by the federal government, but the prosecution alleged that she was fourteen years old. It was stated in court that Janice had no relatives save an eighty-eight-year-old grandmother in Yuma, who not only could not find a birth certificate but had lost her memory and could not quote Janice's age. Somehow the prosecutor came up with the age of fourteen, which stuck throughout the trial. It came out in court that Janice had checked into the Delux Hotel with money she'd earned as Club Bandstand's hostess and either chose to or was coached into prostituting herself. The prosecution entered a statement that Janice had told them I had brought her to St. Louis from El Paso, but had abandoned her.

My defense was that I had brought Janice to St. Louis to employ her as a hostess in my nightclub. Also, when it came out that Janice had been engaged in prostitution in El Paso, we contended that this showed I had nothing to do with corrupting her since she was just starting up again something she had already been doing.

Newspaper coverage of the trial was intense. Each day they

wrote about my hair, my clothes, my attitude and business, not failing to insert any of my song lyrics that could dramatize the trial. I must admit, some of my hundred or more songs did fit parts of their clippings, but I never saw in any where I would have gotten credit for predicting the event. For instance one of my tunes being played then, "Sweet Little Sixteen," got a workout. One writer took the angle that the "sweet little Indian girl" was not quite "sixteen" but bored with the routine of her street life and had chose the glamorous rock life.

The trial took almost two weeks and in the end I was found guilty and sentenced to five years and a five-thousand-dollar fine. The bias of the trial was obvious to the spectators as well as the media, and as a result I had little difficulty in winning an appeal.

It was late May of 1960 when Ms. Mathis took the stand in the French trial. The federal district attorney attacked her with ridiculing and leading questions about my "real" reasons for letting her travel, such as "How aggressive was he?" or "How did he approach you intimately?" When my attorney would post an objection to such "leading on" of the witness, the judge would somehow wake up suddenly and sternly overrule. Fortunately for me, Joan answered slowly and deliberately and, as questioning progressed, the prosecutor began to fall behind in his attempt to prove me guilty of intent.

The last point-blank question by the district attorney was, "Well, are you in love with him?" The answer Joan gave was, "Well . . . yes I am." And at that instant the prosecuting attorney tossed his yellow tablet on the lawyer's table and retired his argument. The two attorneys met at the bench and with a short discussion decided the closing of the case on June 2, 1960, with a not-guilty decision and dismissed.

Two days later I received a call from Joan, congratulating me on the victory and wishing me good luck on the Apache trial. I never heard from or of her again, but I will always know of one girl who to my own estimation, and I should know, did not actually love me but was bold enough to conceive the injustice that was flowing in my direction, and chose to open herself to what was then considered indignity by declaring that she was in love with a Negro. Joan—Thanks.

Things were close to good but far from over. I had rocky reservations about the way the Indian affairs would roll. It would be an unlikely miracle for a black to be in the lead on the road in a race that was that white. I had but little faith in my attorney, seeing many opportunities in the course of the trials where he had missed in rebuttal or could have intervened with a pertinent point, challenging the prosecution.

Meanwhile, Francine was getting a backlash trying to maintain the operation of Club Bandstand. The city came down with all sorts of ordinances about fire protection orders, and complaints were said to be coming from businesses a half block away about the noise and prowling late at night. When the liquor license was threatened because of an owner being involved in criminal activities, I decided to pull stakes and split.

The course of the Indian trial was not promising and Leonard Chess was anticipating a negative result for the appeal. He wanted to get as many songs on tape as he could before I should have to go off to prison so he could keep some product on the market. He advised me to immediately write some more songs and come up and record. That suggestion brought about a recording session that compiled some eleven run-through tunes done in a couple days. Most of the songs were cover tunes that I had always done at the Cosmopolitan Club and, with the condition my head was in regarding the trials, it shows I was less concerned in the results of what was going down then than in what was coming up.

The second Indian trial came up October 28, 1961, and the courtroom was jam-packed as if I was indicted to strum out a string of rock 'n' roll hits. The Indian had ten times as much publicity as the French trial. Janice was the first to take the stand and was questioned for almost two hours. The future for me looked truly unappetizing. Her testimony, though coaxing could be detected, nevertheless was harmful in that it generated much pity in her favor. Next, Fran testified in my defense. The prosecuting attorney shouted insults and ridiculed her, using phrases like, "This blonde claims to be a secretary," then asking, "What kind of secretarial duties do you perform?" and "Did you tell your people you work for a Negro?" My attorney, with his mild voice, weakly sounded objections now and then, winning some, losing more.

The Indian heat was beginning to create more smoke for my defense as the recesses came and went. Unlike the French fry, the

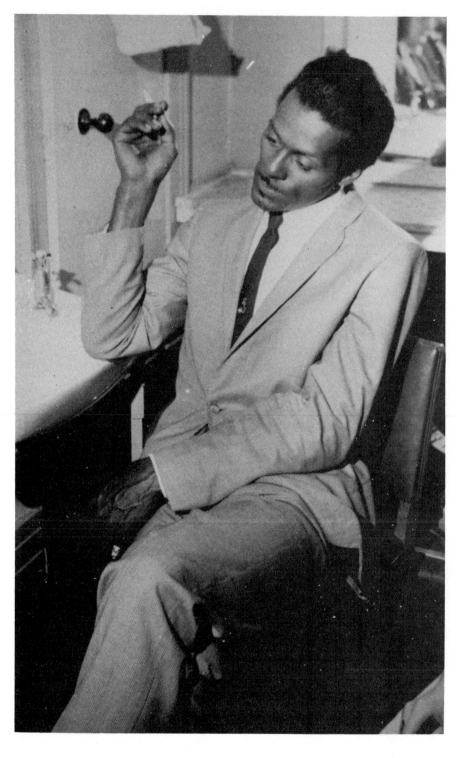

CHUCK

Indian summary was coming to the favor of the prosecution. The closing statement of my attorney sounded to me like a plea for mercy. The thought of the twenty thousand I paid him for finally begging for leniency sent me to the john again. Boiling in the bathroom, I further reasoned that I could have begged for mercy myself. I swore if I ever paid in advance again, I would be certain I would not be purchasing tenderness when I expected technique.

Guilty was the verdict. I was sentenced to three years with a ten-thousand-dollar fine. I was granted thirty days to round up any business at hand and went home still on bond.

I had enough savings to care for my family during the time the penalty would be paid. My flight to popularity had encountered great turbulence, with a pilot who was too weak to navigate the storm and who had landed me in a medical prison somewhere near the Ozarks of Misery. Some three trials, two years, and one verdict before, I had been jetting my own craft, flying high. Now it had all come to a conclusion in what I took as an unwarranted conviction, bad publicity, and over half my savings.

But it wasn't bothering me as much as I thought it would. Themetta voiced her intent to take care of the home front until I could again. The children were our major concern, but the family livelihood was out of danger, with our savings and the two cars and home owned clear of debt.

The Medical Center

When I was sentenced to serve time for what I was convicted of just having the intention of doing, I learned for sure how life can be legislated by the interpretation of laws.

The publicity of my trials came to an end when I was sentenced and the ordeal of interviews dwindled to nil. It was this period of interviews that educated me about reporters. Too many of those who interviewed me left much of the information I gave to them out of their stories, and most of the balance, twisted out of context, left a story of dramatic hardship and horror facing my situation.

When I would read what I was supposed to have said, I was amazed at the difference between the niceness of the person who had asked the questions and the nastiness of the text that had been written. It was about then that I became averse to giving interviews. I thought I would stand tall against the accusation that befell me about the Indian girl by relating the truth in its entirety but it wasn't printed as such. Instead, what was mostly printed were allegations and little of my information. Where before it had always befuddled me why movie stars or anyone would be so upset about what the newspapers printed, I was beginning to realize why people felt that way.

Toddy wasn't too pleased with the news clippings, in fact she could never understand how reporters would arrange things to look so dramatically absurd instead of just telling it like it was. I tried to explain to her my analysis of it. The reporters had to make a living and, in their attempt to get ahead in their position at the newspaper or radio station, they would write a story with as much controversy and scandalous drama as possible in order to capture the attention of the reader or listener of their column or program. In turn they likely would be promoted if they acquired a name from having a widely read column.

I told Toddy it was the American way, a systematic way to bulldoze toward the "Great American Dream" and retire successfully. The only thing wrong about that dream is the way it makes you twist and turn in bed from dogging someone else, awakening you and disturbing the peace and plans of other people. Daddy once told me, "You never have to put a top on a barrel of crabs, because when one of them climbs near the top to escape the lowly status of crabs beneath it, another crab grapples with him to gain the same high status, pulling the top one down." Consequently, few American crabs will ever climb to the top under the existing system some people dream and seem to follow.

Toddy's system was local. She was only interested in family affairs and she announced that a son might be on the way. Through all the turmoil of court and the publicity, she welcomed the birth of a baby boy on August 5, 1961, at 1:15 in the afternoon while I was on my way back from a concert at the Jimmy Menutis Club in Houston, Texas. His name was identical to mine, Charles Edward Anderson Berry, except for the added title of "Junior" and the little dude looked just like my father must have at his birth. Junior was a big one and Toddy declared, "That's it! From here on we party 'family-planning' style." It wasn't too hard to tolerate the diminishing bedroom festivals with the trial and legal expenditures always interfering with a romantic mood.

The month they gave me to finish up my business passed quickly, and when the morning of February 19, 1962, came I took a taxi to the Federal Building in St. Louis. I was fingerprinted, photographed, weighed, wished well, and wooed for autographs. Handcuffed from behind in a sedan, I was chauffeured 210 miles to the Federal Penal Institution near Terre Haute, Indiana, by the marshal and a driver. They stopped at a roadside coffee shop, inviting me in also, but I chose a cup to go, which they settled for since they couldn't leave me waiting alone outside the truck stop. When we arrived at the maximum-security institution, it seemed some of the guards and most of the inmates were expecting me and were lined in the corridors, some peeping from behind secured areas but greeting me a welcome. After a half day of paper processing and medical examination I was settled in a typical jail cell, which I thought was to be my home for three years.

On April 22 a federal prison transport bus rode a bunch of us back through St. Louis to Leavenworth Federal Prison in Kansas. The bus route was via Interstate 70 through Wentzville, Missouri, passing within four miles of Berry Park, where in my office Francine was no doubt writing me letters.

The long-timer prisoners at Leavenworth immediately persuaded me to do a performance. They knew my stay there would be short since I had requested the federal prison in Missouri and would be headed there soon. *Rock* was a dirty word around there, due to the stone walls separating the prisoners from the free world and the punishment of working in the quarry, but the concert was billed as the Leavenworth Rock Festival, and the assembly hall was jam-packed with everyone there in identical dress.

The experience was worth the two-week whistle-stop while awaiting the scheduled north-to-south prison bus to pick up any inmates being moved southward. The 730-mile trip finally terminated 225 miles southwest of St. Louis in the Federal Medical Center at Springfield, Missouri.

It was spring 1962, I was thirty-five years old, really set back, out of contact, feeling more black but still intact, and determined to make the best of it. But as I lived, I learned that "Nothing Remains the Same," things always change, and that every action causes a reaction. I could always know that something, be it good or bad, would replace what may not be presently desired. So it would only be a matter of time for the different state of existence to be. While waiting to be processed with prison clothes and quarters, I wrote

Down from stardom, then I fell, to this lowly prison
    cell.

Far from fortune, far from fame, where a number
   quotes my name.
I, among these men in grief, must be firm in my belief,
That this shall not be the end, but my chance to rise
   again.
So with patience day by day, I will move to prove a
   way,
Back to freedom, maybe fame, clearing my encumbered
   name.

I had expected to see the same prison life-style I had observed watching movies. Instead, there was this typical Missouri red-brick administration building with only a double chain-link fence to offset the resemblance to a regular hospital. I found it to be a well-equipped hospital, but with only a few patients within. Believe it or not, I thought about the great amount of federal income tax that I'd paid out when I observed over three hundred able-bodied inmates, many of them just walking around, doing nothing but being housed, clothed, and fed. What an expense to the tax-paying citizens. Mother's teachings made me feel that I should be earning my way but, considering my tax bracket, the government wasn't losing any money on me.

After registration, my first stop was a single, barred cell in a section called Admission and Orientation. It was rumored that it existed to determine if an inmate should be separated to the area they called the homosexual quarters. Literature about rules was issued. Meanwhile, the newcomers were chaperoned to the main dining room for meals with the rest of the population. The mandatory month's stay in A & O was the most isolating and thought-provoking of any period there.

Had it not been that my recent past life was full of things to recall, the idle time might have overtaken my determination to conquer it. At the same time, for the first time, I sensed I'd be doing time for a long time.

I was growing a bit weary after I'd seen the entire prison complex but I was determined to live faithfully to my philosophy. A good mind can never be in bondage nor its body in less than liberty. I would survive. As with the sun, I thought, it's out of sight for days sometimes but always returns to rise and shine again. The Medical Center was now home.

Before I was in the Medical Center a week, I was informed that I didn't have three full years to serve, for there was "good time" awarded prisoners who behaved themselves. Five months was deducted from each year of a sentence, which in my case figured only three times seven months to serve. But that's almost two years! I wasn't at that moment feeling very philosophical in my cell looking at 630 days there. Come to think of it, the Algoa trip had been well over a thousand days. This shouldn't pose too big of a roll for a rocker. No big alligator, just a little old crocodile. I decided to take the classes I needed to complete high school and to learn to type. I could continue to write songs; I could learn the functions of a corporation; I could do all sorts of wonderful things, except get some "Satisfaction," as sung by the Rolling Stones.

I decided what I really wanted then, more than freedom, religion, love, or money, was the knowledge to maintain them. At that time, I was capable of withdrawing over fifty thousand dollars, had a home housing a wife and family of four and two corporations, which Francine had introduced me into without my having the least understanding of them. My dreams were varied, but my determination was to build my knowledge for managing my affairs, and I was serious about it.

I set out to use the Medical Center for gaining these goals and walked into what came to be the remaining sixteen months of schooling, in prison, that I had abandoned in my teens. I spent all my off-duty time studying business management, business law, accounting (which I really got into, since it has to do with math), typing, world history (which I hated with the truest of ill passion), American history, American government, and speech. Most of these were the credits I needed to complete my twelfth grade of high school.

My first duty job was in the kitchen, mopping the mess-hall floor. Then I got promoted to washing pots and kettles, receiving a good ribbing from the guys for both swinging the mop and slinging the slop. The half-ass jobs consolidated my social relations with the long-timers, because my taking it on the chin from them consequently made their time easier to bear and thus brought favor between us. Although the kitchen was aggravating, it only called for four work-hours a day, leaving me three more hours per day than all other duties would have, thus allowing me additional time in classes.

After six months passed, I was made an aide in the physical-therapy section of the hospital under Dr. Hanzlick. The duties were handling patients, administering their sitz baths, applying hot packs on bruised areas, directing exercises, and such. All went well until on the third day I was scheduled to pick up a patient named Sharp and bring him down to therapy. I found immediately that he was an arrogant and belligerent paraplegic. I soon was assigned to him exclusively and I think I would have sooner enjoyed a summer in hell. I had to walk him to and fro everywhere, spoon feed him lunch, apply hot packs, give him sitz baths, and even assist him to, fro, and while at the john. He realized how much I hated doing this and began infuriating me with signifying and ribbing remarks such as "Not so loosely, brother!" or "Hey, man, a little higher."

After desperately seeking it, I was granted the newly vacated position of physical-therapy ward secretary. This relieved me of any nurse duties and stabilized me in clerical work. A farmer from southern Alabama became heir to the care of Brother Sharp and it almost drove him mad.

Things began looking up. I was doubling my typing ability at the secretarial work and at the school. The correspondence course of accounting that I was taking took up most of my evening hours along with the bogged-down periods when I enjoyed learning to play the game of chess. Sometimes on holidays the fellows encouraged me to bring the guitar, which the school superintendent had allowed me to have sent from home, into the recreation room where I fiddled a few folk or country songs. Rock lovers were scarce in that area and the Springfield disk jockeys did not seem to bother recruiting rockers, favoring country music.

"No Particular Place to Go," "Nadine," "Tulane," "You Never Can Tell," and "Promised Land" were all written while I was in Springfield. I remember having extreme difficulty while writing "Promised Land" in trying to secure a road atlas of the United States to verify the routing of the Po' Boy from Norfolk, Virginia, to Los Angeles. The penal institutions then were not so generous as to offer a map of any kind, for fear of providing the route for an escape.

I would often have to sing aloud while arranging these songs and sometimes I would look around and find an audience of two or three guys listening to my practicing. Once, while improvising in the gang shower where I was granted the privilege to practice, I looked up and saw the Birdman of Alcatraz standing watching me strum. I'd seen him in the corridor walking to and fro but had never exchanged words with him. I said, "Hi, Birdman," addressing him as I'd heard others do. He just smiled, then turned and walked away.

One Sunday while I was playing chess, an announcement sounded for us to stand at attention in the eighty-eight-bed sleeping unit. We did, expecting some government official would be observing the quarters. Who walked in looking around, but a guard and Burt Lancaster! Later we learned that Burt was orienting himself for a film he was starring in that was to be *Birdman of Alcatraz*. I couldn't believe it, but the three-quarter sly smile, so characteristic of him, was being cast around as he paraded through the aisles of cots.

For a long while I'd thought I wouldn't want Toddy to visit me in Springfield, but, as things were looking so uphill, I consented and anticipated the visit. "Charles Berry, visitors' room!" I heard announced the Saturday afternoon my wife and father arrived. In getting ready for the visit I had to undress on one floor, go up in an elevator half nude, and pick up a pressed white cotton suit; then redress and cross out into the parlor where the visitors were. Returning to the quarters was the same nude trip back down.

I spent the afternoon relating my achievements through the months so far. I was surprised at my not being sexually excited, after not having any for so long. From the anticipation of being near her, I assumed I would have stolen freaky rubs and naughty pinches between kisses, which were all the guards allowed in the visiting room. To my surprise, I was a perfect gentleman and regretted it immensely along the time the moon rose that summer night.

As the weeks rocked in and the months rolled on, I typed the attendance and progress reports of the inmate patients in the physical-therapy ward. I counted the days and watched the Alabama redneck take the Michigan black to and from the white lavatory. Many days I sat at a desk beside Dr. Hanzlick, drawing the floor plans to a dream house he had described to me during slow periods when no patients were present except for the daily two-hour treatment of Sharp.

Heavy was the frustration that two female nurses caused within me when they began visiting Hanzlick in his office every other day. They were the only females in the institution and it seemed like they stayed out of sight and only were seen at their position in the medical ward. Suddenly they were coming to see Hanzlick, sitting in front of his desk (facing mine) chatting with him and some times directly with me. The chatting was okay, but the casual squirming and leg-ly laughter lured my lascivious lacking to longing lust. Miniskirts weren't in yet, but many skirts were up to where a guy in the joint would get high in the joint, just to see them. Those two nurses made it very hard, but I typed away at nine words per minute. Believe me, to do some time without seeing anything is far less disturbing than to see sometimes without doing anything.

When I finished the credits and the extra courses in business management and accounting I was ready for graduation. Toddy came to hear me deliver the valedictory speech and witness me receiving my diploma and extra certificates. One of the more pleasant memories, yet a bit sad, was that she wept as I was nearing the close of the valedictory address, causing me to stumble over some lines. Later she told me her sorrow was caused by the location of the occasion within the confines of a prison.

I came to the close of my stay when I was successful at my first chance up for parole. With my diploma and credits, Toddy, my father, and my brother Hank picked me up on my birthday, October 18, 1963, and we traveled back home. I was free again but did not feel much different than the week after I was registered in the place other than I knew I had many more obligations and responsibilities. It may be odd to some but I've always believed that no place or condition can really hinder a person from being free if he has an active, imaginative mind. There is one thing for sure, I did cheat the government of my imprisonment by way of the achievements I accomplished while there. Sorry, great white father, you can't indict me for that.

Back Home

I t was a real thrill to get into my own Cadillac, after not even seeing one for sixteen months, and drive myself sixty miles per hour up I-55 for 255 miles to my own home. Hank and Dad were fatigued after driving down and Toddy and I had the journey back all to ourselves after the first twenty minutes of the four of us reminiscing about things occurring during my absence.

Francine had been staying alone at Berry Park the entire time, looking after things, with the assistance of some 331 censored letters between us. The contentment Fran was enjoying, according to her letters, was long overdue after the hassles she had encountered from bigots and city authorities in St. Louis. So as the days went by, Francine had waited with white dreams for me to return in black reality.

> At last they had released me, one bright and sunny day
> So happy and so cheerful, I proudly walked away
> And drove up through Missouri, northeastward to a
>   home
> Where there remained a young girl, still living all alone
> Caring for the estate, of whom my dad had said,

"She has become a part of, the haven you have made."
Too bold and soon we started, in vain to try and build
A showplace that most any, could walk into at will
But some great city fathers, whose hearts seemed still
    too cold
Caused her to bear some burdens, that soon destroyed
    our goal
At last I'd come back home, to gaze upon my prize
Where she stood there awaiting, and looked into my
    eyes
Then offered me a hugging, while tears began to flow
That made me vow to never, cause her to see me go.

I was back home for sure and not feeling offended at the system for whetting me down for going against the racial barrier of practiced tradition. I adjusted swiftly back to the general trends of society's majority and settled down with friends in the subtle minority. In fact, from meeting and reading different personalities at the prison, I began to understand just why some people could justly feel envy or even hatred for others on mere grounds of looks or position. For instance, there was an inmate named Preston who gave me a package of forty-three song lyrics he'd written during his stay, assuming I'd be honored to get them to my recording company for waxing. After over a dozen letters that insisted I was messing around with his product, as he hadn't heard any of his tunes done by me, his wit then hit the fan and I was reminded I was slack, black, and lacking in the ability to push his tunes into the music market.

After October 18, 1963, I started all over again and quickly got into the swing of rebuilding the business. As soon as I was released I began phoning all my business associates to inform them that the prodigal son had come back home. How glad they were to know this appeared in their immediate readiness to get me back to work as soon as engagements or sessions could be arranged.

I had spent twenty-two months away from the business. The parole officer I was assigned to was at the threshold of retirement and went by the book, which required me to request permission to travel out of the St. Louis City district. This was crippling in negotiating with producers and booking agencies. Many concerts

were lost because of the time it took to clear the paperwork required to process the travel. I was denied permission to travel to Chicago to record. Leonard, seeing still a value in the product, suggested I have my parole transferred to Illinois, where he knew people who knew others who had the authority to allow leniencies to be given in "hardship" cases, as they called it.

By the turn of 1964, my transfer was arranged and I went to Chicago to live. The parole officer in the Illinois district was much more liberal and even allowed me to come back home since I hadn't brought my family to Chicago. It was expensive to create a home away from home, but it paid off; I could go anywhere without the Chicago parole officer demanding that I first register an account of my intended travels. He told me to state only afterward, on my monthly report, when and where I'd gone. I was on parole for fourteen months. It took me a week to get all the papers signed to go up to Chicago in order to record a session of the new songs I had written at the Medical Center.

In May, the Chicago federal parole officer granted me my first travel across the Atlantic, to England, to fulfill a tour for Don Arden Limited. The English tour had mostly bus and trains for transportation. There were two singer-dancer performers on the show, Jamima Smith, a buxom seventeen-year-old blonde, and Atard, a raven-black-haired skinny French peer of Jamima's who was questionable but beautiful, I thought. I can't deny it was those two who persuaded me to begin the tour traveling with the show bus. Peter Meade, the tour road manager, arranged to have the dancers seated directly across from my seat at the very front of the bus. English buses are extremely plush, with reclining seats like those of large air liners. Atard always wore slacks but Jamima seldom was seen not in an exciting blouse and skirt.

A jump between Bristol and Southampton was an all-night drive and everyone slept. I was awakened by the bus driver telling Jamima to move her leg from in the way of his driving. In doing so she and Atard exchanged places. Atard then seated herself on the floor in front of their seat and initiated an exchange of affection such as I had never before seen being awarded a companion. From my vantage point the driver's dash lights provided just enough illumination to distinguish what was taking place. I was nervous that the driver would stop and disrupt the administration of devotion that was being offered to Jamima, according to her expressions. I tried to improve my French with Atard, who looked a bit more mature than Jamima, but throughout the entire tour I could not break the bond of their behavior.

A second European tour came for me in November '64 that paid much more than the first. They sent two round-trip tickets with the engagement deposit but Toddy objected to leaving our three-year-old son, Charles Jr., under the care of anyone else. So I took Francine along. Toddy has never been too comfortable about my traveling alone, unlike other artists who have their managers, valets, roadies, and bodyguards. Plus, she wasn't fond of flying that much.

A teenage boy ran up to me as I was entering the Grand Hotel in Paris, France. The boy asked not my name but pronounced it, and requested an autograph. He introduced himself as Jean Pierre Ravelli and began telling me every recording, by title, of every single and/or album that I had ever made. He was a Frenchman, but his English was clearly understandable. I invited him into the lobby and on into my room after checking in. I could get around pretty well, I thought, with someone so interested in me who spoke English that well.

I got bored quick with all the music talk and no Paris, so I suggested we go out and eat somewhere, knowing I would get into some Parisian provocations perhaps per se. My most memorable experience of our meeting was when he was leading me into the toilette and a raven-haired paragon of femininity strolled past on her way out. What a difference one minute could have made I remarked to Jean who said, "Oh, that's the way it is in Fraunz," (as he pronounced it). We had snacks at various restaurants the greater balance of the evening and I kept trying to replay the earlier occurrence only to find later that such unions were only possible in the entrances of the restrooms and not at the resting moments.

Jean went to every concert I performed on that tour, confirming to me that our friendship was one that would live on. He swore, while he saw me at the Music Hall in Paris, November 11, then all the way to Orly Airport, that this was only the first of many live visits that would never come to soon end.

Meanwhile at the Grand Hotel in Paris, I received a phone call. "You are Shuck Berwee, no?" "Yes, I am." "Okay, me are Nadia Ovincia! Unstand me?" "Yes, I *comprends*," I answered, remembering some French. She continued, "Me . . . no . . . I come to you *chambre* now. Okay?" "Yes, you come now," I said. I didn't hesitate to welcome the visitor, hoping I would get the best French lesson I ever had.

Who arrived was a five-foot, two-inch, hazel-eyed, frosted-blond girl around twenty-eight years old, rushing into the room riddling more French. I interpreted only the last couple of words. "*S'il vous plait le téléphone?*" "*Oui, mademoiselle,*" I responded. She made a short call ending with "*au revoir*" and sat across from the soft chair I'd settled in.

Turning to me she spoke, "Shuck, speak no too good English but I talk to you some. Shuck, you verwee importan person for Paris people. Shuck, I must talk much wiz you tomorwow for my work to do. You unstand, Shuck?" My ears were in a heavenly state of shock, yet my brain overcame the obstacle and caressed each word. "Yes, I understand you well—go on!" The mademoiselle continued, "Shuck, when I can I tomorwow talk about you for me. When the time you zink I come?'' It was one o'clock in the afternoon and I had nothing to do but walk the streets. I was enjoying this to the hilt so I slowly replied in the best pronunciation of English I could muster, saying, ''Why—not—this—afternoon?'' She frowned in a confused manner. I rephrased my best English saying, ''You can no talk today?'' She caught it, confirming: ''No, Shuck. No possible today, I work more today. Tomorwow I no work all day, unstand, tomorwow.'' ''Yes,'' I answered, ''tomorrow you come ten hundred hour. I see you and talk.'' She bounced up smiling, having comprehended each word and kissed me on the cheek saying, ''Verwee gud, verwee gud, Shuck, I come to here ten hundred tomorrow.''

The next morning I waited from 8 to 10 A.M. for Nadia to phone and continued to wait throughout the morning for her to arrive; but no Nadia. I walked the avenues of Paris from 2 to 4 P.M. then came back to the hotel. As I passed through the foyer the bellman handed me a call slip. She had phoned at 2:30 and at 3:30 left a message of her apology and new arrival at eighteen hundred hours. I went to the restaurant for a spot of tea and deliberated upon the possible advantages of the interview. I anticipated that interpretations throughout the interview would carry us over into sundown. Dinner in the room would be no more than a courtesy. I even speculated that in concluding the dinner, surely we would get back to finishing the evening engaged in more French business. It was 5:40 P.M. when I left the hotel restaurant and was ready when she came in a more elegant dress, a little longer than the mini she first appeared in.

I understood her request to phone for ''zum food.'' The sight and sound of her ordering intoxicated me with desire to intertwine in passion with this female. There was little said before or during our dinner for two. We enjoyed the meal, our eyes meeting and causing exchanges of smiles while each would be busy chewing. After dinner Nadia used the wash room, but left the door ajar. With the tap water flowing I could distinguish the sound of a breaking stream. I peeped in to find that she was rinsing her face, so I crept in and kissed her on the neck. She mumbled what seemed to be some endearing words. I left her and somehow I had the feeling she would stay the night. I quickly undressed and got under the

CHUCK

covers with my feet, fingers, legs, and arms crossed that luck would be with me and tonight I would really know a true French-woman. There had been nothing attempted or said about the important interview so far, and the outlook seemed favorable.

When she emerged from the bathroom, she was disrobed to her slip. I had never felt Paris more than at that moment. Slowly I felt her entire body as she nestled in bed. I sank deeper into intoxicating passion when she unconsciously muttered some French words of emotional excitement. As hard as I tried to find out what she was trying to say I couldn't for the love of want decipher their meaning. Not until I was delirious with desire did I turn to climb into paradise. I heard her sweet voice whispering. My ears must have deceived me, for what I then understood the rest of my body misunderstood: "C'est no possible, Shuck." A complete paragraph of extraordinarily large French words ended with, "Nadia sorwee, Shuck. . . . Shuck . . . tomorwow night is gud, no possible tonight, Shuck." She lay the whole night in my arms. My heart beat in disbelief that I spent the entire night, and did not spend, with Nadia Ovincia.

The following day I was scheduled to leave Paris at 9 A.M. I had to do so to make Marseille by 6 P.M. that evening. I kissed Nadia good-bye that morning with her "unstanding " we'd be lovers that evening and flew away to Marseille. It happens to the best of 'em.

Upon returning to the U.S., I found there was a growing demand for my act due to the sellouts while on the English tour. Through trade magazines I suppose, word was getting around that Chuck Berry was definitely coming back on if not strong. The song "Nadine" was being played considerably on the air. My assets were being maintained through the jump in performance salaries that had occurred during my absence. My bookings were rating two thousand dollars per show against an average of seven hundred dollars when I left the stage for the stir.

Lloyd Thaxton booked my appearance on his TV show in Los Angeles on October 30, 1964, and it looked as though the album *Chuck Berry's Greatest Hits,* which included "Nadine" as well as some of my other hits, was catching on strong. When I returned from L.A. I purchased a double-brick flat at 4410 Holly in St. Louis for my mother and father and they prepared to move in. After twenty-eight years living at 4319 Labadie, it took them almost three years (it seemed) to pack up and move to the more modern dwelling.

The Beatles were then in the stratosphere of popularity and still soaring higher as my "Nadine" and "No Particular Place to Go" hit the market. The media quoted their mentions of some of my songs that they had recorded, which naturally was a great help to my then-sleeping repertoire.

I was booked onto the 1965 tour of the Biggest Show of Stars, with such entertainers as Joe Tex, Little Anthony and the Imperials, Betty Everett, Ronny Dove, Walter Jackson, King Coleman, Solomon Burke, Dionne Warwick, the Ad Libs, Alvin Cash and the Crawlers, the Orlons, the Shangri-Las, and the Imperial Show Stopper Band.

Fran somehow convinced me to take a vacation: the first of my career. She suggested Hawaii be the place as she had long wanted to go there. We went in November of 1965 and stayed three days loafing around. I had never stayed overnight in any city without working and playing music. I couldn't imagine or dream that I would enjoy it, but in boyish delight I watched the girls on the sunny beaches and Fran shopped in the hotel stores. She was so overcome with leisure that she had me fill up an empty coffee can with white Hawaiian sand and bring it back to the park for safe-keeping.

On June 17, 1966, after much negotiation, I signed with Mercury Records, obtaining a sixty-thousand-dollar advance on future royalties. Mercury insisted I rerecord all my hits of the past but at a faster tempo than the originals. They released these recordings along with one new tune, "Club Nitty Gritty," on the album *Chuck Berry's Golden Hits*.

During my concerts in the middle of the 1960s, multitudes of young university students and festival-goers were indulging in smoking grass. There seemed to be a unanimous acceptance of the use of marijuana as opposed to liquor. I was being offered joints at the foot of the stage between selections, already lit and christened for me to take a drag. I can think of one concert at a religious college where faculty members were lined along the walls of the auditorium, I thought for maintaining order during the show. I had seen an abundance of smoking and the smell was all over the place, becoming heavier during the latter portion of the show, when two different guys sprang from the front row and walked up holding a lit joint intended for me. The entire audience resounded with "Yes!" Considering the two police officers and the many sisters in habit standing throughout the room smiling, I leaned over and drew a puff, raised up, and blew it out, only to receive a standing ovation for the chance I thought I was taking. However, when telling this story later I was made aware of the implication that it might have had of advocating the use of grass. Being a person in the limelight, I was advised to refrain from going along with the "party playing," so to speak, or to openly reject any favor of it whatsoever.

I traveled to San Francisco to do a recording session for Mercury Records backed by the Sir Douglas Quintet. During the session, naturally, mistakes were made by most of us, but the greatest inadequacy came when the whole quintet would go off to the corner of the room in a huddle for eight to twelve minutes. It was the third huddle before I discovered what was going down in the corner. In unequivocal attention, around a small cloth-covered table where lay a package of neatly placed herbs and several wee little folders, were standing the quintet in their glory. As if in reverence to a Buddha altar, they were staring at the herbs on the table in sheer contentment.

When I suggested we continue the session they did so very politely, only to have a blunder at the same place in the song and return to the altar as for repentance. Over two dozen trips to that altar had my patience at an unbearable point, so I sought retaliation in the control room, where the producer from Mercury could give me help. When I entered the engineer's room I was greeted by the same aroma, heavier than in the studio, plus the wide smiles of both producer and engineer. I was invited to relax and join them and would have accepted if they'd have promised it would be the last interruption.

On January 24, 1967, I took Fran to the Soul City Club in Dallas, Texas, where I was to perform for three nights with Janis Joplin as the supporting act. She was not well known to me then and I thought she was rather bold to appear on stage with a drink in her hand and sing so well.

While doing my performance on an unusually small stage I had

just completed two scoots forward and proceeded to scoot backwards and scooted right off the two-foot-high platform into a
pocket of the stage construction just large enough for my rump to
wedge into. The spotlight followed me into the useless space. The
piano player stood up while still playing (as I continued to do
though sitting in the hole), smiled, and said, "Far out, man! You're
the greatest." I told him to play a solo and tell the spotlight to
move off me so I could crawl out. No such luck. The piano player

was in stitches admiring my fall (a gimmick he thought) and the
spotlight didn't miss a limb with its concentrated beam. I crawled
out in the spot with a sore behind and finished with a smile and
applause.

March 16 of the next year I bought a new 1968 Caddy. It had
become a ritual to purchase a new car every year and ship the
previous year's car to be used by my dad or an employee. I discovered it was less costly to keep my old car than to trade it in and
lose the deduction of depreciation. Consequently, at the end of a
year I would be owner of up to six Cadillacs.

As long as I was working I had a good income. However, 10
percent off the top went to the booking agency, 50 percent off the
same top went to the Internal Revenue, and 6 percent off the top
of the first top to the state tax collector, left a balance of 34 percent
as my share of the effort in performing; minus half of the expenses
to do the job. Royalties, when they do come (sometimes they're
just not sent from disreputable record companies), are taxed 70
percent, leaving only 24 percent net after the 6 percent state tax.
Nevertheless, ever since I was school age I had heard talk of Joe
Louis's taxes not being paid and other celebrities being cleaned

out for avoiding or nonpayment of taxes. I decided to pay the taxes since it was inevitable and a must to everyone.

There is no such tax on real estate, which attracted me to investing in property. When my bank account rose to a height that half of it could purchase 75 percent of a building I had chosen, I'd buy it. I seldom bought into an investment when the balance due after the payment would not be still remaining in my savings account after the purchase.

On August 2, 1968, I closed a deal for the purchase of a small country theater building complex for sixty-three thousand five hundred dollars. It was located in the center of the city of Wentzville. The theater was being operated four days a week when the exchange of proprietorship took place. After hiring a contractor to bring the interior décor to a more presentable level, Fran and I continued the business to see what progress would develop as time passed. In the beginning the local people were delighted to have the improvements: repaired auditorium seats, new carpet, twin soda machines, and the upgrading of featured films. Fran took over as manager under the apprenticeship of Elmer Unland. Fran gained knowledge of where to obtain reels of movies and procure the latest films for the patrons to enjoy. The theater was open seven days a week, projecting the images upon the big screen of Hollywood stars such as Elizabeth Taylor, Richard Burton, Clint Eastwood, Paul Newman, and many others to this little town for their viewing pleasure. The theater put Fran in direct contact with the country people of Wentzville City, who had seldom faced an integrated business.

We soon found out that the local Wentzville adults were unable to cope with the thought of a black man, right there in their country town, having a Caucasian wife (which they assumed Fran was). To them this was unforgivable in their town or in their country, on land or at sea, but the show went on in Wentzville, Missouri, population 3,213 and all but 13 were farmers. Fran and I maintained our black and white smiles regardless. The theater did pick up business for a while with the kids, until the local authorities claimed we were dispensing alcohol from the orange and grape soda-pop machine.

After a summons to court, nothing was found illegal or out of the norm. Though victory of the ordeal was proof of innocence, the allegation caused Francine once again to suffer loss of time and embarrassment. When it falsely became the talk of talks around the small town that she was not my secretary, but my wife, it showed up in the theater attendance. Soon there were only enough patrons, mostly children, to run shows three days a week.

Fran had moved her office to the annex of the building complex that the theater dominated for a change from the Berry Park office. Moving the office simplified film pickups, movie ad changes, and city business, which had caused her to make the four-mile trip into town two and three times a day. She enjoyed the new business. It was different and gave her something to do since the fan mail and engagement transactions had dropped.

A few months later a brick crashed through the bay windows of the office. That vandalism and the shouting of vicious remarks when persons unknown passed her office, brought a close to the office. Shortly thereafter, we shut down the theater because attendance was dwindling and it was running at a loss. Not having been raised in a racially biased section of the country, Fran detested the bigotry that was being practiced in the town of Wentzville. She saw the true light of character from the merchants and so-called friends once they saw me around the theater and the office she had set up in the city.

Not only were these intolerable threats toward Francine happening, I, too, had been causing her grief. Failing to realize her admiration for me intimately was still strong, I'd been indiscreet about bringing women around Berry Park. Their involvement with me had nothing to do with business, though I argued with Fran, knowing she was right in crediting them with little interest in my welfare. She implied that their only interest was in my exposure and popularity. I hadn't listened, and I suggested she leave rather than tolerate what I saw as my freedom. I lost Francine on January 6, 1969, when she took my advice and moved back to Pennsylvania.

Besides the loneliness of losing someone so dependable and loyal, my mistake in relieving her surfaced soon. I was in chaotic befuddlement on February 13, when Ed Deutch, my CPA, came out to audit my 1968 taxes and found me trying to supply files of information necessary to prepare the tax return.

In utter desperation I called a Canadian friend of mine, Rona Pfeffer, requesting she come to Berry Park to help me out of my jam. I continued to perform as many concerts as I could, while Rona did her best at answering phones and sorting out the mail. On April 1, 1969, I bought a twelve-by-sixty-foot trailer and had it installed on the grounds of Berry Park as a permanent dwelling for Rona. As an investment, for twenty-five thousand dollars, I bought another building in Wentzville, at 14 East Main Street. The upstairs of the duplex had two apartments. I kept one for myself for an office and leased out the store downstairs. Acquiring this building along with previous purchases of complexes within the city started a rumor that I was buying up the town.

One of my concerts during this period was on a dual bill with Little Richard at a school in Connecticut where we shared the same locker room as a dressing room. I've always, when convenient, made it a habit to drop in on the supporting act and pay a little professional courtesy, so I did.

This was Little Richard, who boasted of being the "King of Rock 'n' Roll." Though he was second on the bill he didn't yield from his proclamation to be king of whatever. It hardly meant anything to me, nor did headlining a show, as long as I was satisfied with the fee. Nevertheless, I went over to say hello to him (this was our first time on the same billing) and to my surprise he was not a boasting biggie as his stage talk while performing made him seem. I wasn't surprised to see there were no girls hanging around outside nor within his dressing room, just an entourage of guys.

When I entered he raised his hand and ordered, "Everybody out! I want to talk to Chuck." As soon as his request was granted he, with the biggest smile I'd ever seen across his face, held out both arms saying, "I'm so glad you came over, Chuck. I've been wanting to meet you ever since I first heard 'Maybellene,' and here you are." I acknowledged the compliment, reaching for one of the extended arms to shake his hand and he grabbed it. Pulling me onto the chair he sat in he asked me to come to his room in his hotel for a party. I knew Richard was gay and asked him right out was he referring to only him and me having a party. He said, "Chuck, I've always wanted to perform with you since the first time I saw you on television and have thought about it ever since." I thought I saw a certain gleam in his eye and replied, "Richard, I'm frank as fake is phony," and then asked him without pause, "You mean to make love?"

The smile on his face settled so relaxingly broad, he was almost whispering his answer, "You'd love it, it's like no other performance in the world."

I tried to match his smile and then I suddenly excused myself in a rush to get ready for the show, but he bade me farewell in a contented voice and that was that.

I've been on the same show many times since with Little Richard and even chatted at length a few times but he never made another approach (if that was one), nor brought up the occasion again.

A Chance in Millions

A t the Jimmy Menutis Club on 3236 Telegraph Road, at the southern end of Houston, back in August 1961, I met a multimillionairess whose charms and business advice I came to value for more than a decade.

I was walking around through the audience, being hit with questions about the Indian trial and socializing, as I always have, with fans and patrons. At a particular elegantly situated table, a rather well-dressed woman stood and introduced herself and her company, then asked if I would accept an invitation to breakfast at her home after the show. I accepted and as arranged they were all waiting at my rented car afterward in the parking lot. I followed the party of two Cadillacs to a huge mansion in the suburb of River Oaks.

The rich man of the mansion was abroad at that time and the lady of the house, whose name was Candace Mossler, was hosting a family of seven plus four servants and a personal secretary. At 3 A.M., in the gigantic playroom in one wing of the mansion, the family and I were served bacon and eggs by the maid, who shared my hue of the color spectrum. She gave me a typical "who are, what for, why are you here?" look.

After dining and chatting I was invited to stay over in a guest room but I declined even though I was itching to see what the rest of the night would bring to light. There was music playing and we danced and snacked but it died away into dawn with this lady arranging for me to play at a party she would be giving at her mansion, paying me my usual fee.

August 20 of the same year, I was scheduled to play the Galveston City Auditorium and the lady phoned and informed me she would be attending. I couldn't believe she was so enthused over my music. Then she further suggested I stop by on the way to rendezvous and travel along with her. I had to upgrade my ticket to save embarrassment, knowing she would be traveling first class. It backfired because she was traveling coach thinking I would be flying so. She upgraded and we departed from Hobby Airport and talked in flight about my legal situation.

In Galveston she paid for two hotel accommodations and the return plane fare to Houston, where her daughter picked us up to drive to her mansion. The stay in Galveston deepened my courage to respond to the casual kisses that she boldly stole in public places such as when I'd return to her table after a well-applauded performance with everybody in the place still watching me exiting from the stage.

The trip to Galveston closed with only an additional phone invitation to come to her room for breakfast the following morning but opened a sound expectation of intimate relations back at her home when she told me she wanted to spend some time with me alone very soon at a hunter's cabin she'd spoken of.

The same atmosphere was evident, with amplified intentions on her part, during a later engagement at Lou Ann's in Dallas, where, after the show, she invited me to her room and spent half the night talking over room-service snacks of her personal actions of benevolence for the underprivileged then suddenly bade me good-night with a kiss that promised much more should the surroundings recur.

It wasn't until Candace suggested I fly to Houston especially to visit her that we realized her contemplations. Her daughter picked me up at the airport and I walked into her home to find her husband sitting at the kitchen table. Never had I feared being in the South more than when I entered to be introduced unexpectedly to the husband of a wife whose lips had touched mine beyond mere friendship. My nerves were as loose as a bucket of juice until gradually the husband's very intelligent conversation eased my anxiety a bit. I really became at ease when he terminated our chat by telling me he had to leave immediately for Paris.

Upon his departure, I was ushered out of the kitchen while Candace excused herself. For nearly an hour I sat waiting in the gigantic living room, until she returned tiptoeing in a gown, whispering, "Come with me, I'll show you where you will retire."

In a guest room, she turned back the bedding then turned back to me and surrounded my neck with two multimillion-dollar arms and a pair of southern belle lips whose words were determining the direction of that handsome sum as well as my lonesome behavior.

My total worth had just cleared only that of a half million, which caused her suggestions to be of great interest to me. Whether they were professional or personal or even passionate, I believe I would have succumbed. But she was summoned away by the home intercom, and when she returned to the guest room she started talking about her plans to build a recreational complex for the underprivileged boys of Houston. She said she wanted me to see the site she had chosen for it while I was there. Another kiss and my curiosity was standing straight up in need of her effective attentions.

We left to visit the hunter's cabin she'd spoken about, which I found was merely a sort of hideaway camping quarters. Before entering, she hit lightly on the layout she planned for the boys' home, then welcomed me into this big one-room playhouse, as it appeared to me. It was generally untidy except the king bed was made up. She beckoned for me to sit on the luxurious tiger-fur sofa facing a low burning fireplace, perhaps argreably in. I thought, I also thought, this couldn't be what it looks like, still doubting that she could possibly have any interest in me intimately, at least according to my father's philosophy, and have half of Houston's dignitaries flocking to her backyard to honor her gala parties.

Provoked was I, under those surroundings, to approach her with positive response and, with great expense to my courage, I secured ample breath and told her I couldn't believe that she wanted me as it appeared. She replied, "Greater admiration could no one have for someone who feels they are not worthy of it."

In silence her hands began to move about me. I was not prepared for direct contact and further shrunk in disbelief of what was ac-

Candace Mossler at a party in her Houston home.

tually happening. I told her again I just couldn't believe I was about to receive the gratification, anticipating that I would likely be reversed, as so many times women in power have taken advantage of males unable to resist yielding to their will. Is it really to be, I pondered, and if so, why me?

After minutes Candace must have sensed my passive state of mind and raised in noble triumph telling me of the actress, Virginia Mayo, who once had a fan who became so infatuated that he'd unfailingly purchase a front-row seat for her every performance, live or on screen. In time she began to notice the same man night after night at stage plays and public appearances.

She went on to tell me that Virginia had told her that his presence continued until their eye contact developed into smiles and waves from the stage. Finally he found the courage to seek the chance of an autograph. His success did not come then but did a year later in England where she noticed him there at her performance in London and had him summoned from the audience to visit her backstage. It aroused her that he would travel that distance and she wondered if it was only to see her performance. Virginia had her manager invite him to join her at her hotel for a dinner she was hostessing after the show. During the dinner, Virginia grew to admire him and came to desire his company. She arranged for him to meet her in her suite alone.

She said Virginia pulled every ladylike trick she knew to persuade her admirer to seduce her. She became so overcome with desire for him that she finally gave up and openly asked him if he would like to spend the rest of the night there with her. He mumbled yes, lowering his head in disbelief until Virginia walked to him and kneeled before him, pleading that he not think of her as so great that she was out of his reach. She spent the rest of the night trying in every way to stimulate him to readiness for satisfying her inflated desire for him but finally had to resort to explaining to him that he had an incurable case of awe versus desire.

Candace went on to explain that such was my condition regarding her. The story made me feel a lot better but I was still in the part of the country where fear was the direction of my trip. She had amazed me for ten minutes yet only glazed a phase in ways that pay. She began apologizing and suggested we try at a more relaxed time. I returned an apology for my not responding, and we embraced a while and soon left.

My next visit to her mansion was in broad day, a rendezvous we had planned by telephone. I was much more composed as she led me into another room I had not seen. I sat in the only chair that did not have some sort of feminine lingerie draped over it. She disappeared, then returned from the bath wearing a thick fur-trimmed bed gown, tiptoed across the room, arms extended. We embraced without words, pressing body to body. "Come," she whispered, pulling me to the round bed, "and undress me." She turned her back to me and I lifted the gown from her shoulders. I'd often seen the cleavage of her enormous breasts from low-cut dresses she'd worn but never the lower hemisphere of her voluptuous bosom as it became exposed.

She stood silent as I saw my father's expression amid the cleavage of her lily-white bosom, weighing the curves of her anatomy against the cost of his advice. She twirled and lay on the bed, covering her treasures completely. "Hurry," she whispered, "I want more of you today." In dubious perplexity, I yielded, to become more relaxed when approached, and I heard minute moans of a million-dollar approval.

For a while, neither my fear nor my father ever entered my

mind. Neither vulgarity nor virtue was dwelling in my thoughts for the few moments I lingered. Only the voluptuousness I had anticipated over the months I had known her mattered in those minutes. Little was heard except the sound of human pleasures passing.

Later I was hired, for professional fees, to play (music) at two of her lawn parties. We had several rendezvous about the country over the years, including at my fiftieth birthday party when she stayed overnight at Berry Park.

Soon after that party, Candace phoned me at my home (as she customarily did when I wasn't at my office) and asked Toddy to have me call her about a Thanksgiving party she anticipated giving in Houston. Toddy was curious about our affiliation as I kept her abreast of the flow of actions. After Toddy gave me the message, I returned her call, which was an invitation to immediately come to her home. I was on the next Delta to Houston and spent all afternoon in the west wing alone with her. Under a mink spread, she sat up in her gown and talked of the possibilities of our coming more closely together as far as the relation between us had been (it was just that vague to me also). But finally she sounded confessional in informing me of feelings she felt toward me. I must have seemed dumb to her, but I couldn't believe she was really referring to marriage, as she once had during a call from Houston which I had recorded and replayed for Toddy to hear. Finally Candace directed the conversation to momentary pleasures and suggested I attend to her desires. After hours of bedside talk, she tugged at the covers, sinking deeper therein and whispering that I should join her.

The afternoon culminated in intimate moments. While I was moving from my place, I reached down and switched on the pocket audio recorder that I tape song thoughts onto (which I had brought from fear of her misusing my visit). I have since then closely listened to the tape and found the footage incredibly clear and deeply satisfying. She seemed to find the folly irregrettably dear and I likewise.

I saw Candace one more time, in 1977 in Los Angeles. Then the next thing I heard of Candace was that she was holding on to life itself. Our relationship and the reason for her choosing to befriend me so dearly became lost with her death.

Candy

O n September 20, 1969, as I was approaching my Hertz rental
car in front of the Fenway Hotel on Beacon Street in Boston,
Massachusetts, a young girl ran toward the car calling me. I
was with a student of the University of Chicago, Margarette
McCain, whom I'd arranged to take to the concert that night. As
Margarette and I were getting in the car, the hippielike girl handed
me a note with her name, address, and phone number and asked
me to phone her that night. I promised to if it wasn't too late, then
took off with Margarette to the concert at a club called the Boston
Tea Party.

The Boston concert was crowded and I noticed the girl, Candy,
walking around mostly watching my maneuvers. Margarette,
whom I called Marg, was a dancer who enjoyed every selection
played. She was five feet, ten inches tall, yet well built with long
hair, and she perspired freely, slinging her thirty-inch brown mane
around as she danced. Candy was watching every move Marg was
making and I was watching Candy observe the action. Afterward I
took Marg to the Fenway and Candy was again on watch in the
lobby until the elevator door closed off her surveillance.

I called Candy the next day and invited her to the last night of
the Tea Party engagement. The bellman told me she was waiting in

the lobby forty-five minutes before the time we'd planned to rendezvous. I learned from our first long conversation that she was pure Irish, twenty-one years of age, and born in Boston. Her mother and father, though separated, resided locally and corresponded frequently. She had only lately abandoned her enrollment at Boston University.

Even though her driver's license confirmed her age, nevertheless when she told me she was twenty-one my thoughts jackknifed to El Paso and an Indian girl who claimed to be the same. But Candy was really twenty-one though her baby face and pug nose made her look not a day over fifteen. We shared an evening together and a trip to Logan Airport, where I shot a Polaroid of her as I departed Boston.

Candy questioned me about my future concerts and promised she'd be at my Long Island concert the following night. She was there. I escorted her as my guest; the concert went down normally and she spent the night in New York. I took a liking to what I'd found out about her and criss-crossed her with questions trying to discern her future aims and desires. Her major concerns seemed to be to gain and maintain close contact with my music or me.

When I told her about Berry Park and the possibility of her working there she seemed highly enthused. She informed me that she could type and file, and was good at it, having studied it for over two years in Boston University. What interested me most was that just as openly as she stated her abilities, she confessed that her mother was a pronounced alcoholic and didn't want her around.

As we talked of her past she seemed sorry for herself, considering herself a sucker and a loser, until she got a little next to my better virtues I suppose and I promised her the living place and employment at the Park. I purchased her a one-way air ticket from New York to St. Louis and gave her round-trip bus fare from New York to Boston and back to New York to get her things. I explained I would meet only that particular flight arriving in St. Louis and if she chose meanwhile not to come, to then have a nice weekend. I went on then to continue my next concerts.

Around this time, I became interested in the life-style of hippies and what they were doing to society. Berry Park seemed to be the place of the future in business as well as in enjoyment. Many hippies came and stayed at the Park during the summers and secured room and board by helping out only an hour or two per day. A friend of mine who evidently sought a more carefree life even sent her thirteen-year-old daughter, Carol Capone, to live at the Park for over two years and finish high school in Wentzville.

Candy was on the plane she'd booked and I picked her up and settled her in a hotel near Berry Park. I gave her some money to support herself for a week and encouraged her to get around and observe the area and people of Missouri. Two days later I returned to find her contented with some magazines, a hard-back book about the Ozarks, and some snacks lying around. After chatting I left for three more days and found the same contentment and circumstances, excepting this time she asked me why I did not want to make love to her. I didn't answer her positively although I, too, wanted it to happen but instead I took her in my arms and enjoyed the excuse to hug and kiss her as well as the knowledge of the open invitation to do more. As I was leaving she asked me if she could help me at the Park. I told her soon I would be taking her there to live.

I figured her personality was such that she could get along with my folks at the Park. My sister Bennie was living there with Rona and Carol, all pitching in domestically like a little international family. Rona was staying in the main building with little Carol and my relatives whenever they visited. The teenage dances we held at the club building on weekends were the highlight for everyone living there as each had a position of authority in helping to handle them.

When I did bring Candy to the Park, she molded right in with what was expected of her. Candy was always eager for people to befriend her. Another typical trait of hers was that she'd tremble like an elderly, nervous person whenever she was either happy and delighted or heavily depressed and hurt.

During the night of December 1, 1969, we had a big fire at the Park that totally destroyed the quarters where Rona stayed, the room I stayed in when I was there overnight, Carol's quarters, and the room my little thirty-two-year-ol' sister Bennie was using. Only the basement was spared. When the local fire department came their deliberately casual interest in fighting the fire was truly saddening. They fought it from behind the direction it was traveling, allowing the salvageable portion of the structure to be consumed as they watered behind the blaze. Many of the local neighbors who could not give the least in help were gathered around on the dead grass watching the blaze sweep across the building.

The firemen calculated that Bennie had left a cigarette on her bedside nightstand that carried over enough to catch on to the window draperies. No one was injured. When the insurance adjuster came, he looked at the fire damages for about four minutes and declared it a total loss. I immediately booked contractors to construct a new main building while I had other contractors setting up a five-room double trailer.

On the way home from Montreal New Year's Day I met Fran at

Little Candy at sixteen.

the Greater Pittsburgh airport. It had been a year since she'd left
the Park and it was rapidly deteriorating in style and status. There
had to be a change. But she and I were at a stalemate that had to
be broken. That break was to change the conditions confronting
her with my involvement with other companions. In other words
it was my indiscretion more than my involvement that caused me
to lose such a loyal companion. Such was our conversation for two
hours on the balcony of the lobby in the terminal that morning. I
promised myself as well as her to alter my habits to concur with
the way she was raised to believe life should be lived. As a result
of our talk New Year's Day, I went to Lambert Airport January 15
to meet Fran. On my promise of change, she had decided to return
to the Park to live and continue to handle my business.

Candy's interest in helping Fran around the Park was far in excess of what we expected. She was very apt and quick to catch on to the paperwork that Fran thought she could handle. In months she came to be called upon by others there, including members of my family, for various functions unfamiliar to anyone else. Candy seemed to always know where tools and supplies were and could fetch them in a flash.

The most advantageous thing that happened to my business during this period was that I affiliated myself with Attorney William Krasilovsky of Feinman and Krasilovsky, New York City, who started reconstructing, or better still, constructing my scattered financial status that was sprinkled all over the world. The very first thing Bill did was to consolidate me with Broadcast Music, Inc., getting all my tunes registered properly with adequate recognition. Isalee Music Company was far behind current listings, with Fran and me the only ones to look after music clients for licenses and keep up with the royalty fees. Bill Krasilovsky seemed most eager to set us on the right track, but it still surprised me when he came to my next concert in Manhattan.

I re-signed with the Chess Record Company on May 9, 1970. But the recording sessions became more foreign than ever, full of red tape and requirements for permission from other departments of the company for any changes, as opposed to the family-type, small-business settings of the earlier sessions. Leonard was never there anymore and his brother Phil was not a man who could replace Leonard's authority or humor. Nor did I feel Phil ever cared about how the tunes turned out. Half of the sessions were not even done at the Chess studio in Chicago but instead at different hired studios across the country. The reason, I conceived, was that if someone in the Chess facility wanted to go to some particular city, they would book the session there and attend to their interest during the intervals of the recording session. Nevertheless, I went where they chose and recorded.

December brought Phil Chess to finally acknowledge in writing that no songwriter royalties had been paid for three years on my Chess Records product. In a settlement it was agreed that ARC Music would make these collections from then on and I received a check to make up the difference. When Francine and I reviewed the Chess establishment's manner of earlier payment, I was sur-

prised to learn that I had been paid the same songwriter's royalties for an LP as I was receiving for a single record. Chess claimed to be unaware of this "mistake," as if they had never noticed that LPs had between eight and ten songs on them. I also suffered the surprise to find, during that audit, that foreign royalties, which were supposed to be collected through ARC Music, were claimed mysteriously delayed in transit from important countries such as Germany, France, and Japan. This meant that my share of song-writer royalties on U.S. receipts just accumulated (with interest, for others) until whenever "received" in the U.S. Further I was told that the German subpublisher, which was delinquent in paying, was really just a subsidiary and was acting under the directions of ARC Music. I had joined the American Guild of Authors and Composers (AGAC), which was able to obtain prompt redress and assurance that restitution would be forthcoming.

The Chess Records/ARC Music settlement also provided that my writer royalty statements would be in detail in future reports. I had been unable previously to distinguish what monies came in from the U.S. as opposed to from foreign sources. These are separate from the revenue received for printed uses as distinguished

Going onstage at a Berry Park Festival, July 1972.

C H U C K

from phonograph or movie uses. Such are the perils of not having a manager or representative who claims a portion of royalties to curb these losses.

Bill Krasilovsky drafted the settlement that cleared up most of the deficiencies in registrations and directions of royalties and helped me start recovering the copyrights of songs I had assigned to ARC Music before I knew that I could set up my own music publishing company.

The Park had its first rock festival on August 28, 1970. It was a one-day affair starring me and a local musician, Ron Balducci. By noon 250 hippies had gathered in vans, tents, and on foot. The admission was four bucks a head, with the Park receiving the first five hundred dollars from the gate, which was promptly brought up to Fran's office on time. Four bands played well into the night, including a forty-minute show I did around 10 P.M. What we didn't realize in the bargain was the magnitude of the rubbish left to remove to restore the Park to the beauty in which it usually was kept.

Candy went wild during the festival among all those people her own age. Likewise when the Park would give dances on the weekends, Candy would enter her room looking like a poor peasant at four o'clock in the evening but would glue herself into her ticket-taking position at 6 P.M. sharp as the young beauty of the Park.

The weekly dances thrived for a couple years, until Fran had to get two auxiliary officers to patrol them for open and bold marijuana smokers. Then some county deputy got ambitious and came out one night and smelled the telltale aroma in one of the corners and arrested Fran herself.

Fran had long since had a friend in the city of Wentzville who was unlike most of the local residents—she had a Ph.D. and a career in music education. This friend, Nancy Reynolds, was then the mayor of Wentzville, and with a phone call from her the little county-deputy office flung the door ajar and Fran walked away unharmed. The deputy never heard the last of that unnecessary arrest and later lost a reelection to county office. Fran and Nancy celebrated with a barbecue the day the votes returned and he lost.

We finally terminated the dances after a pair of boys who brought a pistol with them to a dance got into a dispute that led to the discharge of the gun. The bullet grazed the arm of one of them.

The mother of the injured kid then filed a suit against Berry Park for one hundred thousand dollars on the grounds that the Park had insufficient protection for the dances. She wound up with an eight-hundred-dollar attorney fee and a court order of $450 paid by Berry Park for her injured son's doctor bill. It just goes to show you, you can't squeeze blood out of a turnip.

On September 7, 1970, I took Candy to Boston to see her mother while I did a concert at Paul's Mall on Boylston Street. There on the second night I met her father, who was among the audience, and sent a note of invitation to his table. During intermission, I met him and his female companion in brief conversation. I also met her mother, Priscilla, whom I'd spoken with several times by phone since Candy had left Boston. She paid me a visit at my hotel room during intermission, unannounced and intoxicated as she'd always sounded on the phone. I remember her flinging her fox fur stole on the bed as she strolled across the room Bette Davis–style, saying, "I'm so happy for Candy and so proud of you for looking after her as you are. She's had it so hard with all the problems between her father and brother." As she walked close by talking, I could see tears in eyes that must have claimed the charms of many men. She spoke lightly, "Charles, I wish there was something I could do to show appreciation for your kindness. I've never known a person like you. How is Candy doing?"

She then planted a quick kiss on my cheek and suggested I allow her to grant me dinner after the show, which I did. The show was late starting in the dinner club, so I spent time chatting at her table. It was weird to be in her company with Candy socializing with the band boys and the father sitting not three tables away. I have but once, with a certain multimillionaire, had a more dignified setting amongst the public with a lady so elegantly displaying herself as did I that night in Candy's mother's company. I listened to her plea of desire after the dinner, assuming she was bombed, yet she followed me back to the hotel and remained the balance of the night.

The morning found me alone in my part of the suite with my companion departed and Candy just in the adjoining parlor room with the connecting door partly ajar. We flew back to St. Louis with Candy seeming happy that I had met and talked with her mother and father.

Golf-carting around Berry Park.

At the Newport Hotel on November 30, 1971, I met Rachel Spindler, a grade-school teacher who claimed to have never heard of my music or me. After we talked throughout the intermission of my show, deciding I held a worthwhile conversation, she granted me the courtesy of a friendly correspondence. Two weeks later she flew from her home in Chicago to St. Louis to visit me at the Park. Six months later she severed her marriage and moved to employment at the Park. Six years and seven countries later she left to settle in California. What her life was meanwhile has yet to be reaped from the acres of seeds she sowed on the grounds of the

Hanging out by the pool with the festival bike crew.

Park where her intelligence left a mark. As hippie-type as Candy was, the two of them spent much time together playing games during the cold winter months.

Rachel told me once that her ex-husband referred to himself as having lost out to a field hand. Nonetheless, on the banks of the Seine, once she told me she was in love.

I needed someone to manage an apartment complex I owned in Hollywood, and Candy was the only one in my employment who could fill the position, so we let her. That went well for a few months until the tenants learned how kind and soft-hearted she was and finagled their payments, getting behind due dates with sad stories to her. Shortly thereafter, she was raped by two guys while returning from a show on Sunset Strip one night. The two culprits were seen jimmying an automobile lock through its window by cruising police officers. The officers questioning the two guys noticed Candy running back across the street to expose her assailants. Her childlike features and her clothes still in disarray encouraged the officers' belief in her story and they arrested the two on the spot for rape and attempted burglary.

I placed another in Candy's job and flew her back to Berry Park with Francine, her play mother, who took her in as before without hesitancy.

In July 1972, our second festival, running four days and produced by Bold Swimmer Productions, was held at the Park. They presented several local acts such as Free Flight, White Horse, Spoon River, Ace, Zachary Beau, and Parchment Farm. There were sixteen motor-bike club members for security personnel. We made the swimming pool available at no extra charge for the festival customers. It went well considering the bikies dominated the pool and in the heat of the afternoon shed their clothing to skinny dip, which of course ran all the conservative patrons out of the pool. Surprisingly enough though, as mean and aggravating as bikies are said to be, they otherwise patrolled the Park in shifts and obeyed Fran's every request as if she were Bike Queen. Most of the bikies were all right, I guess. Candy was extremely comfortable with them. They, being just her age group, had created good "vibes" that helped Fran to manage the group. Candy was intermediary for whatever Fran wanted done.

Independence Day, July 4, 1974, Fran leased the Park out for the third and last festival, which was twice as large as the other two combined. Just for a rundown: it was on thirty acres of the Park surrounded by a six-foot enclosed fence; there were twenty-six portable johns set up, a thirty-by-fifty-foot bandstand fourteen feet high, and four dressing-room trailers; a fifteen-hundred-amp power line was installed and buried; there were ten bands, some sixty thousand beautiful people, and two different helicopter news teams coming in and out. From 4 P.M. Thursday the flow of traffic, feet, and wheels began. The Park gates opened at 6 A.M. and the allotted parking lot was filled overnight. Two adjacent small farms were rented for additional parking. The admission was ten dollars for the three days.

The star of the show, Leon Russell, was not paid by the promoter and consequently did not show up. The promoter then fled without paying the balance owed the Park and some late arriving artists. Some of the kids then took their revenge and did some damage to a couple of the wooden portable johns, threw bottles toward Fran's home, then finally strolled away.

Everything that has happened at a festival must have been repeated again at this one. On Monday morning there were sixty-some cars left and on the grounds mounds of debris. Fran and I, seeing the appearance of the Park, agreed "Please—not ever again!" Of course the St. Louis news media gave the festival a bad time, alleging it was a multitude of marijuana smokers, drunk, with nudity as usual at a festival, but the teen idol Chuck Berry shouldn't have let it occur with children among them.

As the cleanup operations were in progress with countryside teens picking up some dollars, faithful Candy instructed them for days in how, where, and what to do with the festival rubbish. To help I purchased a '74 International pickup truck with a dumpster and a tractor with a brush hog. Repairs to the windows of Fran's dwelling were made and it seemed then that all would be peaceful and quiet again at Berry Park.

Candy surprised me once when I arrived at NBC in L.A. for a TV show. Candy had long proved to me that she could gain admission to any affair that had doors manned by males. She had not only gotten into the audience of this show (the Dinah Shore show), but she had gained employment and was to dance, on camera, with others in fifties costumes. I never saw her happier in the seven years she lived at the Park than she looked then.

The reason for my chapter on Candy is that she had been wandering around Boston, dabbling in drugs, but she chose to come to the Park and dry out. She didn't seem to miss the drugs or pot that she'd mentioned being accustomed to in Boston and never complained about the little room she was given to live in. In fact, she bragged about it and took pride in personalizing the walls with mementos of her rock music idols. There were several posters of Elvis Presley on the ceiling and walls—a couple of me—one of Gary U.S. Bonds, a few of popular groups like the Rolling Stones and the Beach Boys. Candy roamed Berry Park on a golf cart, then would settle to watch television at night. She obeyed Fran and myself to the T and fitted into a position there that was indispensable. I advised her as I would a child of my own and was proud to see her take on confidence in herself.

Candy was a big help as we endeavored to put the Park and much of my musical affairs in order. Leave it to Candy, she knew every song. Even those that caressed the bottom of the charts. We always asked her when we were in doubt on a title or date or when a song was popular and she'd come up with it, so few times wrong that we relied on her to be none short of correct. I miss her being around.

CHAPTER   SIXTEEN

My Ding-A-Ling

U p to 1972, my career and success had not registered to the point that I believed I was a "legend," as had been stated here and there in articles on my music and performances. I had been so elated with the possessions I'd accumulated that whatever fame had accentuated the achievement was greatly underadministered due to the attention I paid to the income I was collecting. Many of the things I'd dreamed of in life were coming to me and I was determined not to let loss come to what I'd obtained.

By the only wife I've ever had, I now had four grandchildren from Ingrid's and Melody's marriages. They seemed to partially pacify Toddy's loneliness at home while I was traveling worldwide in an attempt to stretch the good living to my immediate kinfolk. My five brothers and sisters had granted me nineteen nieces and nephews, who all lived in St. Louis. Up to then I had owned a total of twenty-nine automobiles, most of them purchased new and most of the new ones Cadillacs, which was then the epitome of well-off. During the twenty-two years of marriage I'd purchased twenty-three pieces of property located from Los Angeles to Kitchener, Ontario, costing $677,000 in total.

I was lacking about fifty thousand dollars from having a million in savings, a dream I'd had since I first saw my bankbook rise to six digits. I also lacked the time to keep my wardrobe up sufficiently in show or street attire. The red pants that many fans have seen me in were bought in 1972 at a jeans store on La Cienega in Los Angeles, for eight dollars. Unlike when I started performing, wearing tuxedos on stage or TV, the rock groups of the seventies seemed to be performing in whatever they happened to be wearing at the time, whereby I assumed T-shirts and jeans had become the thing.

In trying to maintain the show-biz attire I was familiar with seeing on stars, I was fast becoming out of style. Many times I was reminded that I looked like the FBI when I would show up in a suit. The same was occurring in the audience that showed up at the concerts and definitely at the festivals, where not only did the spectators come in casual clothing but in some instances none at all. I made my debut signing of an autograph for a nude young lady at a Michigan festival, where she requested I scribble it on her buttocks. So rare was the obligation that I in turn requested a snapshot for my scrapbook.

Since the TWA air travel credit card granted me in 1956, I'd obtained charge cards from Hertz, Visa and MasterCharge, American Express and Standard, which made it unnecessary for me to carry cash for travel expenses. Identity was no problem. In fact recognition was becoming extremely potent. I realized that the extent of fame then surrounding my image would soon take a serious toll on the privacy that at times was necessary to my view of life.

I was not and will never be one who can come to accept the honor or gratitude that is forwarded from those who see in me that which is only an image they conceive. In other words my conception of me is: I am only what I am and not what one may believe me to be from the image he sees of me regarding my works.

This is not to imply that I refuse anyone's opinion or reject the value of his conviction. But my view remains that I do not deserve all the reward directed on my account for the accomplishments credited to the rock 'n' roll bank of music. I've long thought that people who reach beyond their grasp to praise or condemn something that is not worthy of either are knowledgeable of neither.

Nor does it touch me as flattering to be idolized for efforts of my profession. In fact, my profession was to me only a job, a job that I've always performed as if it was overpaid considering the joy I receive in performing it. Therefore, why so much reimbursement? While all others receive monetary consideration, why shouldn't I as well? Many times I have bid too low, not knowing the market price of a show, at a certain place and employed myself for less. For an example: if I did a concert for five thousand dollars and the promoter received twenty thousand dollars at the box office for arranging the gig, though our efforts are different in quality, our returns should not differ in quantity; so those in the business, for years, have said. So, though I play from desire, I feel I should be paid for the hire.

On February 3, 1972, I was performing at the Lanchester Ballroom in Coventry, England, where another tricky tactic of the music industry's way of doing things without my knowledge was under way. At the close of my show, the song "My Ding-A-Ling" was recorded during my performance before thirty-five thousand students who, eagerly but also unaware, were joining in on the recording. I can't deny that it turned out okay but it would have

been better for the band and myself to know if and when the recording was being made.

It is strange when I realize the magnitude that came from the song. I had been singing it for four years prior where audiences were appropriate and suddenly after recording it, it came to be number one on the record charts. What's more strange, at least to me, is that I had not registered a hit in seven years. In fact, after having two surges of popularity, I never expected to reach near the top of the charts again.

After the Lanchester engagement we went to Phillips Records studio, in London, for a recording session. It was different recording in England, hearing the local engineers speaking the King's English with such dignity and excessive politeness. It almost hurts being a bit of an American. We did the entire session, which was to come out as *The London Chuck Berry Sessions,* in about five hours, including a break for lunch, cheerio!

For the period ending December 1972, my royalty statement from Chess showed that there were sales of 1,295,075 singles of "My Ding-A-Ling" and 187,975 LPs of the *London Chuck Berry* album. "My Ding-A-Ling" was big and everybody wanted it, with the exception of some person in England named, I believe, Mary Whitehouse, who wanted it banned.

I signed a different contract with Chess with a royalty rate of 10 percent of the record's suggested list price as opposed to 21½ cents on the $6.94 list price of the hit LP and as little as 10 cents per copy on the LP *Chuck Berry's Greatest Hits.* The new 10 percent rate would more than double the payments per LP on future recordings under the new contract. The recording contract also guaranteed that Chess Records would authorize two LPs a year and absorb the cost of the first fifteen thousand dollars per LP, without following the record-industry practice of recouping those costs from the artist's royalties.

At the time of "My Ding-A-Ling," Chess Records was a division of the GRT (General Recorded Tape) Corporation. "My Ding-A-Ling" was doing so well that a two-hundred-fifty-thousand-dollar check, the largest I'd ever received, was handed to me while crossing Fifth Avenue. I stubbed my toe on the curb at the sight of all the zeros.

This GRT Corporation was heavily involved in manufacturing tapes and cassettes under license from other record companies. Unfortunately, as the market for tapes and cassettes grew to take over more than one-third of the sales of all popular records in the U.S., GRT became so financially successful that its former licensors started retaining these rights for themselves and refusing to continue to do business with GRT. This led to bankruptcy. Before going bankrupt, the GRT Corporation dealt to sell many of its important masters to All Platinum Record Company, Inc., with a turnover date stated to be as of July 1, 1975. This company also

went bankrupt, and between the two bankruptcies, the promotion, marketing, and collections on the Chess catalogue (including Muddy, Bo, and me) have been substantially affected. Eventually, Bill Krasilovsky encouraged suing All Platinum Record Company, and we obtained a judgment in New York State Supreme Court that resulted in my being a free agent, which enabled me to enter into a deal with Atlantic's Atco Records. Nevertheless, the old masters were left in the possession of All Platinum and there was an endless stream of confusion as to who had the rights to own what when the suit was settled.

One isolated success of the hit tune "My Ding-A-Ling" was that my own Isalee Music Company owns it and is the publisher, which is very important in controlling a copyright throughout the world. So along with striking interesting licks on a guitar, chuck squawking, and duck walking, one lives and learns, as time goes by, to take precautions and not make the same mistake again.

On Christmas of 1972, for the first time my father and all my relatives enjoyed our Christmas dinner in a reunion at the Park. The Holy Ghost was present all over the place that day. That "old-

time religion'' was rolling in the studio room of the Park's administration building and that good ol' rock 'n' roll was reeling around
among the young-blooded Berrys in the main assembly room. Baptist hymns rang through the second-floor walls as the Baptist beat
bounded back unbent. I listened to the spirit of the season with
mixed emotions while noticing closely the change in the spirit,
since the inspiration came more from the beat now than from the
blessings. Still the upbringing and indoctrination of religion long
bestowed in me surfaced, bringing tears to my eyes as I realized
how I'd abandoned the frequency of churchgoing. Rock of ages
cleft for me, just what is to be will be.

I started off 1973 exercising a game that people play, spending
some of the fortune that had come my way. I took my wife and
secretary along with a backup band, Billy Peek and his group, on
a tour to England and on to Europe. It was twenty-two consecutive
nightly concerts, beginning in the cold and distant Odeon of Glasgow, Scotland, where the Edinburgh Hotel was maintained at
sixty-three northern degrees with the bathrooms down the frigid
corridor meters away, but the show hit on time with me in my red

pants. Bournemouth was chilly, Birmingham was damp and cloudy, and Manchester, as usual, was overcast with rain. Not until we reached the outskirts of London (in two chauffeur-driven limousines, some trips by rail) did we thaw out coming offstage at the Rainbow Theater.

In Manchester, the promoter, emcee, and stagehands with their ladies followed us back to the hotel, talking about the show. What was irregular about that night was that it was the third night in a row I picked up spontaneous group dinner tabs. So I led off by ordering a short order of Hungarian goulash and hot tea, asking the waiter if it was quick and short, hoping the question would start an ordering trend. The very next order was that of the chauffeur assigned to the limo that carried my party around, who, up to two nights prior, customarily waited in the car. Like the previous two nights he came in and this time had the audacity to order a New York sirloin steak, plus dessert, and he was the only one to accept the bottle of wine a waiter suggested to the group. I sat boiling in temper. My goulash did not come until after the chauffeur's steak had been served to him, which added to the flame.

In Schelsen, Germany, I rented a Hertz car with Dick Alen, who after twenty years was practically my manager/agent with the William Morris Agency, and we drove to the countryside location of a music festival I was to appear in. After being lost for two hours we managed to find the stadium area then migrated our way along the back road through the fans approaching the stage. The balance of my fee was to have been paid at the airport by an agent of the promoter and was now due because the agent hadn't shown up to meet our arriving flight. At the festival location we found the agent, but we had to drive back to the city to collect the balance due.

It was striking 9 P.M. when we parked under the stage, on which some English band was performing at the time. When they finished it was close to 11 P.M. and another act came on before Jerry Lee Lewis was to hit. The long intermission to set up Lewis's equipment plus the two announcements to get his presence on stage took until 1:20 A.M. I was contracted to perform a forty-five-minute show beginning at 11:45 P.M. There I was, sitting in the rented car by the stage all this time waiting for Jerry to come on. I was hungry, cold, bored, and angry when at last he finally showed on stage, high as a Russian kite.

His band started a tune. He inspected the musicians and setup before deciding to stop the tune and start a vocal number. The melodic lyrics to it were sort of spoken in a monotone and occasionally the bottle he brought on with him was visited for a hit between verses. In fact, he was drinking at a rate so frequent he wouldn't have known where he was if the Bells of St. Mary had rung in his ear. It takes a numerator of soberness in a denominator like Jerry Lee to find the quotient of his drunkenness. He was bombed.

This went on for over a half hour while my empty stomach, freezing skin, impatient head, and disappointed heart awaited his exit off stage. Finally fed up, I told Dick I was going on regardless of Lewis still being on, just to make a showing that I'd been there to the audience and the promoter, who we'd not even been able to locate.

For the first time ever I invaded another artist's performance and joined in with my guitar, playing "Great Balls of Fire," and I thought there would be for walking in on Jerry Lee. When I came on stage Jerry appeared confused, but jolly and joyful as could be. He arose and met me mid-stage. He welcomed me on, put his arms around me, and even announced my name as if my appearance had all been planned. I bowed and joined him in rocking out "Great Balls of Fire." We jammed for about eight minutes, in which I danced my duck walk and did my scoots and splits, waving to the audience. I was so elated at his presentation, knowing from past contact that he could care less for a black invader upon his show, that I sang and danced fifty minutes. The fans cheered my exit and I left the show to Jerry. That same evening I closed down and left Germany.

Diane Gardiner, a publicity agent for Elektra Records who had also helped me in my California real-estate dealings, seemed to know half the people in L.A. During our affiliation, getting around from place to place meeting different people, one day she encouraged me to visit Phil Spector, who was then very successful in producing recordings. Diane somehow knew Spector was having John Lennon as a guest at his home in Beverly Hills and suggested I let her bring me there. We went and I met Spector and greeted John, but had little opportunity to chat because of the extremely loud volume at which they were playing some albums. I couldn't believe such a successful producer could realize any comprehen-

sion at that volume, but one usually feels that successful people tend to know the better way of doing or having things and therefore take it for granted. Well, I and those who feel that way are wrong, I must say. John and I looked at each other and he shrugged his shoulders. I learned that Spector was either crazy or deaf. After a short while, I couldn't stand the db's banging my eardrums and went into his john for more than one type of relief. When they started drinking I suggested to Diane that I wished to leave and we did. She explained that she thought, as many others did, that Spector was crazy, but what did it matter if he was successful. Damn! What a business, I thought.

My interest in the visit was because there was talk around that time by Dick Alen of the likelihood of Lennon and me doing an album together but he was unable somehow to get in touch with John.

To celebrate my forty-seventh birthday, Fran had sent out gold cards inviting business associates, music friends, girlfriends, friend friends, my family, and our few Wentzville friends to a gala party at Berry Park. I had the pleasure of introducing the guests to each other. Candy helped with the catered food, trembling before ARC publisher Gene Goodman; my record company owner, Phil Chess; my accountant, Ed Deutch; the mayor of Wentzville, Nancy

Reynolds; the multimillionairess, Candace Mossler; and about eight other dignitaries, Toddy and my entire family, and some sixty-five other closely affiliated personalities. My wife met most of the guests, hardly knowing any of them but having heard of most, especially Candace. I particularly watched out of the corners of my eyes as Candace reached for Toddy's hand. Toddy seemed so flattered that she appeared breathless in amazement.

I was nearly fifty years old and still rocking 'n' rolling among some performers who were still in "Baghdad" when I began. How many times has the thought crossed my mind, when will it end? I hadn't tired of singing, but the waiting that occurs prior to concerts and flights often bothered me since my popularity and recognizability was restricting me from discreetly girl watching anymore.

I took both of my daughters—Ingrid, who performed, and Melody, whose husband was playing drums for the Spoon River group —to a concert at the Aquarius Theater in Hollywood, March 18, 1974. Bo Diddley and Johnny Rivers and his band were guests on a ninety-minute show Dick Clark let me arrange and host for his "In Concert" program. I was so excited about exposing Ingrid and Spoon River, the group she was singing with at the time, that I rehearsed them from 9:30 A.M. through to show time at 8 P.M. that night, at which time I found myself mentally rewarded but physically retarded. The show went spontaneously along in apparently fair response but I forever will claim that had I not been pooped out by show time it would have been one of the best shows that I'd ever performed. At least I enjoyed the privilege of directing the flow of entertainment for once. I had no problem sleeping that night.

Throughout 1973 my accountant Ed Deutch had toiled with a claim by the IRS that the corporation I'd opened in 1958, Chuck Berry Music, Inc., was a holding company and had to be liquidated. Its assets had to be distributed, which dumped over one hundred fifty thousand dollars into my personal income that year. According to the tax structure, nearly all of the distributions to me (the major stockholder) were highly taxed at the 70 percent personal income rate instead of the 26 percent corporate rate, and of course I paid. Up to that time, my tax returns had been analyzed only once, and I had paid around $1.7 million in income tax to the government since 1956. I was having one of my biggest years as far as performance income and could have done without the claim, but I learned that it was a change in law and suffered the loss. However, I immediately sought to incorporate in a manner that would not be a holding company.

So on May 7, 1974, I went to Chicago to a meeting with Van Spaulding, a sales representative for a video company, Corplex Inc., that paved the way to close a deal for my purchase of the furniture and business of a branch they had in downtown St. Louis. The corporation that I'd hoped for was coming into reality. Ed Deutch formed Chuck Berry Communication Systems, Inc., and registered it in Missouri with the four former employees of Corplex and two new ones I'd added, Rachel Spindler and my daughter Melody. One of the city-slick rather red-neck employees was the inherited salesman, who, after a getting-to-know-you relation had been established between us, actually informed me (after I loaned him three thousand dollars on his home) that his wife told him that she never thought he would stoop to work for a black man. In his reluctance, inability, or refusal to make payments on the loan, I had to threaten foreclosure before he came up with the payment, which actions (he claimed) caused his wife to dissolve their relationship.

After the release of *Bio* in 1973, it was getting so GRT wasn't releasing any selections from my sessions at all. They were involved in transactions with All Platinum Records without my knowledge until I was invited to All Platinum's studios in New Jersey to celebrate their ownership of my masters. The term "not transferable" was incorporated in my contract with Leonard Chess's record company, but after Leonard died nobody knew how or even where the company was.

I was contented with the engagements I was enjoying and wouldn't take the time to seek assistance to follow up on the routing of my recording contracts, and consequently I wound up at an International House of Pancakes in New Jersey celebrating where my next recording session was. Strangely enough, a woman I was fascinated with ever since she invited me to a lonely studio on 52nd Street in New York back in 1956, namely Bobbie Prior of Mickey and Sylvia ("Love Is Strange"), was part owner, along with Joseph Robinson, of All Platinum. At the celebration, I believe she wondered if the flame still was aglow. I hopped along, continuing to record but holding the tracks, pending a legal contract with All Platinum that never came.

Beginning around 1973, nearly every year Richard Nader booked me at Madison Square Garden in New York City for the Revival of the Fifties show. I thought the title was dumb because rock 'n' roll never had heart trouble and thus did not need to be revived. Nader was enjoying full houses at the Garden, grossing over nineteen thousand paid admissions, yet he had problems sharing profits adequately. However, he did offer to hand me an additional sum under the table in exchange for lesser amounts being stated on the contract. He had phoned spontaneously sometimes, asking for me to appear at various concerts and quoting me one fee for our contract (sometimes as low as $280) and another amount to be handed under the table. These were unethical transactions that later caused both of us problems.

And so, for over a year Richard Nader and I engaged in "malparamanopo" (that's my word for "bad-two-person-operation"). A lousy practice, I should have realized, and would have had I not been at the threshold of having a million dollars in my bank account. Including real-estate equities, I was worth far past a million, but to have that amount at hand in caressable, cold cash was an unforgettable dream that seemed to possess my intentions.

IRS

T he contract for my January 1973 tour of England was not completed until I arrived in London, whereupon the William Morris Agency revised the figures in the contract to indicate that thirty-six thousand dollars was the balance due. I had already received a thirty-six-thousand-dollar deposit for the tour, but as the revised contract was worded it sounded as if that amount was the entire fee for the tour. This is where the biggest mistake was made.

It was a good tour with great attendance, in fact a couple of nights were added to it spontaneously. I charged the promoter a flat fee for the two additional concerts, which he argued furiously about but submitted to. Because of our deteriorated relation, I demanded the balance for the last couple of concerts in advance and the very last of them was really shallow in attendance. That put the icing on the cake.

The next stage of the mess was when I heard the promoter went bankrupt declaring he had paid me eighty-seven thousand dollars, when the total was really twice thirty-six thousand for the twenty-one nights and four thousand each for the two extra concerts added, totaling eighty thousand dollars. Then a letter arrived at the office introducing a Mr. Smith, who was an agent for the IRS. The letter requested a visit to my office at Berry Park to review my 1973 tax return. After several days Mr. Smith arrived in person with a briefcase in hand. He seemed to be a typical American Mr. Smith, discussing my songs and music (rubbing shoulders) while eating his sandwiches and drinking his coffee for days until he returned completely silent and became businessified.

It still didn't bother me to any great extent because I had since 1958 had a certified public accountant doing my tax returns who seemed to be as strict as any IRS people could be. I had never been audited before, only had a few unreceipted deductions from ten to maybe a hundred dollars in value knocked out that weren't worth contesting.

We drew up a big table and Fran began supplying the gentleman with all the documents he requested. On the second day of his investigation I returned from performing on the road to find he had already come to a confusion in tallying figures so I offered my assistance. Not fifteen minutes into the record, he directed the conversation for thirty-five minutes into a detailed description of his musical career playing trumpet with a local band that went not too frequently anywhere but home after work. Besides asking for various receipts and ledgers, he for the next two months came, greeted, worked, and bade farewell twice a week.

My accountants, Rubin, Brown, and Gornstein, had been assisting with the audit, putting in many man hours to locate various scattered cashier's checks I had purchased on the road. Such purchases relieved me of handling the flow of currency from each engagement. There were a number of "time deposit certificates" I'd purchased on different occasions with cashier's checks. There were also some deposits of foreign currencies from a prior English tour that I had exchanged for dollars with no problem. Rather than be paid in English bank checks, I had accepted the foreign currency in pounds and brought it home to America.

There was no excuse for it, but after the January '73 British tour, I did not exchange the forty-four thousand dollars in English pounds because the contract only mentioned thirty-six thousand dollars. The balance, I invented or at least hoped, would not be known about for taxation. It only required a forty-two-mile trip into St. Louis to an international bank to exchange the pounds, but I didn't. The Queen's smile on the bread was looking so good that I became attached to the ol' girl and decided to hold on to Her Majesty. I couldn't let Fran enter it in the books with my intended plan so it lay dormant for years; in fact, I still have most of it. I've paid the penalty for obtaining it and it's mine now.

Along with these hardships, it was found during the audit that not all of the employees at the video corporation I bought from Corplex were honest. Some of the merchandise that had been ordered missed coming in and at times came up missing. This confirmed to me what my father had often said about staying on the job with one's business. After soaking three hundred thousand dollars into it I began plans to bring the business to a close as inconspicuously as possible.

The next contacts were a series of meetings spanning a period of well over a year, with Mr. Smith searching through my receipts and contracts, wherein he found that I had paid up to then over six million dollars of income taxes. At that point he began talking even more nicely, as if he were bored with the investigation and only had to complete his job, so he joked and scribbled along and I rocked 'n' rolled on with my concerts, not knowing what the IRS was searching for. I left him to finish up his thing with Fran while I hit the road.

The next bit of surprise came from Fran, who walked from her office in wonder handing me two envelopes. One was a nice royalty check from BMI and the other a revenue claim that my taxes were in deficiency. My accountant, Ed Deutch, wrote that he was worried for me about a thirty-six-thousand-dollar difference in the records I reported to them in 1973 and about some freaky payments from a promoter in New York. Well, I knew all hell had broken out then because I had deliberately not revealed to Ed my transactions with Richard Nader.

When Dick Alen began suggesting that I get a lawyer to look after my tax problems, I shook it off, proclaiming I was in good hands with a big firm that did my accounting for me. Dick told me that was all well and good but they couldn't defend me should there be some deficiency somewhere. He informed me that the IRS had spent days at William Morris digging for information about my contracts.

I next heard from Mr. Smith by way of a phone message that postponed his next appointment. The postponement lasted almost a year, and we heard that he had had a heart attack. But he and his little two-sandwich lunch wrapped in Wonder Bread paper returned as sure as pneumonia. He never once accepted a hot cup of coffee, just began asking questions that I knew would lead up to my deal with Richard Nader.

The items that were in question were the lengthy periods between when funds were received and when they were deposited. Caring for my own business affairs on the road, it wasn't always convenient to deposit my receipts into a bank immediately. Also, I would sometimes purposely hold money until the day the bank interest would be at its highest rate. As a result, my accountant had difficulty realizing the source of certain deposits. Thus at the end of the year, at tax time, my accountant would ask me to recall the mystery. I wouldn't have the slightest idea, could hardly remember what had happened just last week.

The receipts from 1973, during the time of "My Ding-A-Ling," were so mixed up that Ed announced a catastrophe and advised me to place funds in their proper place and time. After the horse was out I stabled the practice of inadequately handling deposits. Meanwhile Mr. Smith returned to introduce me to his colleague Mr. Donati, a special agent.

I really began to believe then that there was much more to my tax investigation than disallowing deductions. They would never say more than the normal social greetings; they would just sit there and tally the records produced and take notes. Soon a machine was brought in to copy most of the contracts and records. Finally a list was presented to my secretary and me, instructing us to find the source of certain amounts of deposits and/or cashier's checks. On and on it went.

Several months passed, along with some eighteen thousand dollars in accounting service fees. Then, back home from a concert, my mail informed me that an indictment was likely to be issued for underpayment on my 1973 and 1974 taxes. Even to me there were some mysterious amounts, which enlarged the cloud of guilt that hovered over me. I intensified the search for the amounts missing and the bits that were insignificant began to fall more into line, but two large quantities still remained lost from the source of where or just when they were earned. My philosophy of "as long as you know you have it why bother where it is" was proving to be incompatible with reality.

One day Richard Nader phoned and told me that he had lately declared bankruptcy and consequently had exposed to the IRS the plan he had initiated whereby the two of us could avoid large concert fees and comparable taxes by my showing less earned.

This is how the deal worked. Richard claimed he couldn't pay me my regular fee for performing, but could come near it if I would accept a lower amount on the contracts and a separate payment in cash. The deduction I accepted below my normal fee was equal to the tax I would have paid, but still, from the regular rate, a savings to him. I yielded to the deal he proposed, feeling I could afford to go along with it, since he would benefit and I would not lose.

Soon an indictment for tax evasion was brought forth for the missing British tour income and the Nader monies received, as they called it, "under the table." It seemed that the indictment was especially great news for the hometown daily papers. The news promptly hit the streets of St. Louis that afternoon—live and in color—"The rock 'n' roll star, Chuck Berry, was indicted today" (as if rock 'n' roll itself was a disgrace), then it went on, "who back in 1959 was convicted of the Mann Act," etc., "who some say is the Founding Father of Rock," etc., "who back in 1944 was convicted of armed robbery," etc., and so on.

The daily publications got the ball rolling. It's all generally true, but most of the time it seems that their journalistic efforts are to call rock 'n' roll on the carpet, and rock 'n' roll never did hurt anyone.

If there is any advantage to the publication of the indictment, it shall be this book. I had been lying to the media about writing this book for years. Their publication not only exposed my intention, but encouraged my ambition. Bravo to the media for replaying all the old news in juicy detail, which prodded me to vent the reality.

Through all this I kept performing. I met a country singer named Sandy Hayes working in a restaurant who sounded encouraging and had a nice appearance as well. I let her rehearse with me and the group I was working with locally. Sandy got into it so well and had such a serious attitude about making it big in music that I began taking her out to concerts, letting her sing for the exposure.

C H U C K

After she had performed several concerts on the road with me in 1977, I took her to an engagement at Opry Land in Nashville, a memorial tribute to Elvis Presley. The song they wanted me to perform for the show was "Memphis," and Sandy came along to sing harmony.

Jimmy Dean, of "Big John" fame, was the emcee of the TV production. He mentioned that I would sound better if I didn't have Sandy harmonizing. By the way, Sandy is white and very nice looking. The discussion became very opinionated before I told them I would present my appearance as I saw fit, as always. I didn't know they were going to have no part of our different-complected faces singing together, not in Nashville, not then anyway. Charlie Rich, Chubby Checker, Tanya Tucker, and others were all sitting facing the studio audience when, in a last attempt to separate our two faces, the producers slid a foot-high stool out for me to stand on while singing.

Over the boom mike, I announced in perfect diction for all to hear, "If the production is attempting to shoot the duet over Ms. Hayes's height it will be impossible to pick up the guitar solo in the chorus of 'Memphis!' I slid the stool back to the stagehand and started the song. Sandy sang beautifully and we got outstanding applause as we completed the tune, but!

It's a good thing I was paid in advance because not one of the production staff let me get near enough to thank them for letting me have the setting I had insisted on. I was never invited to the gathering they had immediately after the show and left Opry Land as I would have in 1895. Since then I've had the red carpet treatment there, meeting Billy Carter, who took me to the presidential suite to entice me to play the grand piano but found the room locked.

When the tribute was aired, Sandy called all over the country telling friends to watch, and she set up a party at her home the night of the show. The moment the final credits started rolling, in sheer embarrassment, Sandy phoned Jimmy Marsala long distance, asking what the hell was going on. They had completely deleted the selection she and I did.

Within this time frame, I met a true native Texan, during a week-long engagement in Dallas, Texas, at Granny's Dinner Playhouse, who introduced herself as Yvonne Cumbie and started fraternizing a bit. She then went and got the rest of her party which included her mother, who it became apparent was the real fan. The mother, Willa Dean Holmes, was the daughter of a member of the Ku Klux Klan who was just one step below the rank of Grand Dragon. The two of them seemed to feel free in mentioning the KKK, although during the conversation it chattered my legs on both sides at the knee caps. Plus they had steel-gray eyes which further lowered the temperature.

I was with my daughter Ingrid and her band, my bassist Jimmy Marsala, Yvonne and her husband, and one night at 2 A.M. all of us went to Denny's to eat. I suggested that we sit boy by girl so that all the guys would have a companion to talk to. I directed the seating so that Yvonne would be between Jim and me, with her husband filling in on the other side of the booth. After everyone became busy eating, like a fox I slyly inched my hand under the table and rested it just above Yvonne's knee. She gave me a half fast smile, so I withdrew it immediately only to try again moments after. The second time I tried, the palm of my hand touched something hairy and rough, and my brain instantly knew it was not of a feminine nature. At that split second Jimmy looked over and said, "Damn, is 'zat you, Sam?"

As the meetings continued all week long, discussions about the possibilities of her moving to St. Louis and working evolved and her mother joined in promoting the idea. I got word she'd decided she wanted to look at an apartment unit in St. Louis that I'd mentioned I had vacant.

Yvonne soon made up her mind to come to St. Louis and live and work with Fran and myself. On New Year's Day of 1978, she did and just in time to help in the search for four- and five-year-old records requested by the IRS. Like the KKK, the IRS man seemed a close cousin to the Dragon from the way he was handling the investigation so I told Yvonne to stay out of sight while he was at the Berry Park office. After Yvonne's mother and her father, Garland, both had visited us at Berry Park, I felt better about Mr. IRS seeing her there.

Fran and Von, as we called Yvonne, made a good team. In view of what Fran wasn't happy doing, Von seemed to enjoy the out-of-door things and vice versa. Nothing with a motor or operating instructions was beyond Von's capacity to tackle. "I want to live at Berry Park forever'' was a welcome statement she one day made to me.

At this time I was in the process of fulfilling my new recording contract with Atlantic. Feeling more relaxed in familiar surroundings, I had the recording sessions moved to Berry Park. The Atco A&R person, titled executive producer, came to my Berry Park studios to administer this recording session and be responsible for the recordings. This was new to me since I'd always A&Red my own recording sessions, even during the three years I recorded with Mercury. Artist and repertoire? What was that? And what was an executive producer anyway? I wrote a song, went somewhere with the band and recorded it, and the record company processed and released it. That was that. All these titles and execs were ''new wave'' to me.

A group of Memphis musicians were brought in to jam with my own guys, Jim Marsala, Johnnie Johnson, and Ebby Hardy. The session was completed and mixed for a new album, *Rock It*.

I was determined not to go to trial in my dear hometown. Ironically, I feel there are some certain few, of (no doubt) influencing authority, who love me none too much. Perhaps the same wheels that rolled themselves to get rid of Club Bandstand would once again roll over me. I went to California and finally found an attorney to my liking, Bruce Hochman. I exposed all factors to Bruce, who in turn conferred with his colleague Harvey Tack, and together they planned the strategy to confront the situation I had explained to them. Trips were made to St. Louis to obtain a transfer of the trial to the Promised Land.

Soon thereafter a meeting between the United States and Little Ol' Me was called. I went with my big California attorney; I wanted to see the faces of some of the United States investigators who had been hand-delivering the breathtaking reports of tongue-twisting amounts of taxes still due. The meeting was four minutes long with but one five-foot Uncle Sam, who readily agreed to allow the case to be transferred to Los Angeles, California, if I would plead guilty. ''No way!'' shouted my attorney, ''with the weak case presented on the 1973 and practically no case on the corporation deficiencies.''

Then another meeting ensued that I could see I was too little to attend. The result thereof was announced in the famous Chase

Park Plaza Hotel that night. Bruce Hochman, Harvey Tack, Norman London, the state's legal representative, and I sat down with coffee to discuss the results. They had succeeded in obtaining a transfer to Los Angeles, but the cost was a plea of guilty to reduced charges.

It was up to me to make the decision. Stay in St. Louis with a possibly prejudiced trial or accept the charge actually due though slightly exaggerated out in California with a plea of guilty. The odds were "Go west, young man." I did.

The date of the trial was June 11, 1979. It had been eighteen and a half years since I'd stood before a judge and all the thoughts of what I could say to summarize the information for a truly fair judgment took wings, leaving the cosmic question—why was I even being judged? Patriotism, religion, liberty, and crime all pounded at my statement to intervene for acclamation, but none achieved precedence. The simple thought of what my eighty-four-year-old mother was feeling from my behavior instantly brought visions of her face in sadness. Though a twenty-year sentence could not have buckled my knees, the mere vision of her thoughts of my being arrested for anything did. Only some five or six times in the last twenty years have occasions arisen that have brought tears to my eyes. This was one of those times.

Seconds after I whimpered, I asked if there was any way that the sentence could be kept from reaching my mother? Again I broke tearful at referring to her, knocking over the glass of water set on the table for me. At that action, it came to me not only that I must look stupid standing there in tears, saying nothing that really mattered, but also that asking for clemency after a plea of guilt could aggravate any judgment already in the mind of the Honorable Judge Pregerson. I'd learned that a judge observes all data about a case prior to a trial and the live statement during court only finalized his direction of judgment, so my uncomposed "statement before sentence" was brought abruptly to a close and I erected my stance to face another style of music.

The courtroom was pin-drop silent. His honor spoke softly, mentioning that he had sentenced others of my status in the public eye and that they, the public, should take it as a "deferral to such behavior as you've shown." Then he delivered the sentence of three years (a petite pause) with all but 120 days suspended. I would serve it at a Lompoc Camp and then remain on a four-year probation to render one thousand hours of community service.

There were many more words to the sentence but even this much I had not understood precisely. Even my attorney did not have a clear conception of it. The mallet had sounded and the court was dismissed, so we strolled to the exit with three or four years wrapped around 120 days and one thousand hours. The judge had granted my passport returned and permission to travel to Europe during the thirty days before the sentence commenced.

In the month interval I had a European tour that had been set up prior to court. The Newport Jazz Festival, produced by George Wein, contracted my performance for several days in France, one day in Germany, and the last two dates in London, England. I had to leave August 11 for Nice, France, where the tour was to begin. When I landed at Heathrow Airport, I was greeted with sympathy as the news of my fate had been exposed by the British media.

Quite different was the response in St. Louis after the Concorde zipped us back to America. Landing at Lambert Airport, I received far less sympathy. As a matter of fact, some first-time-meeting chats had a farewell of "I'll be seeing you," said with a definite connotation. I summoned my car, returned a smile at the parking-lot lassie, and set out home to Berry Park.

A tour was over again and the chorus to the music of my behavior was rounding up at a rapid tempo. There were a lot of notes to attend to with few rests to enjoy being home, plus there were questionable bills and personal transactions to close. I had to program the show to go on without its main attraction and tune my music business to a key that would harmonize with the absence of the melody. The symphony would have to continue its tempo while the conductor paused to write. The staff and I knew it was only momentary. Life is but a day. Dream it not away. Carry me back to old adventures.

It's thirty miles from the 'port to the Park. I thought deeply as I drove, wondering if all this travel would ever stop. Had my love for travel, my playing music, my watching girls, my saving earnings, my writing songs come to a sudden halt or would I actually still be doing these things yet? I'd been retired by the government before and these habits had not vanished. I wrote music while at the Medical Center. I played music although my body was confined. I traveled in my mind to many places. I had even managed some girl watching. The staff at Berry Park was asleep when I rolled in off of my Interstate Dreaming. I was tired and sleep came easy. The next morning out of sheer enthusiasm I started this book.

Lompoc Prison Camp

Wednesday, August 8, 1979, with everything in order at my home and at the Park, I bade farewell to my family and staff and took the red-eye special midnight TWA flight from St. Louis to Los Angeles. Arriving in the wee wee hours of the morning I took a taxi to my Hollywood property and hit the hay. I visited the bank the following morning, arranged last-minute affairs, and went on to the William Morris Agency, where I talked to Dick Alen outlining strategies for concerts pending cancellation. Then I visited my attorney, my real-estate manager, arranged for the forwarding of my mail, looked at a few videotapes of brighter nights, then retired for the last day.

The morning of August 10, I headed up the Ventura Freeway toward Lompoc in an Avis station wagon. Under an overcast California morning, I drove north constantly staring at the drivers headed in the opposite direction, wondering if they could realize how wonderful their direction of travel could seem to some people.

The weather grew drearier after Santa Barbara. Turning on to the county road, leaving U.S. Highway 101, the 101 came to mind as being nineteen digits short of the days until I would be turning back on the same highway going home. I turned the station wagon in at Avis in Lompoc and the rental attendant took it as a privilege to come along, letting me drive the last two miles to the camp. As I turned in on the prison grounds many of the inmates were standing along the entrance drive and peering from the dormitory windows. I followed signs to the receiving office and parked the wagon.

The building resembled a typical old unpainted concrete Holiday Inn three stories high with venetian-blinded windows. Over a half hundred inmates and a dozen or so of the staff and photographers were waiting outside on the steps of the office. My guitar, which I was allowed to bring, was my first rapid retrieval from the wagon. Holding my face away from the reporters, I pretended to observe the many inmates on the opposite side, shouting greetings to me. I took swift large steps in the shade of a large helpful tree while moving toward the steps, knowing well that dim light would make it hard for the photographers to get good photos. Meanwhile I gave my face and attention to, "Welcome to Lompoc, Chuck," shouted by a group of inmates. I quickly smiled and waved and walked.

A man in a green suit, sweating profusely and rather frustrated, touched me and asked was I Charles Berry? "Yes, I am." "Well, then," he said as he turned and looked toward the photographers, "if you don't care to, you don't have to talk to anyone." His disappointed expression indicated to me that he was in favor of pictures. The green-suited man then nodded toward a door ten feet away, suggesting I should bring my bags along inside.

All sorts of gimmicks crossed my mind from previous experiences with the press. I thought of running for the door while the cameras would be set for a still shot, which would catch me in a blurring mess; but a fast camera would get a dandy shot, which could be matched to a story saying I was eager to get into prison. Maybe the caption would read, "Chuck Berry raring to seek shelter from that Mean Old World of TAXES."

I walked briskly beside the green suit, on the other side of him from the cameras. His slow pace put me in the lead to open the door that he had indicated. A sudden flash from the bushes that lined the front of the building, as I was about to enter, let me know that some photographer was a real professional. Can't win 'em all, but the bush play was dirty pool.

The green suit turned out to be the camp's assistant administrator, Mr. Allganney, who began explaining the regulations of the in-

My Lompoc Prison Camp building.

stitution to me as I was changing into the civilian clothes inmates were allowed to wear, such as jeans, black shoes, and your own underwear. I had brought $260 covering the $65 a month allowed in spending change, along with two dictionaries, seven new tablets, and my guitar. I was issued a mattress and bedding, then shown to a (or rather my) cubicle, where I was to reside for the next 120 days.

I was kidded by the guys about causing them extra detail work in window washing, hedge trimming, and mowing lawns since the staff was anticipating the press to accompany my surrender. In view of the extra work, the guys declared that I should reciprocate with some guitar playing that weekend. I conceded with the thought of it putting me in good from the start with my captivated California camp colleagues.

Compared to the unpartitioned forty-four-bunk open dormitory at my alma mater, Algoa, the cubicle-divided dormitories seemed almost hotelish. The fellows shared fifteen-by-fifteen-foot rooms, three persons to each, and each inmate had his own desk and locker. Periodically an official walked through the dormitory to count inmates. It dumbfounded me at the change of shifts to see the count taken by a female officer, which brings up another thing. The only real bother about prison, to me, is the loss of love. It was going to be a little harder to do the time with females walking around.

Most of the women had clerical or security jobs except two, a schoolteacher and a recreational administrator. There was a definite change in penal institutions since my Algoa days, both in mood and food. Fran and Yvonne had been trying to economize by eating hot dogs while I was writing home about the T-bone steaks they were serving us in the joint. No inmates need go hungry from rations in a government institution, at least not in that one.

A bell rang in the dorm and I followed the crowd to a room where names were being called off in a high-pitched voice. It was a woman with long hair and high heels calling roll. The officer had a figure that was too much for a public classroom much less a penal camp, yet the other inmates were paying little or no attention to the attraction. Some of the guys were joking with her, bringing laughter sometimes. I had just started on my sentence and was disturbed. I wondered how long some of the guys could work around that much authority and not be authentic lunatics. How could a guy love fish and yet yearn not for seafood? Mine eyes gazed on the glory as the days went dancing on.

"Berry," I heard. I answered. "Report to your case manager," she instructed. "Yes, ma'am," I acknowledged and quickly tried to gobble back the "ma'am," but the guys laughed and so did the officer, realizing I did not yet know my way around. The case manager explained my duties and place of work where I set out to rack back the 120 days of debt for the deed I'd done.

At 3 P.M. I would come in from work, get out the new tablet, and write. It was then that I seriously started writing the manuscript of this book. I planned to write four pages each day to compile four hundred pages by the time I was released. On my third day I received a clipping from the press that quoted my intention of spending my time in prison writing my book.

On the fourth day the man with the green suit told me I could play for the inmates at the Group Activity Center, the camp's recreational building. So the evening of the sixth day I played for 114 guys who seemed starved for a rock 'n' roll jam session. It was a one-man, one-guitar concert, almost like playing on a street corner for a crowd of people who couldn't cross for traffic. Three female clerical workers and two female security officers made their presence apparent and I inherited a dorm full of friends.

After being in the camp seven days, I was sent to get a physical.

C H U C K

The results made me proud of myself. Over fifty years of changes and chances, and there was little that had need of attention other than the need for some attention. The physicians found all my engines functioning properly, especially the carburetor that was ticking slow and sturdy but strongly. I weighed in at 172 pounds, stood six feet, one-half inch with no dents or scratches, had a lot of miles but a good grease job. As long as I could get a little petro now and then, I could plan on cruising in low gear for a good while yet.

I was mailing the handwritten pages of manuscript to Fran at the office, where she and Yvonne would type and proofread them and send them back. By August 25, Francine had mailed back fifty typed pages. I got to know the mailroom officer well from mailing such a quantity of mail, plus answering fan letters that I received. The fan letters mainly requested autographs, which I would sign and send collectively to Fran to distribute.

On Labor Day I graduated, I guess, and was assigned to a room shared by a chiropractor and a chess player who I never once beat. While I was there, our room was only searched once, for a coffee maker the chessman made us hot chocolate in for a fee.

The camp had a holiday, which I didn't think came in prisons. It was like the picnic on the White House lawn that I had attended just a few weeks before entering the camp. The picnic had been given in appreciation of black music, with President Jimmy Carter as host.

That day I was called upon to do a couple of guitar selections for the children of the inmates at their visiting quarters, called Sesame Street. There I tried for a few minutes to hold the attention of the five-year-olds. I tried out their opinion of "Are You Sleeping, Brother John," the only lullaby rocker that came to mind besides Christmas carols and turkey trots. It went over like a bowl of baked beans. When I finished the song they were still waiting for me to start the show. I then tried Belafonte's "Day-O." A kid asked me to sing "My Ding-A-Ling!" I sang it and one little soul brother was singing along the respondent phrases. He knew it well and encouraged the others. Before the end of the song all were singing so loud that parents were gathering around the door and windows joining in. I closed the song and the show and split with that hit.

My sleeping nights were short then, especially when I would write late and drift off into dreams that surfaced in the next writing session. Memories of my past seemed to hover over the lagoons of sleep, tracing chances to approach a possible girlfriend that I had wasted. For spirited stimulation, I often side strided and wrote purely sexual short stories, which I enjoyed while doing and let the fellows read. One fellow, exclusive of my music, came to be a fan of mine in this new field, regularly calling on my cubicle to check for any new "good stories."

I was getting along fine, with the exception of both the personnel and the fellows setting me in the typical celebrity dilemma, with different-from-normal treatment. Being an inmate, I thought like an inmate, and though I appreciated the favors that came unassociated with being celebrated, I wasn't content with favors that resulted from the image the others had of me.

I'm just me, not always doing my duck walk or picking guitar. I sit and think, cry, freak out, or just plain do nothing. Sometimes while doing the first, I've been asked, "What's wrong, Chuck?" I want to say, "You've just invaded my thoughts!" But to a person merely concerned, that would appear rude. They're serious and I suppose without thinking they don't realize that what they have always and only seen me do is but an hour of the days that make the months that compile the years of things I've done.

Sometimes at the camp, while in deep concentration, I wouldn't hear a greeting. But woe be unto a celebrity, I've found, who misses responding to a greeting—he's stuck up. However, in time most of the camp inmates mellowed down to, "Hi, Chuck" instead of, "Hello, Mr. Berry," which was the most relaxing change.

The guys had begun inquiring about the possibility of my doing another performance for the population some evening. The recreational officer, Pam Bookman, was one of the most attractive women who worked in the camp, and the only one who dressed in feminine attire. Pam had me summoned to her office at intervals regarding the paperwork for getting amplifiers and equipment brought into the camp. It had been weeks since I'd been alone around a female. I entered her office and was asked to close the door. I daresay that she did nothing whatsoever to provoke me to become aroused but while talking of no more than the arrangement of the stage, it happened. Uninvited, I took a seat at her secretary's typing desk.

I managed even less composure the second time she sent for me, because she was standing all the while we talked and seemed to realize the tension present in my speech. I was fifty-three years old, an inmate with a perfect behavior record that was close to being jeopardized should I continue to think along the lines I was thinking while back in my cubicle writing.

Each time I was summoned regarding the coming concert, my control deteriorated in her presence. Where most all the fellows that came into the office while I would be there would joke and kid with her, I was paralyzed in fear of falling out of line, not having the ability to say meaningless things or hint at things intended to convey the message of desire. For example, late one afternoon after the sun had finally burned through the smog, a guy came into her office and she casually asked him, "How does it feel outside, Robert?" He answered, "I don't know, I haven't taken it out yet." She just laughed it off. It would have taken me seven years to get that familiar, according to my dad's advice. I made it through the night but not without a rise in my anticipation to be summoned to that office again.

The day of the concert came, and I got my guitar and skipped over to the recreation building to report. One hundred forty-four guys were seated in the small assembly room with the house lights lowered, ready for me. The three accompanying musicians were in place on stage. "All those in favor of rock 'n' roll, let it be known by the usual sign: Ole!" A hell of a roar went up, "Ole!" and the show was on. With all that we had—drums, flute, harmonica, and my guitar—we struck out with "Maybellene." Feet began to stomp approval of what was going down and we followed through as best we could with what would have been a typical Chuck Berry show. We rocked until 9:45 P.M. and were counted in the cubicles at 10 P.M. with hot chocolate.

In the chapel, Monday, October 8, I was practicing on the Hammond Organ, when Jeannene White, a very likable lady who ran Sesame Street, the children's center, greeted me, "Auh-lou, Shuck" (she was French). Walking down the church aisle she explained, "Dah are no shildzen coming today. Dhey are in school, zo I am clozing deh nursery." She came up to the organ and suggested I play a song she knew that wasn't too difficult to follow as I looked into her blue eyes.

She progressed through the song as I was reminiscing through the state of France, climaxing in high-spirited harmony with the organ. It was a duet I'll never forget. Even adult French people, when speaking or singing English, sound like children. Besides loving to hear a French accent, remembering back to when Mother would sing the hymns we were attempting brought moisture to my eyes. Simultaneously Jeannene broke into tears, which then brought the assembly to an emotional end. For a while we talked of the "hows and whys" of the levels of luck in our lives and confessing the reasons for the blue and brown eyes of tears.

She told me that she had been orphaned as a child and, just as I'd been reminiscing, she was having memories of the spiritual environment she was brought up in. We sang again; the title fails my memory but the words I remember: "If I have wounded any soul today/If I have caused one foot to go astray/If I have gone in my own willful way/Dear Lord forgive." My eyes were flowing with forgiving tears at that moment, wondering what my mother was going through as she worried about my welfare in prison. We stopped singing, her head bowed, our hands found each holding the other momentarily, and she left the chapel without a word spoken.

I truly believe a state of love existed from the spirit generated during those few moments we lived together in perfect harmony. I'll never forget.

Francine and Yvonne flew out to visit me and finally got to see the place to which they'd mailed so many pages of this manuscript. Prior to then I had thought it dumb to have any folks come all the way from Missouri to visit when I was handling the 120 days so well. I told Fran when they arrived, "Well! So you've come to see the boss in his federal retreat." I thought, what's to visiting? Hour after hour, people just walked around the floor doing nothing once the news from home was exchanged. Walking you over the floor is almost as nerve-racking as walking the floor over you! So I sent them into Sesame Street, after a bit, to visit Jeannene. I was summoned after a few minutes and, Behold!

As I entered, I crashed a surprise birthday party for me with a

Outside Lompoc. My bassist, Jimmy Marsala, holds open the door of my Cadillac, which he brought up for my release.

guitar-shaped cake that had icing strings attached and was centered on a table with everyone around it singing "Happy Birthday." The few extra minutes that I thought Francine and Yvonne had spent visiting the rest room, actually were spent finalizing Jeannene's own surprise (bless her *voulez vous* heart) in Sesame Street. I cut the cake under a bombardment of flashing bulbs while Fran helped serve ice cream and the party was on.

October 24, at 1:30 P.M. I stopped smoking (for twenty-two days to be exact) and suffered like a dog with nothing to do during the intervals habitually enjoyed with a light-up. During that smoke-out I began to notice smokers and their manner in handling their cigarettes, the unconscious flipping of ashes here and there and what things were happening at the instant they were prompted to reach for one. I had quit "cold turkey" twice before, but this time no empty-stomach feeling followed, just boredom. I started smoking Lucky Strike (Greens) at fourteen, eleven cents a pack, and stopped for twenty-one days the first time at age forty-eight, then stopped again for twenty-four days when I was forty-nine. My present landlord (the government) warned me that cigarette smoking was dangerous to my health yet they offered the cancer-sticks

free in the joint. May I enjoy another thirty-four years (grandpa's example) of smoking and you not touch another smoke as long as you live!

October 29, 1979, was my thirty-first wedding anniversary and I stood in line to call home to the first and only lady, wife, and mother to my children.

Dick Alen visited and I informed him that the first draft of my book was finished and that I was scheduled to be released on November 23, 1979. It was then Saturday, November 10, and the 'morrow was scheduled for a farewell concert with a visiting Los Angeles group, Peter Gun. We were to play on a bandstand outdoors near the visitor area. We nicknamed the small stand the Penal Bowl.

That Sunday, a line of inmates, triple deep along the redwood fence that separated the visitors' area from the inmate yard, watched the first musical concert there in years. I opened the show with "Roll Over Beethoven." Officer Bookman came and sat beside me before the entire staff, visitors, and inmate population during the visiting band's performance. Had she had the ability to read my mind as we watched the Peter Gun band performing, she would have felt far more uncomfortable than she seemed—maybe just the opposite. The last selection was a song entitled "Big Ten

Inch" and, during the course of the song, Officer Bookman leaned over and asked me, "What are they saying, 'ten inch'?" I answered, "Yes! Do you remember it? It was pretty big a while back." She said, "I know, but it seems they'd have better taste than to play that here." I didn't touch that.

I was nearly a total wreck from the close association with Pam Bookman by the time my last day of the stay came around. By this time I had been allowed to do most of my writing in her office on the typewriter. She was fond of chestnuts and kept a setup to make hot tea that she would share with me. The closest I came to joking with her as the other fellows constantly did was once when I managed to ask, "Do you want me to crack some of your nuts today, Mrs. Bookman?" She only laughed as she did with all the others.

On the last day, as I was turning in my GI bedding and articles and clearing papers for my release, Jeannene offered to bring my car from the little Lompoc Airport parking lot where my bassist, Jim Marsala, had brought it and left it for me the day before. During some hours of the last day, there were moments I actually didn't want to leave. Thirty-six minutes after noon on Monday, November 19, 1979, I was set free for the third time, right at seventeen years apart. My next fall is due around year end of 1996, so I have a while yet.

Driving down U.S. Highway 101 alone, I had to stop and fill my tank with petrol. Somebody recognized me in the filling station and spoke. I wondered if they had any idea I had just left prison less than an hour before.

When I reached Los Angeles and turned off the freeway the sunset was streaming down Hollywood Boulevard. I rolled uphill to my office and called it a day. While setting my business in order, I realized I was truly free, and ten minutes after midnight I was lifted up into the clouds over Los Angeles flying back to my home in St. Louis.

Since Then

A fter my release in the winter of 1979, I had to brace for the cold shoulder some of the press was giving me. But I was back on the road and doing my thing.

Since Lompoc, I have performed 334 concerts within the U.S. and I guess about two dozen more benefits that went with my release requirements. I was obliged by the courts to perform community service to fulfill my parole, which took me on December 7 to Santa Maria, California, to play a benefit concert. After some of the media printed this requirement was unfavorable and trucker was calling Fran to book me at their benefit. The album *Rock It,* which I had recorded at Atco of Atlantic Records, was my latest release, which came slowly out while I was "in" and was trickling along in the record shops. I had a songbook with a couple dozen piano selections that hit the market just before Christmas, and it didn't seem too bad starting out again.

Within weeks from the turn of 1980 I purchased a Xerox 850 Page Display Word Processor in L.A. and spent much time in my Hollywood place compiling the manuscript I had begun in Lompoc. The model changed immediately, and so did I, to their new 860 model. The typing course I had completed in Springfield was a

great advantage to me in creating the stories that helped build the chapters that make up the book.

Between working on "the Book," as we came to call the project that it turned out to be, I added to Berry Park, putting more asphalt roads through the wooded area. That area has now been developed into picnic grounds by pruning the many black oak, silver leaf maple, and cottonwood trees. I must admit that administering these improvements carried my soul back to Lompoc, when I would sit across the road within the complex and reminisce about the many foreign places I had been and wonder if I would have the chance to return to the music world and perform on stage as I had been doing for so long.

People seem to feel, when they don't see me on television often, that I have stopped performing or retired. When I'm asked whether I have, I only smile and say, "Never, I couldn't do that." In fact I shy away from television because it has always seemed so restrictive to me. It locks the performance into a schedule, usually with stock music, and leaves no room for the innovation and spontaneous inventive creation which, to me, are the main glory in the thrill of performing.

If it wasn't for the feeling I get while performing, I think it would have been impossible for me to have continued as long as I have. It is also difficult for me to conceive what on earth people see in my act that has caused it to linger as long as it has. So far as the scoot (as opposed to the "duck walk"), if there ever was anything that I have been branded with, that is it. Why it seems to be liked so much will always be beyond my conception, since anybody could and many guys have copied the scoot on stage.

In July of 1980, my mother passed on, leaving my dad with the five of us. Since then Yvonne's father in February 1981, Fran's father in June of 1982, Yvonne's mother in June of 1985, and Fran's mother in October of 1986 have passed.

In November of 1980, I played South America for the first time, in Santiago, Chile, then Manila in April of 1981 and on to Nagoya, Osaka, and Tokyo, Japan.

The same month I jumped off a roof that my brother Paul and I had just repaired and gave myself a herniated disk requiring traction and seven days in the hospital, my first stay since my circumcision back with Alma. Oy vey! While suffering with the pain, I

Intermission with Bob Hope and Johnny Cash backstage at Billy Bob's in Fort Worth, December 1981.

completed an engagement in the Chicago Hyatt Regency that was booked prior to the injury. The employer (a radio DJ convention) pleaded for me to come, if at all possible, even if I could just sit and sing a couple of selections. The DJs and patrons were so amiably considerate that, in spite of my condition, I left the barstool they had placed for me to perform on and had the audacity to try to do my duck walk. After two steps, I had to stop and ease back up to a standing position to finish "Maybellene." I shall never in life forget the standing ovation I received for the feeble two steps I did manage, which strengthened my courage to complete the forty-five-minute set.

Also since Lompoc, all three of my daughters have welcomed me with the sum of four more grandchildren, which now brings me to father a grand total of ten huckleberries from the Berrybush of four that Toddy and I have rooted.

CHUCK

In December of '81, I had the distinct honor of playing on the same bill with someone I consider a star. Like I once heard the comedian Clay Tyson say as he came on stage at the Howard Theater in Washington, D.C., "Y'all don't have to clap, I'm just the moon; the star's waitin' to come on." I still consider the heavies, like Davis, Gable, Crawford, Burton, Taylor, Bogart, and Hepburn as stars whereas the Dominos, Joplins, Presleys, Richards, Lynns, Jacksons, and Mandrells, as well as the Berrys and Ronstadts and Diddleys, are all moons and satellites so far as I'm concerned. In other words the first category of artist will go down in the history books of even Russia, China, and Arabia—where we moons might circle a few years in the foreign magazines and then fade away in the next conventional war. Oh! By the way, the star I was on a bill with was Mr. Bob Hope, New Year's Eve, 1981.

March 1982, I did the film *Class Reunion,* and in October '82, Fran arranged another big surprise birthday party for me. She naughtily invited all the females that she thought I admired, and I was swamped and had to stay on stage playing nearly all the evening. Her success with the fest was at an all-time high but my liberty with the guests was at an all-time low.

I have to admit, simply because I can't deny it, I've had a lazy feeling come over me since '83 that has caused me to care much less for anything beyond actually performing on stage and creating lyrics. Well, among other things, I'll go into my next book. I've decided that after writing the book I must get out and stir more than I needed to when I was busy building the Park. It's typical for a man to get fat and forty, well fat at least for me, sitting around a desk getting blobby. I don't jog or play golf or do much else other than maintain my manhood, nowadays. I'm not treating myself properly.

In 1984 and '85 I went to Budapest for the first time, where the kids and adults came with tickets or rather government coupons that allowed them admission to the concert. During the performance I couldn't tell the difference from being in Miami or Denver so far as them singing along and applauding at highlights of the show. Since then, with the taking of hostages and terrorism that have spread through Europe, I have declined any engagements abroad.

January 23, 1986, I was inducted into the Rock 'n' Roll Hall of

*Between two heavies: Ahmet Ertegun and Keith Richards
at the Rock 'n' Roll Hall of Fame induction ceremony.*

Fame, although I remember Ella Fitzgerald presenting me an award for a Rock 'n' Roll Hall of Fame at the Santa Monica Civic Auditorium, August 9, 1975. Since then I was inducted into the Songwriters Hall of Fame and "Johnny B. Goode" was hauled off on the famed *Voyager 1,* past Jupiter and Saturn and on his way toward Neptune, some four billion miles away, thanks to Dr. Carl Sagan.

Also in January '86, I went to New York to survey the prospect of doing a video production and was introduced by Bill Krasilovsky to Stephanie Bennett of Delilah Films. During a concert at the Lone Star Café on February 23, Ms. Bennett came and discussed in detail the making of a video celebrating Chuck Berry's music.

A moment with Marvin Hamlisch
at the Hall of Fame induction.

jected we came to an agreement.

Before we got far, we merged the video musical production agreement into a full-length motion-picture contract for over double the fee and proceeded to arrange for the concert that was to be the apex of the movie. It was decided that we would shoot the concert in my hometown at the Fabulous Fox Theater, just a city block from where I had tried to break the black-and-white ice in 1959 by running my "mixed" nightclub, Club Bandstand.

After much filming of Berry Park, of my father at home in St. Louis, of the Cosmo Club in East St. Louis, and interviews at the airport as well as during flights, the concert came off on my sixtieth

CHUCK

*Keith Richards adding Jagger riffs
to "Johnny B. Goode," Chicago, June 6, 1986.*

birthday, October 18, 1986. To the amazement of most, I guess, it sold out in hours nearly two weeks prior to the night it was scheduled. The first show alone was over three hours long, what with the stopping and starting for loading cameras and explanatory breaks. The second show that was added after the first sold out lasted over two hours and was said by many to be the most enjoyed although I was nearly pooped when it began.

February 17, 1987, I went again to the Big Apple to do some dubbing and looping for the final editing of the film, which is to be called *Hail! Hail! Rock 'n' Roll*. While there I was given an award at the City Hall honoring my musical contributions and in support of efforts to combat sickle cell anemia. I also sat for a photo session for the cover of this book and finally, that evening, met over dinner with my book publishers.

After eight years, I am finally pecking away at the last chapters of this book. Now that I know much more about the writing of a book, strangely enough I intend to go for another. One that I will enjoy, the true story of my sex life. It shall not infringe on anyone or thing but me and my excessive desire to continue melting the ice of American hypocrisy regarding behavior and beliefs that are now "in the closet" and only surface in court, crime, or comical conversation.

Another book, the companion to this one, will be a songbook, complete with the dates and data of all my songs and concerts as well as Fran has kept them throughout the years.

It's Saturday, February 28, 1987. This morning my father passed and just yesterday I looked into his sleeping eyelids as I visited my sister Thelma. A ninety-one-year-old companion is not an easy pal to lose but his teachings shall be practiced long during his rest until he is joined by his offspring. I was surprised to be reminded that my father left a sister-in-law, a cousin, plus a battalion of two daughters, three daughters-in-law, three sons, one son-in-law, twenty-three grandchildren, and thirty-eight great grandchildren. When told he had passed, my only thought was, say hello to Mom.

Heroes and No-Nos

A t sixty years of age a guy has had time enough to decide whether he likes or dislikes a particular thing. I'm right at the halfway point in my life, so I'm taking the liberty to let all my dos and don'ts hang out.

First of all, I do not like liver. It dries my throat and feels and tastes like a mixture of cardboard and sour-pickle patties. I don't get near okra or gumbo because it's just the opposite, slimy and gooey; I can't even hold it in my mouth, let alone swallow it. At a point of starving I'd eat celery, carrots, cooked onions, eggplant, grapefruit, or salami, but only as survival nutrition. I'd rather my taste buds suffer than my heartbeat flutter.

I especially have a taste for pork though I'm not too fond of hog jowls or chitlins; I enjoy beef as in T-bone steak or stew, but absolutely no brains, tongue, and all that. I like fillet of catfish and salmon best of all freshwater fish, sweet and pungent shrimps of sea foods. Peaches are my favorite of all fruits; home fries and/or candied yams of vegetables; soupy chili of all bowl portions; date- or apple-filled oatmeal cookies of the cookie kingdom; ''pea'' in the nut field; raspberry in preserves (never jelly) and grape in soda pop. The only sandwiches I care for are egg and bacon on lightly toasted bread or apple butter thickly spread on lightly toasted white bread. I like Butternut or Snickers in candy bars; pineapple in fruit juices; and I drink orange juice all the time, anytime. White sliced French bread, soft vanilla pound cakes, and Dutch apple pie are especially good for treats at any hour of the day. For hot cereals it's oatmeal and for cold cereals it's corn flakes with a very ripe banana. I prefer fried (fresh) rabbit over chicken, duck, or turkey. To finish off things I like assorted mints, Colgate toothpaste, and well water. Darn, I'm getting hungry.

Aroma! The scent of burning oak leaves in October in Missouri. Next, and following respectively, would be an oncoming breeze laden with the smell of mint plants, a Chinese restaurant while waiting in line for a table, a passing pipe smoker using rum-and-maple tobacco, the uncontaminated breasts of a female companion, the brewing of coffee in the winter, the interior of a new automobile I just purchased, and, although I detest the smell of liquor, somehow I'm carried asunder by the surprise of liquor on the breath of a strange lady.

What really turns me on now is recalling an experience that has greatly stimulated me. Reviewing thoughts is nearly as intense as the physical effect of the reality. I also like the period of the approach of a pleasant experience and the triumphant solving of a problem through strategical effort. I greatly enjoy (but have yet to master this totally) the quelling or subsiding of a physical discomfort or psychological depression through concentration. I like to play music, softball, twenty questions, chess, croquet, house, and around. I like highway driving especially with a companion. I crave the feeling that I get from a performance when I hear the response of one or more to that which I have delivered. The greatest highs I've ever had in life have come from a mob of as many as sixty-two thousand voices, and also from the moan of one.

Over the years I have had plenty of opportunities to study the various manners in which people approach me to ask for an autograph. The most exciting ones to me are southern white children who obviously are sent by their parents. No doubt the innocent child has been trained in historical southern attitudes toward race relations but now, through the "encouragement" of his parents, is being confronted with approaching a black man. Peering nearly toward the floor the child in speechless silence holds out a pencil and a piece of paper. I wait. I realize I shouldn't blame the kid for not having the courage or talent to handle the situation. I give in and ask if he wants something. Scared stiff and looking to his parents for advice and help, the kid doesn't speak until I ask if his parents sent him over. I ask him to point to his mother and father. Without hesitation he does. The child and I then approach the parents, where I confirm his (their) wants and give the autograph. The parents seemingly rationalize that I am "one of them good ol' boys" and then thank me, telling me how the child loves my music. The poor kid is practically under his mother's skirt.

Then there's the shrewd hometown dignitary who comes up face-to-face with me, silently looks directly into my eyes for fifteen seconds, then with a smile asks, "Don't I know you?" which is a question no one can answer but him. But most uncouth of all approaches is when a person hands me a pen and a piece of paper, then says nothing and waits. Once I tried to wait it out and the guy picked up his pen and paper and excused himself declaring, "Oh —I thought you were Chuck Berry."

When people recognize me I can tell how rapidly the realization is progressing. After seeing so many kinds of responses I have learned to handle many different circumstances. For instance, someone walks along; he thinks he recognizes me; his recollection is evolving; then it develops until he is somewhat confident of my identity. I try to confirm his conclusion by raising my eyebrows and smiling. One time I wiggled my eyebrows too late and it was taken as a fresh gesture by a lady who immediately wiped her smile off. Sometimes I give a courteous nod of my head when an on looker has recognized me without hesitation. There are people who voice their spying of me loud enough to reach my ear as I pass them, communicating their discovery to a companion: "Isn't that Chuck Berry? Yes it is. Naw. YEAH, IT IS!" Sometimes the other will say, "Go ask him." "Are you crazy? You ask." If I'm walking, standing, or waiting in line I give them a smile and nod.

I have found that as a result of my exposure in photos, television appearances, and the couple of movies I've done, I can't be just another guy on the street, not even in places as far away as Berlin, Glasgow, or small-town U.S.A. I can swallow almost any ap-

CHUCK

proach when I'm recognized except when it's too lengthy, such as when a guy starts out, "Are you Chuck Berry?" and I reply yes. He then gets real informative, forgetting that I have many things on my mind and I don't know him from Adam, saying "I saw you at . . . I grew up on your . . . I wrote some songs . . . I have a group that . . . and I was wondering if you would" etc.

When a drunk comes up and asks me my name, I say, "What do you think it is?" He answers, "Are you Chuck Berry?" I reply, "Yes." He starts then, "Do you remember me?" I say, "Yes, how are you?" He says, "Fine. Well, what's my name, though?" I really don't remember the guy or girl and I've already lied and now I'm cornered. So if they're not very drunk, I'll apologize, but if they are real drunk, I make a scary face and walk away.

They have no right to pump me for memory when most times I only shook hands with them or spoke briefly at a party. This sort of thing has happened all through each week of my career.

In 1971, the great John Lennon mentioned once that I was his hero. This was one of the most stimulating statements that had ever been bestowed upon me. On my forty-fifth birthday, the only time we stood side by side performing together the music we both loved so well, though sixteen years apart in age, we stood sixteen inches apart sharing the lyrics of "Johnny B. Goode." I believe somehow in heaven, he now reviews those moments with Yoko and Chuck in Philadelphia doing the Mike Douglas show. Oh yes! he was the hero of the whole show in Toronto with Yoko at Varsity Stadium when he raised his hand, holding it up more than sixty seconds under the cry of well over sixty thousand fans in plea for cessation of the applause so he could begin his performance.

As I sat in prison for a no-no seed I sowed, I thought of the manner in which we lost Dr. Martin Luther King and John F. Kennedy; but I never would have dreamed that music would lose Lennon's genius in the same manner. Tell Yoko you love his music, for in this world of today, what more can be done but to declare to Yoko his place with the Heroes. Janis Joplin, Jimi Hendrix, Clyde McPhatter, Elvis Presley, and others we lost from a cause unlike John, were heroes in relation to rock music but were proven wrong in taking too strong and rolling too long.

The Palladium in Hollywood was jam-packed for a 1972 concert. The wings of the stage were loaded with music lovers. Some of the music that I jitterbugged to in my school days was being sung by the artists who first made the records. When they would finish, coming offstage hot and sweaty, I'd be standing there to congratulate them. Of all people to drop in, T-Bone Walker, a favorite guitarist/blues singer of my own teen-tone-tune-time, was walking around backstage. Later Mr. Blues himself walked by my door, and I shouted for him to pause a second and drop in. I wanted to personally pay my respects as some have paid them to me. It was Big Joe Turner, the first to "Shake, Rattle and Roll" in "Chains of Love" with "Wee Baby Blues."

A flashback to a May-day in his heyday during 1943 when he was appearing one night at The Rum Boogie nightclub in Chicago on 55th and South Parkway (now Dr. Martin L. King Drive). I climbed up to a window of the club where I saw and heard him sing "Rock Around the Clock," a tune Bill Haley copied ten years later.

Big Joe Turner walked in saying, "Hello, Chuck," as if we'd met many times before. I embraced him heartily, for it was now I who was overthrilled and speechless while meeting "one of my heroes."

Big Joe's incredible belting of the blues had me climbing the walls as it had done some thirty years earlier. I followed Joe's performance with my four-piece studio group. About midway through my show another musician appeared on stage and exchanged places with the guy on guitar. All was well, the more the merrier. It was getting too loud but going good until the sound man working the stage monitor turned the guitar up even more, causing him to miss the breaks in the song. After I had signaled twice for him to mellow down, I terminated the selection, turned, and asked for my guitarist to return to the stage.

There came a murmured "Aw!" from the audience as they realized the guy sitting in was leaving, but the show continued on to a festive climax and closed with a standing ovation. It was not until I reached the dressing room that Francine whispered to me, "Do you know who that was on stage?" "No. Who?" She said, "You just put the Rolling Stones guys off stage!" "Aw shit." I went straight away to try and retrieve them or make some sort of an excuse and get them back for an encore or something. In sheer trauma I searched backstage with the ovation from the audience still yelling for more. It was Keith Richards playing guitar, and other members of the Stones were waiting to come on, but, to my sorrow, they had immediately left. Since then, I have never invited anyone off the stage without asking (if I don't recognize him) who he is.

The Stones, Keith and Jagger especially, have mentioned being Chuck Berry music fans as well as I have mentioned being a Stones fan, but many articles have been written about that night. Let it be known that if I had known it was them playing on my set, loud or not loud, I surely would have let my audience tolerate the nobility.

I have always found awards shows comfortable to be a part of, in that they're comprised primarily of show people in a similar category. On August 9, 1977, I participated in a rock awards show in Santa Monica, California. I was running around meeting artists I hadn't met before, mainly to see if they were just as I'd assumed them to be. I was standing in the wings of the stage when I looked around to discover Dolly Parton was observing the rehearsal progression just behind me. She greeted me and I returned the greeting with surprise. She started to say, "I want to speak . . ." but was interrupted by her aide summoning her onstage. The suspense of what was to follow is well and alive yet today, having lived through *Nine to Five* and other views of her on TV.

The same memory lingers from an awards show at the Palladium, where everybody was milling around and meeting and drinking with each other. In the middle of the auditorium, I was introduced to Loretta Lynn by someone with her. I was stunned when Loretta immediately turned to face me and planted a two-lipped kiss on me. It didn't strike me as unusual upon meetings between show people, but still she was a southern white woman such as my father had laid a lifeline of caution against. The smacker straight away swept my memory back in time to Mrs. Cockrell beckoning me to dance with her at Algoa when my dad's training was still ringing in every note of the music. Loretta will never know the software of that kiss or the double density of the program that it stored in the document of my main memory.

On September 4, 1975, I made an appearance on "The Sammy Davis Show" with my favorite female comedian, Lucille Ball, as the guest star. After I was announced and did my selection, I walked over to Sammy, surprised that he was not as tall as I thought, and picked him up in my arms. He immediately yelled, "Put me down! Are you funny or something?" I thought I was pulling off a laughable fatherly gesture, and it did get a laugh from the audience—unfortunately not from my gesture but from Sammy's plea. I walked over to the talk-chair seating and sat beside Lucille Ball, reached for her and held her hand through the talk portion of the set. She has been my idol since "I Love Lucy" first hit the TV tubes. I knew I'd never have the chance again and I took the liberty to squeeze her hand, which she either ignored or forgave my stupidity for, because she never even blinked either of those beautiful aqua eyes. Forgive me Gary (and Desi), I love Lucy as well.

Any word read or heard only conveys the meaning that is available to the person reading or hearing it from his individual understanding of that word. This meaning is based on the values that his entire life's experiences have brought to that word up to that instant. But his understanding of that word could immediately be altered to a different conception from that hearing or even during the very next phrase heard.

With that in mind, it is easy to believe that no word could possibly register precisely the same meaning in any two individuals whose lives have not consisted of identical experiences, which is impossible. Although two people's different conceptions of a single word can register as an extremely minute variation in the understanding of those two people, most communications are made up of many words, each of which is understood uniquely by each person. The number of words that are to be heard or read multiplies the complexity of the message and therefore greatly diminishes the probability of identical conceptions being reached by two different minds.

So a letter of the alphabet is most likely to convey the same thought pattern to a great many, not all, persons. A word will have less chance to convey the same meaning because it first must rely on the exact conception of each letter within. A phrase or surely a sentence read or heard into two different minds, is at great risk of not creating precisely the same understanding. It is realized that only in extremely critical circumstances such as contracts or intricate mathematics, where a great deal of value depends on exact analysis, must such a message be so precisely conceived. The greater the gain or the larger the potential loss, the more pertinent it is that precision should prevail.

Such perfection has long been achieved with numbers and fairly so with alphabets but poorly yet with symbols or words, and surely not with phrases. As for sentences and paragraphs, let alone stories or books, it is not unlikely that any two individuals reading the same page of a script come away with entirely different conceptions. But then how and why should it be proven, unless huge benefits or enormous losses depend on the analysis?

Thus as you read this book, remember, it may not necessarily be what my thoughts were because I, as well as you, cannot be sure I've written a precise account of what dwells in my memory. So what is seen, felt, or thought cannot possibly be transferred to another without a difference born from the journey.

As far as society has come with language, this way of corresponding is the best way so far to communicate. Just remember, my accounts of actions I've experienced are the fourth generation of communication. First, it happened; second, I conceived what happened; third, I reproduced what I conceived; and fourth, you will conceive what I have reproduced. My created songs, like my opinions, come to you only in the third generation because they were not delivered from a foreign source into my conception but were born in my concept.

I shall not believe that any words I've used to depict my thoughts will be conceived by you in the identical context of those in my thoughts, but only hope they will be found as intended. What more is imagination but that which flows into consciousness from where we do not seem to conceive? A thought from within is like a chip on a stream or like a straw in the wind, like a vaguely known dream. Where do they come from?

In the early years of my career, I used to tell everything in interviews. When I started being interviewed after my first hits in the fifties, I took it for granted that I would be quoted exactly as I had spoken. In answering a question I gave information freely, while staying with the facts. Seeing the results later I soon learned that interviewers would add an opinion or description that would give the quote an entirely different meaning. They would alter my remarks by creating new phrases that changed my meaning or they would insert comments that would imply another slant on what I said.

My desire to be interviewed dwindled over the years as I would read back what I was supposed to have said to reporters. The changes and alterations I detected in reviewing the articles were sometimes better than I could have said it and other times worse, sometimes with southern dialect added. Francine has several extensive interviews printed by magazines like *Rolling Stone, Gallery,* and the *Village Voice,* that have all chosen to insert quotes that have yet to be said by me. Also, some of the quotes I did say were rendered in dialect to stereotype black speech. Yet in another part of the same piece would be a mention of my distinct diction!

Then I thought it smart to let journalists record what I would say so that it couldn't then be mistaken in the article. But a few of these recordings started coming back edited, sometimes with the interviewer inserting questions unlike the original ones I answered. I've heard radio interviews, which I had simultaneously recorded with my pocket recorder, replayed after being edited. The edited interview was altered to the extent that some of the questions that were later (in the editing room) inserted around the original answers (I gave to different questions) were replies to a subject never raised originally!

It's like taking the head from one photo and fitting it to the body of another. Then who is who? Neither is real or true. That is my opinion of interviews (recorded ones) that are all edited.

TV interview. Okay. Beautiful and live, also a challenge of wits between the "ask" and the "shall be given," plus people can form their own opinion of the truth, whether they want it or not, from visual expressions and so forth.

Seeing how all this was done, I revamped my shrewdness and only allowed visual-sound consultations that were too costly to conduct for just the audio and thus likely not to be edited. I saw to it that they wouldn't edit it by waving my hand before my face while answering questions to make it too obvious if they cut the scene to insert or omit anything.

Interviews that are taken down in notes or written from memory are less real than taped ones because if quotes are not taken down word for word, they are reconstructed under the influence of the writer's opinions. But again, it must be that some people don't know or even care about the truth or what is real anymore. If that be so, why do journalists bother to seek interviews at all, particularly nonrecorded ones? The interviewer could do his thing on it anyway, and usually does. I know many who did and for a long while this caused me to renounce interviewing. I told them that I was not interested in dramatics, only music, and I wrote my own.

The rejection of interviews prompted the reputation that I was negative to them and interviewers. The rumor spread quickly throughout the business. Reporters would come to the dressing room of a concert and start their salutations with, "Hi, Chuck, I know you don't like to interview, but . . ." I would try to explain to them what I'd learned about habits they followed. They would declare they were not like that and if I would just answer a few questions, they'd be satisfied. Sometimes I would yield, then later, when reading the clipping, the same ol' sheet would be hitting the fan club.

Sometimes the questions asked were routine and could hardly be answered with new or exciting information. In such cases, with my answers being quite similar to those in previous interviews, the writer would juice up the story, likely under pressure of his superiors. Actions and comments would be described that I'd never done in habit. As a result I limited myself to the same repetitious material. These similar stories published about "Chuck Berry" were not satisfying to the more professional interviewers whom I'd begun to recognize by then. Consequently, the pros pressed for new data that I freely came forth with, due to their respect and consideration. The student reporters and small-town reporters were mainly interested in returning with something different on Chuck Berry. They in turn sought juicy stuff on the personal side like controversies, the jail sentences, marriage versus divorce, and would welcome anything on the kinky side pertaining to just what made the man tick. These little interviewers seemed not to care

Ingrid Berry Clay.

about the manner in which they obtained their story as long as they could get some point or statement to launch their preplanned ingredients.

Interviewers have asked me questions on topics I could not for the love of Jesus connect with music. They want details on my hobbies, fantasies, frolics, foods, measurements, father, and family. Other than discussing my daughter Ingrid's activities in the music field, I wonder why would anyone want to know I am married with a total of four children and have tinkered around with a hundred thousand dollars' worth of video. Why would they be interested in finding out I have had a desire since childhood to be a houseboy on a southern plantation, preferably during the Civil War? (Don't ask me why.) Why would they want to know I am an ardent girl watcher? That I love the taste of chili, strawberries, and oranges, wear a size 42 jacket, 32/34 trousers, and in terms of best or preferred, have no favorite songs or artists? Do they need to be informed of my everlasting underwear to maintain an interest in the music I have created?

There were times when the press was so determined to get something on my incarceration background to add to and/or distort, that at first I merely mummed up about it. Later I began to request that they refrain from digging for information about it because it did not involve music.

My desire to write an autobiography originated during the early sixties when, to my surprise, the reform-school episode of fifteen and a half years back was elaborated on more abundantly than the allegations I was then confronting. I knew it was I who had to write it if the truth was ever to be known.

As time went by the press often saw need to bring up the misfortunes I endured during my career. Time after time the teenage reform-school bit was used in closing an article, be it for blame or acclaim. Their desire to write (and readers' desire to read) of the heartaches of others, especially celebrities, confirmed to me that bad news travels first class where good news must take the dirt road. Let me live in a house by the side of that road and be a friend to good news. Sometimes I wonder whether the facts straight from the horse's mouth are as winning, on the track of entertainment, as the fantasies constructed by the media in their race for advancement.

I suppose it is up to a reporter to use his skills to construct a product that is sympathetically observed or somewhat ridiculous to make a story interesting, humorous, or even hysterical. Assuming this is the case, it seems most American readers enjoy the most entertaining stories, even if they pervert the truth. Such dramatized and twisted versions frequently outsell the facts. The more prominent the individual, the more spectacular the fabrications. Whereas if the subject is a nobody, there is little interest. As long as the writer stays within set legal boundaries his interpretation is accepted.

For myself, I admire the person who can create these fantasies. But I admire even more those who do not believe everything they see or hear in the media. For those with the intelligence to take it as entertainment, it is cheaper than a movie or recording. My advice for the ambitious person is not to use only the media for information. Even if it is leather-bound and gilt-edged, the contents of the book can still be invalid. I'll likely be quoted by the media as saying, ''Honor thy column and thy by-line that thy analysis be equal to the lovely load of litter laid before thee.'' Then employees of the media may say, ''Our Media, whose art we offer, hallowed be our message; the daily post shall prove as close to truth as it does to drama.'' So be wary of the media is what I'm stressing. Thank God it isn't just one person.

I cannot remember all the things that bother me about the press. But a lack of true values is my biggest complaint. And God knows I have suffered less than many other public figures from the exploitations of the media.

This very book of my own true writing will no doubt be partially rewritten when reviewers and critics again inject their personal opinions, thus altering my trend of thought as an adjective changes the following noun. As I have reviewed the press, so the press has the right to review me. So be it.

Just as it bothers me to be overpraised or condemned, it annoys me to be misunderstood, which is a problem when interviewers ask me a question that I feel no one person can answer. For example, ''Where is the music fad going in the future?'' or ''Is the audience the same as they were back in the fifties, more or less?'' Both questions have been asked more than a half dozen times by reputable reporters. The first thing that hits me (about the first question) is "where is where?" since music is only heard every-place, even in space. If I answered only in ears, it would be rudely stinky but rightly stated. The next thing is how in the hell do I know about the future! Even if I had some experience in predic-tions, what right (truly) do I have to forward my (one person's) opinion to the many (maybe easily indoctrinatable) people who rely on what a person says just because they may cherish or wor-ship him in another capacity? As for the second question, the fifties were ten years long, which makes the summary of audiences com-putationally complex—yet the question was asked. And which group of people, where, and when is "the audience," who are never the same even on the same night of two shows? My response was "Oh, about the same."

I have been asked in many interviews, "Why don't you have your own band?" Well, the reasons are few but potent. To start with I did have; Johnnie Johnson on piano, Ebby Hardy on drums, and myself from my first recording, "Maybellene." Then I went to five pieces, adding Alvin Bennett on bass and Leroy Davis on tenor sax. But drinks and drugs were never my bag, nor were they an excuse for affecting the quality of playing so far as I was con-cerned. A few ridiculous performances, several amendments to our band regulations, and the band broke up, never to be recon-structed. Whenever I've assembled other groups and played road dates, similar conditions have prevailed.

More than once I have had the intention of again forming a group of top-notch musicians with female singers, including my daughter Ingrid, for another score to my multigenerations of fans. I know I shall do so soon, as Ingrid is persuading me vigorously to hang in there and sock it to 'em.

Interviewers often ask why I do not rehearse with a group that is to play behind me at a concert. I do rehearse sometimes, but not nearly as often as I don't. When I do it is because I've not played before with that particular group, I have not heard them play, or I have a program of lesser known tunes planned that evening. I don't rehearse if the group has played for me before, if I know they are competent musicians (studio bands, jazz groups, or artists them-selves), or if I've heard them do my tunes many times before.

Encores also come up as an issue during some interviews. Often one is expected either because of the tradition of the place or

*Ingrid and me on stage
under the Arch in St. Louis.*

because the promoter has misstated the length of the performance
and hopes to have it extended with the performer doing encores.
Most artists work forty-five minutes to an hour on stage, giving an
encore mostly if their popularity could use the recognition or to
encourage a return date. The more stable artists I guess sometimes
do it merely for the pleasure of a responsive audience.

My contract specifies the time of each performance as forty-five

minutes with or without an encore. More times than not I go over-time and come off without doing an encore. Ninety percent of my performances carry over to an hour and some have been two hours. Usually the audience becomes enthused near the climax and responds for more at closing.

The reality of an encore by me rests entirely on my condition after exiting. I get so enthralled at the high vibes that exist in the latter moments of my act that I exert unpossessed energy and my fatigue is unnoticed until exiting. How I feel then determines whether I return for more action or even a bow.

Repeatedly some writers claim that I have a bitter attitude about this or that, but mainly toward the circumstances and verdict of the Indian girl case. The conclusion is drawn that my state of mind is uncontrollable. And yet I finished my time at the Medical Center with several diplomas and the information to administer two of my corporations, whose potential I had not previously recognized. Another story rehashed a few times stated that my marriage was ruined. I have now been married thirty-five years with no separation or divorce.

When I progress to the point where I can write as well as a professional journalist I'll try for a second book that might not be all facts, but won't be written at the expense of an individual or group or of the truth. Until then, I hope for the sake of those in the writing business who missed an interview that this book answers your missing questions. Love ya.

CHUCK

What Now?

L ife must go on. Sixty years have gone by and I'm feeling fine. No words can describe how fortunate I believe I am to be (as I will put it) still kicking.

I must admit the first thing I want to do as soon as this eight-year-ol' book is published is to go somewhere for a vacation and the locations that are the most interesting to me are Hong Kong and South Africa. Why the latter I'll never admit but maybe the heat will settle to a mild toast soon. Anyway, since I've pretty much seen the world, I want to live in some places that have intrigued me most. Maybe my father's teachings will become essential in the south of Africa while in Hong Kong they'll be least necessary.

I've written a book and have only read six hardbacks, in full, throughout my life. Paperbacks by the dozens but only for stimulation. Now I'll have time to really find out how I am because I'm going to watch you and other people for the rest of my life. That's the only way, I believe, to know about yourself, and, since you know a little about me now, I won't feel that I'm invading anyone's castle by walking around watching his character.

I intend to continue to perform now and then, since continuity is a big part of my psychic anatomy. If the movie *Hail! Hail! Rock 'n' Roll* does well, maybe I'll try doing another, but it would have to be a drama and I could enjoy writing the script for it. That's about the only way I'd find a screenplay that did not have within it stereotyped black characteristics from bygone years. I never accepted the few roles presented to me during my career for just that reason; they overplayed traits and customs of the American black person, especially the male and too often the black female. The time is coming, though, when all races and nationalities in the United States will be merged into, let's say, "Americanese" people.

Now, wouldn't that be real nice? A one-race, normal-face, average-shade, medium-made, balanced-weight, open-fate society with no disturbing variants. As my father used to say, "It won't happen in my lifetime." But I can see the great change that has happened in mine, such as being turned away from the door of the Fox Theater as a child and being paid what I consider a fortune to be featured there forty-five years later.

But there's no way people would be content with such monotony. It just wouldn't work.

Many people rely on religion in the latter years of their lives, but it was vice versa in my life. I got that old-time religion during youth. What you see now is what I'll be later. I haven't changed that much in my thirty-five years of show biz. I'm still drinking screwdrivers (without the driver) and yet smoke Kools ('bout a pack a day). I still weigh 180 pounds as I have since age eighteen (naked, drippin' wet). So the future looks fantastic and I'm forecasting my welfare as fine.

I know for sure that there are many things I have failed to remember to put in this book, but the highlights of my life are here. I am also sure that my autobiography would have been much more complex had the time and attitude of the public been right for the exposure of truly explicit information about my personal adventures. But it shall come as time goes by.

> Now let me leave you with these rhymes, that life has
>   shown me through the times.
> Though life is long, it seems abrupt, and thoughts like
>   these help sum it up.

Once in history, reigned a king, who upon his noble
 ring
Carved a statement, true and wise, which when held
 before his eyes
Gave him counsel at his glance, of his life of change
 and chance
Truth in words? Then these are they, Even this shall
 pass away.

Trains of camels through the sands, brought him gems
 from foreign lands
Fleets of sailships through the seas, brought him pearls
 to match with these
But he counted not his gain, of his treasures mine nor
 main,
"What is wealth?" the king would say. "Even this
 shall pass away."

Fairest woman ever seen, was his choice to be his
 Queen
Sprawled upon his noble bed, whispering to her soul,
 he said,
"Though no man has ever pressed, softer bosom to his
 chest
Mortal flesh does turn to clay, Even these must pass
 away."

High above the village square, rising ten yards in the
 air
Stood his statue, carved in stone. As the King stood
 there alone
Gazing at his sculptured name, he asked himself, "Of
 what is fame?"
Fame comes fast to slow decay, even it does pass
 away.

In the revel of his court, at the zenith of his sport
When the palms of all his guests, burned with clapping
 at his zest

He, among his figs and wine, cried, "Oh, loving fans of
    mine,
Pleasures come but not to stay, even this must pass
    away."

Fighting on a battlefield, once a spearhead pierced his
    shield
Comrades hurried as he bade, them to carry him for aid
Tortured from his bleeding side, "Pain is hard to
    bear," he cried,
"But with patience, day by day, even pain will pass
    away."

Sick with cancer in his spine, moments from the finish
    line
Spake he with his dying breath, "Life is done, so what
    is death?"
Fell, in answer to the King, rays of sunbeams on his
    ring
Flashing words back from the ray, "Even this shall
    pass away."

Those who don't know and *do not know* they don't
    know, are awful, avoid them.
Those who don't know but *know* that they don't know,
    are awkward, assist them.
Those who know but *do not know* that they know, are
    asleep, awaken them.
Those who know and *know* that they know are alert,
    accept them.

A man there was—of unusual gift—who bore such a
    good honored name.
Life came to him—filled to the brim—offering him both
    wealth and fame.

But turned he his head—in choosing instead—to follow
a leisurely trend,
Thinking that he—was never to be—the genius he well
could have been.

When opportunity—knocked at his door—there came
no compliance at all.
Long did it wait—with patience that fate—would bring
him to answer his call.
Day after day—time wasted away—in pleasures he
took as devout.
Intrigued with the thought—that fun, as he sought—
was what life was all about.

When opportunity—knocked once again—it found his
ideal still unbent.
Over and over—it knocked to uncover—his talent
from trivial content.
But gloried name—and chance for fame—were lost
from lack of will.
So as it went—his life was spent—his genius
unfulfilled.

May your days be filled with good music
And your nights with pleasure as well,
While the thoughts that become so confusing
Will shake off like ringing a bell.

Some days are like hours of music,
Some songs are like stories you'd tell,
Some views that came down from the hippies
are now classics, like rock is as well.

Sincerely,
Chuck

Songs are listed below in the order Chuck Berry recorded them. The dates and other information are based on his memory and files.

The single numbers are all Chess releases except where indicated by the abbreviations MC (Mercury) and AT (Atco).

SESSION	RECORDED	SONG NUMBER	SONG TITLE	SINGLE NUMBER
1	5/21/55	1	Maybellene	1064A
		2	Wee Wee Hours	1064B
		3	You Can't Catch Me	1645A
		4	Thirty Days	1610A
2	12/20/55	5	Together We Will Always Be	1610B
		6	Roly Poly	
		7	No Money Down	1615A
		8	Down Bound Train	1615B
		9	Berry Pickin'	
3	4/16/56	10	Roll Over Beethoven	1626A
		11	Too Much Monkey Business	1635A
		12	Brown Eyed Handsome Man	1635B
		13	Havana Moon	1645B
		14	Drifting Heart	1626B
4	1/21/57	15	School Days	1653A
		16	Deep Feeling	1653B
		17	Blue Feeling	1671B
		18	Low Feeling	
		19	La Jaunda	1664B
5	5/6/57	20	Oh Baby Doll	1664A
		21	Reelin' and Rockin'	1683B
		22	Rock and Roll Music	1671A
		23	How You've Changed	
		24	Thirteen Question Method	
		25	I've Changed	
6	1/6/58	26	Sweet Little Sixteen	1683A
		27	Rock at the Philharmonic	
		28	Guitar Boogie	
		29	Surfin' USA	
		30	Night Beat	
7	2/28/58	31	Ingo	
		32	It Don't Take but a Few Minutes	
		33	Johnny B. Goode	1691A

		34	Around and Around	1691B
		35	Surfin' Steel	
		36	Blues for Hawaiians	
8	6/12/58	37	Carol	1700A
		38	Hey Pedro / Lazy Pedro	1700B
		39	Beautiful Delilah	1697A
		40	House of Blue Lights	
		41	Time Was	
		42	Oh Yeah	
		43	Vacation Time	1697B
9	9/28/58	44	Sweet Little Rock and Roller	1709A
		45	Anthony Boy	1716A
		46	Jo Jo Gunne	1709B
		47	Memphis	1729B
10	11/19/58	48	Little Queenie	1722B
		49	Merry Christmas Baby	1714B
		50	Run Rudolph Run	1714A
		51	That's My Desire	1716B
11	2/17/59	52	Almost Grown	1722A
		53	Away from You	
		54	Back in the USA	1729A
		55	Do You Love Me	
		56	Blue on Blue	
		57	Say You'll Be Mine	
		58	Let Me Sleep Woman	
12	7/27/59	59	Too Pooped to Pop	1747A
		60	Betty Jean	
		61	Childhood Sweetheart	1737B
		62	Broken Arrow	1737A
		63	Let It Rock	1747B
		64	I Just Want to Make Love to You	
		65	One O'Clock Jump	
13	3/29/60	66	Bye Bye Johnny	1754A
		67	Worried Life Blues	1754B
		68	I Got to Find My Baby	1763A
		69	Drifting Blues	
		70	Don't You Lie to Me	
		71	Run Around	
		72	Jaguar and the Thunderbird	1767A
		73	Our Little Rendezvous	1767B
14	4/12/60	74	Down the Road a Piece	
		75	Confessin' the Blues	
		76	Mad Lad	1763B
		77	Diploma for Two	1853B
		78	The Way It Was Before	
		79	Little Star	1779B
		80	Sweet Sixteen	
		81	Stop and Listen	
		82	Still Got the Blues	

		83	How High the Moon	
		84	Lucky So and So	
		85	Crying Steel	
15	1/19/61	86	I'm Talking about You	1853A
		87	Route 66	
		88	Rip It Up	
		89	No title	
16	8/3/61	90	Come On	1799B
		91	Go Go Go	1799A
		92	All Aboard	
		93	Trick or Treat	
		94	The Man and the Donkey	
		95	Adulteen	
17	1/14/64	96	Nadine	1883A
		97	You Never Can Tell	1906A
		98	Things I Used to Do	1916B
		99	Brenda Lee	1906B
		100	Fraulein	
		101	Dust My Broom	
		102	Crazy Arms / Lonely All the Time	
		103	I'm in the Danger Zone	
		104	O Rangutang	1883B
18	2/25/64	105	Promised Land	1916A
		106	Big Ben Blues	
19	3/26/64	107	No Particular Place to Go	1898A
		108	You Two	1898B
		109	Liverpool Drive	
		110	Hey Good Looking	
		111	Chuck's Beat	1089A
20	8/16/64	112	Little Marie	1912A
		113	Go Bobby Soxer	1912B
21	12/15/64	114	His Daughter Caroline	
		115	Dear Dad	1926A
		116	Butterscotch	
		117	The Song of My Love	
		118	I Want to Be Your Driver	
		119	My Blue Christmas	
		120	Lonely School Days (Slow)	1926B
22	1/9/65	121	She Once Was Mine	
		122	After It's Over	
		123	You Came a Long Way from St. Louis	
		124	Jamaica Farewell	
		125	Why Should We End This Way	
23	1/31/65	126	My Little Love Lights	
		127	I Got a Booking	
		128	St. Louis Blues	
24	9/1/65	129	Run Joe	

CHUCK

		130	Every Day We Rock and Roll	
		131	One for My Baby (And One More for the Road)	
		132	It's My Own Business	
		133	Right off Rampart Street	
		134	My Mustang Ford	
25	9/2/65	135	Welcome Back Pretty Baby	1943B
		136	Vaya Con Dios	
		137	Merrily We Rock and Roll	
		138	Wee Hour Blues	
		139	Loving You in Vain	
26	9/3/65	140	It Wasn't Me	1943A
		141	Ain't That Just Like a Woman	
		142	Instrumental	
		143	Forgive Me	
27	4/13/66	144	Viva Viva Rock and Roll	
		145	Ramona Say Yes	1963B
		146	Lonely School Days (Fast)	1963A
28	9/20/66	147	My Tambourine	
		148	Mum's the Word	
		149	Campus Cookie	
		150	Laugh and Cry	MC 72643B
29	9/21/66	151	Sweet Little Sixteen (Re-rec)	MC 30143B
		152	Memphis (Re-rec)	MC 30144B
		153	School Days (Re-rec)	MC 30144A
		154	Maybellene (Re-rec)	MC 30143A
		155	Johnny B. Goode (Re-rec)	MC 30146B
		156	Rock and Roll Music (Re-rec)	MC 30146A
		157	Roll Over Beethoven (Re-rec)	MC 30145A
30	10/26/66	158	Around and Around (Re-rec)	
		159	Back in the USA (Re-rec)	MC 30145B
		160	Thirty Days (Re-rec)	
		161	Club Nitty Gritty	MC 72643A
		162	Misery	
		163	Oh Captain	
31	10/27/66	164	Brown Eyed Handsome Man (Re-rec)	
		165	Let It Rock (Re-rec)	
		166	Almost Grown (Re-rec)	
		167	Carol (Re-rec)	
		168	Reelin' and Rockin' (Re-rec)	
32	3/21/67	169	Back to Memphis	MC 72680A
		170	I Do Really Love You	MC 72680B
		171	Ramblin' Rose	
		172	Check Me Out	
33	3/22/67	173	It Hurts Me Too	MC 72748A
		174	Bring Another Drink	
		175	So Long	
		176	It's Time to Go	

34	3/23/67	177	Sweet Little Rock and Roller (Re-rec)	
		178	My Heart Will Always Belong to You	
		179	Oh Baby Doll (Re-rec)	
		180	Flying Home	
35	6/27/67	181	Rocking at the Fillmore	
		182	Every Day I Have the Blues	
		183	C C Rider	
		184	Drifting Blues (Re-rec)	
		185	Feelin' It	MC 72748B
36	6/29/67	186	Johnny B. Goode and Closing	
		187	Hoochie Coochie Man	
		188	Fillmore Blues	
		189	Wee Baby Blues	
37	12/21/67	190	Louis to Frisco	MC 72840A
		191	Ma Dear Ma Dear	MC 72840B
		192	The Love I Lost	
		193	I Love You, I Love You	
		194	Little Fox	
		195	Rock Cradle Rock	
		196	Soul Rocking	
		197	I Can't Believe	
		198	Good Looking Woman	MC 72963B
		199	My Woman	
		200	Too Dark in There	MC 72963A
		201	Put Her Down	
		202	Concerto in B. Goode	
		203	Funny That Way	
		204	If I Was	
		205	Get a Little	
38	12/22/69	206	Tulane	2090B
		207	Have Mercy Judge	2090A
		208	Gun	
		209	I'm a Rocker	
		210	Flying Home (Re-rec)	
		211	Fish and Chips	
		212	Some People Live	
39	1/8/71	213	Oh Louisiana	
		214	Let's Do Our Thing Together	
		215	Your Lick	
		216	The Festival	
		217	Bound to Lose	
		218	Bordeaux in My Pirough	
		219	San Francisco Dues	
		220	My Dream (Poem)	
40	2/3/72	221	My Ding-A-Ling	
41	2/5/72	222	Let's Boogie	2136B
		223	Mean Old World	

		224	I Will Not Let You Go	
		225	London Berry Blues	
		226	I Love You	
42	6/3/73	227	Bio	2140A
		228	Hello Little Girl Goodbye	
		229	Woodpecker	
		230	Rain Eyes	
		231	Aimlessly Drifting	
		232	Got It and Gone	
		233	Talkin' 'bout My Buddy	
		234	Roll Away	
		235	Tell You about My Buddy	
		236	Roll 'em Pete	2140B
		237	One Sixty-nine A.M.	
		238	You and My Country	
43	8/26/74	239	I'm Just a Name	
		240	Too Late	
		241	Turn the Houselights On	
44	8/27/74	242	South of the Border	
		243	Hi Heel Sneakers	
		244	If I Was (Re-rec)	
		245	Jambalaya	
45	8/28/74	246	Swanee River	
		247	You Are My Sunshine	
		248	My Babe	
		249	Don't You Lie to Me (Re-rec)	
		250	Dust My Broom	
		251	Together Again	
		252	J B Blues	
		253	The Weight	
46	8/29/74	254	Rockin'	
		255	I Just Want to Make Love to You	
		256	Baby What You Want Me to Do	2189B
		257	A Deuce	
		258	Shake Rattle and Roll	2189A
		259	Sue Ann? Sir	
		260	Here Today	
47	2/14/79	261	Move It	
		262	Oh What a Thrill	AT 7203A
		263	California	AT 7203B
		264	Pass Away (Poem)	
		265	Boogie Tonight	
48	2/15/79	266	I Need You Baby	
		267	If I Were	
		268	House Lights	
		269	I Never Thought	
		270	Havana Moon (Re-rec)	
		271	Wuden't Me	

The recordings and films of Chuck Berry appear in the order they were released or presented to the public.

For the LPs, only those cuts appearing for the first time are listed. All records that do not bear the prefixes LP or EP are single, 45 rpm (or 78 rpm) records.

Peak chart positions are indicated as follows:

◇ = highest ranking on *Billboard* "Hot 100" chart

□ = highest ranking on *Cashbox* "Top 100" chart

○ = highest ranking on *Billboard* "Rhythm & Blues" chart

Film dates indicate time of first world showing, and only those films in which Chuck Berry is seen on screen are listed.

1955

July	Maybellene ◇5 □5 ○1 / Wee Wee Hours	Chess 1604
September	Thirty Days ○8 / Together We Will Always Be	Chess 1610
December	No Money Down ○11 / Down Bound Train	Chess 1615

1956

May	Roll Over Beethoven ◇29 ○7 / Drifting Heart	Chess 1626
September	Too Much Monkey Business ○7 / Brown Eyed Handsome Man ○7	Chess 1635
November	You Can't Catch Me / Havana Moon	Chess 1645
December	LP: *Rock, Rock, Rock*	Chess LP-1425
	NEW SONGS: none. Also includes songs by The Flamingos and Bo Diddley	
December	FILM: *Rock, Rock, Rock* (DCA) SONG: You Can't Catch Me.	

1957

March	School Days ◇5 □3 ○1 / Deep Feeling	Chess 1653
May	EP: *After School Session* NEW SONGS: none.	Chess EP-5118
May	LP: *After School Session* NEW SONGS: Roly Poly; Berry Pickin'.	Chess LP-1426
June	Oh Baby Doll ◇57 □45 / La Juanda	Chess 1664
September	FILM: *Mr. Rock and Roll* (Paramount) SONG: Oh Baby Doll.	
September	Rock and Roll Music ◇8 □14 ○6 / Blue Feeling	Chess 1671

C H U C K

| c. November | EP: *Rock and Roll Music* | Chess EP-5119 |
| | NEW SONGS: none. | |

Chess EP-5119 was reissued in December, 1957, with two substitutions, neither new.

1958

January	Sweet Little Sixteen ⟨2⟩ [2] (1) / Reelin' and Rockin'	Chess 1683
March	Johnny B. Goode ⟨8⟩ [11] (5) / Around and Around	Chess 1691
March	EP: *Sweet Little Sixteen*	Chess EP-5121
	NEW SONGS: Guitar Boogie; Rock at the Philharmonic.	
March	LP: *One Dozen Berrys*	Chess LP-1432
	NEW SONGS: How You've Changed; Ingo; It Don't Take but a Few Minutes; Blues for Hawaiians; Low Feeling.	

Low Feeling is Deep Feeling (Chess 1653) at half-speed, slightly edited.

June	Beautiful Delilah / Vacation Time	Chess 1697
August	Carol ⟨10⟩ [31] (12) / Hey Pedro / Lazy Pedro	Chess 1700
October	Sweet Little Rock and Roller ⟨47⟩ [52] (13) / Jo Jo Gunne	Chess 1709
c. October	EP: *Pickin' Berries*	Chess EP-5124
	NEW SONGS: none.	
December	Merry Christmas Baby ⟨71⟩ [97] / Run Rudolph Run	Chess 1714
c. December	EP: *Sweet Little Rock and Roller*	Chess EP-5126
	NEW SONGS: none.	

1959

January	Anthony Boy ⟨60⟩ [76] / That's My Desire	Chess 1716
March	Almost Grown ⟨32⟩ [31] (3) / Little Queenie ⟨80⟩ [91]	Chess 1722
April	FILM: *Go, Johnny, Go* (Hal Roach) SONGS: Johnny B. Goode; Memphis; Little Queenie.	
June	Back in the USA ⟨37⟩ [49] (16) / Memphis, Tennessee [87]	Chess 1729
July	LP: *Chuck Berry Is on Top*	Chess LP-1435
	NEW SONGS: none.	
September	Broken Arrow ⟨108⟩ / Childhood Sweetheart	Chess 1737
November	Say You'll Be Mine / Let Me Sleep Woman (as by the Ecuadors)	Argo 5353
Unknown	FILM: *Jazz on a Summer Day* (New Yorker Films) SONG: Sweet Little Sixteen (live).	

1960

| January | Too Pooped to Pop ⟨42⟩ [56] (18) / Let It Rock ⟨64⟩ [60] | Chess 1747 |

April	Bye Bye Johnny [64] / Worried Life Blues	Chess 1754
August	I Got to Find My Baby / Mad Lad	Chess 1763
Summer	**LP:** *Rockin' at the Hops*	Chess LP-1448
	NEW SONGS: Down the Road a Piece; Confessin' the Blues; Betty Jean; Drifting Blues.	
October	Jaguar and the Thunderbird ⟨109⟩ [93] / Our Little Rendezvous	Chess 1767

1961

February	I'm Talkin' About You / Little Star	Chess 1779
c. September	**LP:** *New Juke Box Hits*	Chess LP-1456
	NEW SONGS: Rip It Up; The Way It Was Before; Away With You; Don't You Lie to Me; Route 66; Sweet Sixteen; Run Around; Thirteen Question Method.	
October	Come On / Go Go Go	Chess 1799

1962

| c. May | **LP:** *Chuck Berry Twist* | Chess LP-1465 |
| | NEW SONGS: none. | |

1963

April	Diploma for Two / I'm Talking about You	Chess 1853
August	**LP:** *Chuck Berry On Stage*	Chess LP-1480
	NEW SONGS: Brown Eyed Handsome Man (Re-rec); All Aboard; Rocking at the Railroad; Surfin' Steel; I Still Got the Blues; I Just Want to Make Love to You; The Man and the Donkey; Trick or Treat; How High the Moon.	

Surfin' Steel is the same as Blues for Hawaiians (Chess LP-1432), and was labeled Crying Steel at least once by Chess on a later issue.

1964

February	Nadine ⟨23⟩ [32] / O Rangutang	Chess 1883
April	No Particular Place to Go ⟨10⟩ [9] / You Two	Chess 1898
May	**LP:** *Chuck Berry's Greatest Hits*	Chess LP-1485
	NEW SONGS: none.	
May	**LP:** *The Latest and Greatest*	Pye (UK) LP-28031
	NEW SONGS: Fraulein; Lonely All the Time.	
July	You Never Can Tell ⟨14⟩ [15] / Brenda Lee	Chess 1906
August	**LP:** *Two Great Guitars* (with Bo Diddley)	Checker LP-2991
	NEW SONGS: Liverpool Drive; Bo's Beat; Chuck's Beat.	
September	Little Marie ⟨54⟩ [51] / Go Bobby Soxer	Chess 1912
September	**LP:** *You Never Can Tell*	Pye (UK) LP-28039
	NEW SONGS: Little Girl from Central High; Big Ben Blues.	
November	Promised Land ⟨41⟩ [35] / Things I Used to Do	Chess 1916
November	**LP:** *St. Louis to Liverpool*	Chess LP-1488

NEW SONG: Night Beat.

1965

March	Dear Dad ⟨95⟩ [90] / Lonely School Days	Chess 1926
April	FILM: *The T.A.M.I. Show* (AIP)	
	SONGS: Johnny B. Goode; Sweet Little Sixteen; Maybellene.	
May	**LP: *Chuck Berry in London***	Chess LP-1495
	NEW SONGS: My Little Love Lights; Butterscotch; She Once Was Mine; After It's Over; I Got a Booking; You Came a Long Way from St. Louis; St. Louis Blues; His Daughter Caroline; Jamaica Farewell; Song of My Love; Why Should We End This Way; I Want to Be Your Driver.	
September	It Wasn't Me / Welcome Back, Pretty Baby	Chess 1943
November	**LP: *Fresh Berrys***	Chess (UK)
	NEW SONG: Sad Day, Long Night.	LP-4506

1966

c. April	**LP: *Fresh Berrys***	Chess LP-1498
	NEW SONGS: Run Joe; One for My Baby; It's My Own Business; Every Day We Rock and Roll; Right off Rampart Street; Vaya Con Dios; Merrily We Rock and Roll; My Mustang Ford; Wee Hour Blues; Ain't That Just Like a Woman.	
June	Ramona Say Yes / Lonely School Days	Chess 1963

1967

January	Laugh and Cry / Club Nitty Gritty	Mercury 72643
March	**LP: *Golden Hits***	Mercury LP-
	NEW SONGS: Re-recordings of Maybellene; School Days; Memphis; Sweet Little Sixteen; Johnny B. Goode; Roll Over Beethoven; Rock and Roll Music; Carol; Thirty Days; Back in the USA.	61103
March	**LP: *Chuck Berry's Golden Decade***	Chess LP-1514
	NEW SONGS: none.	
May	Back to Memphis / I Do Really Love You	Mercury 72680
September	**LP: *In Memphis***	Mercury LP-
	NEW SONGS: Ramblin' Rose; Check Me Out; Bring Another Drink; It's Time to Go; It Hurts Me Too; So Long; My Heart Will Always Belong to You; Oh Baby Doll (Re-rec); Sweet Little Rock and Roller (Re-rec).	61123
October	**LP: *Live at the Fillmore***	Mercury LP-
	NEW SONGS: Rocking at the Fillmore; C C Rider; Drifting Blues; Feelin' It; Every	61138

Day I Have the Blues; Flying Home;
Hoochie Coochie Man; Fillmore Blues; It
Hurts Me Too; Wee Baby Blues; Johnny
B. Goode.

November	Feelin' It / It Hurts Me Too	Mercury 72748

1968

July	Louis to Frisco / Ma Dear Ma Dear	Mercury 72840
October	LP: *From St. Louis to Frisco*	Mercury LP-61176

NEW SONGS: Mum's the Word; My
Tambourine; Misery; Oh Captain; Rock
Cradle Rock; The Love I Lost; I Love
Her, I Love Her; Little Fox; Soul
Rocking; I Can't Believe.

1969

August	Good Looking Woman / Too Dark in There	Mercury 72963
c. November	LP: *Concerto in B. Goode*	Mercury LP-61223

NEW SONGS: My Woman; Put Her Down;
Concerto in B. Goode.

Unknown	FILM: *Sweet Toronto*	

SONGS: Rock and Roll Music; School
Days; Johnny B. Goode / Carol / Promised
Land; Hoochie Coochie Man; Sweet Little
Sixteen; Reelin' and Rockin'; Johnny B.
Goode.

1970

Early	Tulane / Have Mercy Judge	Chess 2090
November	LP: *Back Home*	Chess LP-1550

NEW SONGS: Christmas; Gun; I'm a
Rocker; Flying Home; Fish and Chips;
Some People; Instrumental.

Unknown	FILM: *Toronto Pop* (Pennebaker Films)	

SONGS: Johnny B. Goode; Sweet Little
Sixteen.

This film was re-released in 1972 in edited form as *Keep on Rockin'*.

1971

September	LP: *San Francisco Dues*	Chess LP-50008

NEW SONGS: Viva Viva Rock and Roll; Oh
Louisiana; The Festival; Let's Do Our
Thing Together; Your Lick; Bound to
Lose; Bordeaux in My Pirough; My
Dream; San Francisco Dues.

1972

c. July	My Ding-A-Ling ◇ 1 / Johnny B. Goode	Chess 2136
October	LP: *St. Louis to Frisco to Memphis* ◈185	Mercury LP-6051
	NEW SONGS: none.	
October	LP: *The London Chuck Berry Sessions*	Chess LP-60020
	NEW SONGS: Mean Old World; I Love	

	You; I Will Not Let You Go; London Berry Blues.	
November	Reelin' and Rockin' ⟨27⟩ [30] / Let's Boogie	Chess 2136
Unknown	**LP: *Johnny B. Goode***	Pickwick LP-
	NEW SONG: Reelin' and Rockin' (Re-rec).	3327

1973

February	**LP: *Golden Decade, Volume 2***	Chess LP-
	NEW SONGS: Betty Jean (alternate take).	60023
c. May	Bio / Roll 'em Pete	Chess 2140
August	**LP: *Bio***	Chess LP-
	NEW SONGS: Rain Eyes; Got It and Gone; Talkin' 'bout My Buddy; Hello Little Girl Goodbye; Aimlessly Drifting; Woodpecker.	50043
Unknown	FILM: *Let the Good Times Roll* (Columbia) SONGS: School Days; Sweet Little Sixteen; Reelin' and Rockin'; Johnny B. Goode; Untitled jam with Bo Diddley.	
Unknown	South of the Border / Bio	Chess (UK) 6145.027

1974

April	**LP: *Golden Decade, Volume 3***	Chess LP-
	NEW SONGS: Blue on Blue; Time Was.	60028
Unknown	FILM: *Alice in the Cities* (New Yorker Films) SONG: Memphis (live, Holland).	
Unknown	**LP: *Golden Decade, Volume 3***	Chess (UK)
	NEW SONG: Do You Love Me.	LP-6641.177

1975

February	**LP: *Chuck Berry***	Chess LP-
	NEW SONGS: Sue Ann? Sir; A Deuce; Hi Heel Sneakers; South of the Border; I'm Just a Name; Too Late; Swanee River; You Are My Sunshine; Don't You Lie to Me; My Babe; I Just Want to Make Love to You.	60032
February	Shake Rattle and Roll / Baby What You Want Me to Do	Chess 2169

1977

Unknown	FILM: *American Hot Wax* (Paramount) SONGS: Reelin' and Rockin'; Roll Over Beethoven; Sweet Little Sixteen.	

1978

Unknown	**LP: *Live in Concert***	Magnum LP-
	NEW SONGS: Live versions of Rock and Roll Music; Nadine; School Days; Wee Wee Hours; Hoochie Coochie Man; Johnny B. Goode / Carol / Promised Land;	703

Sweet Little Sixteen; Memphis; Too Much
Monkey Business; My Ding-A-Ling;
Reelin' and Rockin'; Johnny B. Goode;
Maybellene.

February	**LP: *American Hot Wax*** (Soundtrack) NEW SONGS: Reelin' and Rockin'; Roll Over Beethoven.	A & M LP- 6500
Unknown	FILM: *The London Rock 'n' Roll Show* SONGS: Live versions of School Days; Memphis; Sweet Little Sixteen; Mean Old World / Beer Drinkin' Woman; Wee Wee Hours; Let It Rock / Roll 'em Pete / Carol / Little Queenie; Reelin' and Rockin'.	

1979

August	**LP: *Rock It*** NEW SONGS: Havana Moon (Re-rec); Oh What a Thrill; I Need You Baby; Move It; If I Were; House Lights; I Never Thought; Wuden't Me; Pass Away (Poem); California.	Atco LP-38118
August	California / Oh What a Thrill	Atco 7203

1980

Unknown	**LP: *Rock! Rock! Rock 'n' Roll!*** NEW SONG: Let It Rock.	Mercury (German) LP-6463.044

1982

October	**LPs: *Toronto Rock 'n' Roll Revival, 1969,* *Volumes 1 & 2*** NEW SONGS: none.	Accord LPs- 7171, 7172

1983

Unknown	**LP: *Chess Masters*** NEW SONGS: I've Changed; Rock and Roll Music (demo); Thirteen Question Method (version I); 21; 21 Blues; Sweet Little Sixteen (demo); Childhood Sweetheart (alt. take); Reelin' and Rockin' (alt. take); Brown Eyed Handsome Man (1963 version); One O'Clock Jump (undubbed); How High the Moon (undubbed).	Chess (UK) LP-CXMP- 2011

1986

March	**LP: *Rock 'n' Roll Rarities*** NEW SONGS: Johnny B. Goode (alt. take); Come On (alt. take); Time Was; Little Queenie (alt. take); Sweet Little Sixteen (alt. take); Beautiful Delilah (alt. take); Rock and Roll Music (overdub); Reelin'	Chess LP- 92521

and Rockin' (demo); It Wasn't Me (alt. take).

| August | **LP: *More Rock 'n' Roll Rarities*** | Chess LP-9190 |

NEW SONGS: Sweet Little Rock and Roller (alt. take); Route 66; Brown Eyed Handsome Man (1961 version, undubbed).

Chuck Berry also appeared on Chess sampler albums (The Blues, *Volumes 1 & 2, both Argo LPs from 1963, and* Pops Origins, Vol-*ume 1, on Chess from 1964) as well as on numerous budget re-issues in the 1970s and 1980s including LPs on Pickwick, Everest, Gusto, Trip, Upfront, and many more.*

Germany, 264
Giant, 179
Gillespie, Dizzy, 110
Gillium, Francine, 163–178, 180–
181, 190, 193, 200, 202–203, 207,
213, 219–220, 222, 226, 227, 230–
231, 244–246, 249, 252–253, 266,
272–273, 278–279, 286, 287, 290–
291, 297, 310, 314
Gillum, Slillum, 66–70
Gleason's Bar, 108
"Going Down Slow," 34
Go Johnny Go, 187–188
Golden Gloves tournaments, 64–
70
Goldenhersh, Robert, 203
Goodman, Gene, 110, 266
"Great Balls of Fire," 265
Gregory, Marion, 36
Gregory, Mildred, 36
GRT Corporation, 261, 269
"Guitar Boogie," 130, 154–155

Hail! Hail! Rock 'n' Roll, 303, 323–
324
Haley, Bill, 153, 310
Hamilton, George, IV, 192–193
Hanzlick, Dr., 216, 218
Hardy, Ebby, 89, 93, 100, 112, 117,
138, 140, 279
Harris, Ira, 42–43, 88
Harry (cousin), 13
Harry, Jr. (cousin), 13–14, 35–36
"Havana Moon," 151–152
Hayes, Sandy, 275–277
Hendrix, Jimi, 309
Hochman, Bruce, 279–280
Hogan, Carl, 88
Holmes, Willa Dean, 278
Homer G. Philips Hospital, 42
Hong Kong, 232
Hook, Jack, 105, 110, 114
Hope, Bob, 299
Howard Theater, 131–132
Howlin' Wolf, 97, 100
Hubbert, Phillip, 76
Hudson, Mr., 59
Hudson, Rock, 179
Huff's Garden, 88–89

Hutchinson, Lawrence (Skip), 37–
38, 49–57, 59, 65, 72, 76

"Ida May" ("Maybellene"), 100,
103, 143
"Ida Red," 143–144
"I Love Lucy," 312
"I'm Tore Up," 105
"In Concert," 186, 267
Intermediate Reformatory for Young
Men (Algoa), 55, 57–72, 76, 285,
311
Internal Revenue Service (IRS),
271–275, 279–280
Isalee Music Company, 246, 262
"It Don't Take But a Few Minutes,"
155

Jagger, Mick, 311
James, Elmore, 88, 97
"Johnny B. Goode," 127, 155–158,
300, 309
Johnson, Buddy, 121
Johnson, Ella, 122
Johnson, Johnnie, 89–90, 100, 112,
117, 138, 140, 156, 190, 279
"Jo Jo Gunne," 161
Joplin, Janis, 227, 309
Jordan, Louis, 88
Jubilee Ensembles, 26

Kansas City, Mo., 49–55
Karrenbrock, Webster, 197
Kennedy, John F., 309
King, Albert, 105
King, Martin Luther, Jr., 309
Kingston, N.C., 123–124
KMOK, 14
Krasilovsky, William, 246, 249, 262,
300
Ku Klux Klan, 278

Lancaster, Burt, 217
Lanchester Ballroom, 259
Leavenworth Federal Prison, 213
Lee, George, 40–41
Lennon, John, 158–159, 265–266,
309
Lewis, Jerry Lee, 93, 264–265